Telling True Tales
of Islamic Lands

To Annie —

For the sincere pleasure
of learning with you.
I'm counting the years
until I can read
your book!

Warmly,

Julia

Telling True Tales
of Islamic Lands

Forms of Mediation
in English Travel Writing,
1575–1630

Julia Schleck

Selinsgrove: Susquehanna University Press

Associated University Presses
2010 Eastpark Boulevard
Cranbury, NJ 08512

The paper used in this publication meets the requirements of the American National Standard for Permanence of Paper for Printed Library Materials Z39.48-1984.

Library of Congress Cataloging-in-Publication Data

Schleck, Julia, 1976–
   Telling true tales of Islamic lands : forms of mediation in English travel writing, 1575–1630 / Julia Schleck.
      p. cm.
   Includes bibliographical references and index.
   ISBN 978-1-57591-158-8 (alk. paper)
   1. Traveler's writings, English—History and criticism.   2. English prose literature—Early modern, 1500–1700—History and criticism.   3. British—Foreign countries—History—16th century   4. British—Foreign countries—History—17th century.   5. Islam in literature.   6. Cultural relations in literature.
I. Title.
   PR756.T72S35   2011
   820.9'3209031—dc22   2010046899

For John

"The wonderful thing about language is that it promotes its own oblivion: my eyes follow the lines on the paper, and from the moment I am caught up in their meaning, I lose sight of them. The paper, the letters on it, my eyes and body are there only as the minimum setting of some invisible operation. Expression fades out before what is expressed, and this is why its mediating role may pass unnoticed . . ."

—Maurice Merleau-Ponty, *Phenomenology of Perception*

Contents

Acknowledgments

SINCERE THANKS ARE DUE TO THE MANY PEOPLE WHO supported me in the research and writing of this project. First and foremost, my thanks are due to the Rachana Sachdev at Susquehanna University Press and the friendly and professional staff at Associated University Presses. They made the publication process seem simple. Their anonymous reader improved the project significantly, and also deserves my sincere thanks for his or her time and thoughtful effort. My initial research at the British Library, Bodleian Library, Wellcome Library, Folger Library and Newberry Library, was made possible at first by a New York University Graduate School of the Arts and Sciences Summer Pre-doctoral Fellowship, and later by the University of Nebraska Research Council, with the awarding of a Maude Hammond Fling Fellowship. I am grateful as well to the many grants-in-aid given to me by the Folger Shakespeare Library and the support provided by the Renaissance Consortium at the Newberry Library. Special thanks are due to Dr. Ernest Gilman and the NYU in London program for facilitating many indispensible hours in the British Library, as well as providing impeccable companionship during the hours the library was closed. While their doors were open, my work was immeasurably assisted by the gracious and professional staff at all of these archives, especially at the Folger Library.

Ernest Gilman, John Archer, and John Guillory were all instrumental in the early shaping of this project. Nabil Matar, Judy Hayden, Virginia Mason-Vaughan, Claire Jowitt, Daniel Carey, Charles Ross, and Mary Fuller have all in various ways supported the development of this book and improved it through the opportunities they offered and the questions and challenges they posed. I owe a deep debt of gratitude for the unflagging friendship and material support Carole Levin has given me since I was fortunate enough to meet her four years ago. Without her, my book would not be what it is, and my life would be less sane. I am similarly indebted to Stephen Buhler, whose guidance and support has made all the difference in these challenging last few years. My general fitness and mental state have been infinitely improved by our epic "health and inebriation" walks. To all of my inspirational and affable colleagues in the Department of English at UNL, and especially to Joy Ritchie, I render my heartfelt thanks.

These acknowledgments would be incomplete without the mention of Katie Sisneros and David Moberly, currently at the starts of their careers in early modern studies. Katie labored for hours on my irregular prose and formatting, striving to bring the chapters of this book to greater clarity and elegance. Both Katie and David provided me with inspiration and intellectual challenge in their spirited debates over the issues and texts discussed in this book, as we met each week at the end of some very long days during the cold Nebraska winter.

There are always a few people who, in a series of small acts of infinite generosity, pour hours of their time into improving the work of their friends and colleagues. I am lucky not only to have had such people pouring their energy into my manuscript, but also to have merited the attention of a group of scholars possessed of formidable intellect and delicate tact. Kelly Stage and David Landreth suffered through endless pages of my prose at the earliest and most inchoate stages of this project, and never failed to make insightful suggestions on how to push my thinking further. Elizabeth Bearden has been an advisor, friend, and indefatigable reader on this project, providing hours of thoughtful suggestions on how best to shape my argument and to handle my struggles with sources and with the writing process. Where I would be without her ready assistance is difficult to fathom.

Finally, although I do not express it often and earnestly enough, I am deeply grateful to my parents, George and Suzanne Schleck, and to my brother Matthew. Their steady love through the years has allowed me to fly far afield in pursuit of my dreams, and yet always to come home once again to the delight of their humor and easy grace.

Parts of my discussion of Hakluyt and factuality in chapter 5 were originally published as "'Plain Broad Narratives of Substantial Facts': Credibility, Narrative, and Hakluyt's *The Principall Navigations*," in *Renaissance Quarterly* volume 59, no. 3 (Autumn 2006). Sections of my analysis of early modern newsprint were first printed in *Prose Studies*, volume 29, no. 3 in the article "'Fair and Balanced' News from the Continent: English Newsbook Readers and the Thirty-Years War." I thank these journals for their kind permission to reprint this material here.

Telling True Tales
of Islamic Lands

Introduction

what is truth?

WHAT DID IT MEAN TO WRITE A TRUE ACCOUNT OF ISLAMIC lands in early modern England? How did authors attempt to craft their material to render it more credible? What formal choices did they make and which generic patterns did they follow? How did readers determine which accounts were "true" and which were less true, or simply false? What work did these true reports from abroad perform for English society?

This study addresses these questions by examining the mediating role played by the rhetorical crafting, generic negotiations between authors and readers, and publication histories of several English accounts of Islamic cultures written between 1575 and 1630. Broadly speaking, this book pursues the "rededication to form" advocated by such historical formalists as Stephen Cohen: it performs a rigorous formal analysis of each text to reveal its place in the domestic book economy and in the social sphere of its author. The emergent formal practices of travel narratives thus function "not simply as containers for extrinsic ideological content, but as practices with an ideological significance of their own."[1] In short, I consider how each of these texts functions as a social document and as part of an emerging genre. At issue here is the way that experience is mediated into text, texts into physical publications, and publications into "true" knowledge about Islamic lands and peoples. Ultimately this book is concerned with the ways in which certain stories achieve the status of truth—information that is actionable and integrated into the political and economic history between England and the various Islamic nations of North Africa, the Levant and beyond—while others are relegated to a more liminal epistemological status, situated outside the realms of power and credit.

"EXPRESSION FADES OUT BEFORE WHAT IS EXPRESSED": RECOVERING FORMS OF MEDIATION

Studies of early modern Anglo-Islamic contact currently focus primarily on dramatic representations,[2] a unique and complex genre that is, without question, a rich locus for investigation into the representations of Islamic societies produced by early modern English writers. But, Matthew Birchwood's assessment of the field is correct: he claims that much of our critical energy "has focused upon the relatively contested field of Elizabethan and early Jacobean drama, also known as the Age of Shakespeare. The gravitational pull of Shakespeare and of his immediate contemporaries

13

separating it from drama.

has therefore tended to warp our understanding of the larger impact of Islam, and particularly the Ottoman Empire, upon the Early Modern period as a whole."[3] Birchwood makes this critique in order to call attention to dramatic representations in the Civil War era and beyond—with a tip of the hat to Matthew Dimmock's work on the place of Islam in early Tudor literature—but it is applicable to the generic pull of Shakespearean studies as well. Stage plays were undoubtedly a compelling way for early modern Englishmen and women to meet Turks and Moors produced by domestic writers, but they were not the only, nor necessarily the most widespread, method of doing so. They were certainly not the "most popular and accessible response to English interaction with foreigners" at a time when broadsides featuring Turks were sung from street corners and posted in alehouses, and news reports and other cheap pamphlets were read aloud outside St. Paul's Cathedral to eager groups of listeners. Furthermore, while dramatic performances may have "brought cultural difference into the everyday lives of Englishmen and women," there is a growing body of evidence that experiences of cultural difference were already an established part of everyday life for Londoners and other city dwellers. As Nabil Matar points out in *Turks, Moors and Englishmen* and Imtiaz Habib's *Black Lives in the English Archives* tracks in great detail, there existed significant communities of Levantine and African peoples living in London during the early modern era.[4]

An essential part of rebalancing our critical resources to cover the whole range of genres in which early modern English writers treated Islamic societies is to recognize prose texts as complex, carefully crafted representations deserving of the same kind of theoretically sensitive analysis as drama or epic poetry. A well-developed literature exists on prose romance but, apart from some recent work on captivity narratives, the mass of short "non-literary" prose texts treating Islam have yet to receive sustained study.[5] This is not to say that they are unrecognized or unmentioned: travelers' tales—such as those by Sandys, Morison, Coryat, Lithgow, the Sherleys, and others—as well as Hakluyt and Purchas's compilations of such texts, are now widely known and frequently cited in studies of early modern English representations of Islam and Anglo-foreign contact in general.

Yet these prose accounts still suffer from what we might call relentless mentioning, a visible symptom of their status as "archival," "nonfiction," or "factual" documents, different in kind from their more "literary" brothers.[6] For instance, this ingrained attitude toward such texts is in evidence in a recent collection of essays about representations of the Mediterranean world, in which the editor's introduction explains: "material that we can classify under the broad category of travel literature has not been dealt with in separate contribution in this volume, but to varying degrees, all the essays resort to a number of travel documents in generating historical contexts for their arguments." This material, listed as "accounts of travel, *2nd to other* merchant-adventurers' records and diaries, border annotations and illustrations in geographical maps, descriptions of places in atlases, manuscript portolan charts, and treatises on trade and shipping in the Mediterranean," may indeed "represent rich resources for our knowledge of the area," but if they continue to serve only as a source for "generating historical context" for arguments about drama and romance, then they will continue to be understudied and occasionally misunderstood.[7] *misunderstood*

The hazards of this practice are demonstrated in the same introduction, when Goran Stanivukovic cites a passage from Richard Willes' *The History of Travayle in the West and East Indies*, a compilation of works on this subject published in 1577. Stanivukovic quotes an extensive passage from the section Willes takes from Richard Eden, part of which I reproduce here:

> What is the matter, you Christian men, that you so greatly esteeme so lytle portion of golde more then your owne quietnesse, whiche neyerthelesse you entende to deface from these fayre ouches, and to melt the same into a rude masse. If your hunger of golde be so insatiable, that onlye for the desire you have thereto, you disquiet so manye nations, and you yourselves also susteyne so many calamities and incommodities, lyvying lyke banished men out of your owne countrey, I wyll shewe you a region flowing with golde ... the greedie hunger of golde hath not yet vexed us naked men ...

Stanivukovic uses this passage as evidence of "an early criticism of the English colonial practice articulated by Richard Eden, as given in Richard Willes's commentary." He further specifies that "Eden's criticism of Christian men's hunger for gold, their self-inflicted calamities and their disruptions of other nations also represents his critique of the thirst for rule that obsessed Christians and spread hatred among them."[8] While the publication of this passage in English at a time when English colonial ambitions were only just stirring and had yet to produce a single overseas colony may indeed represent a very early instance of a counter-colonial discourse within that nation, the text in question is far more complicated than a simple English critique of English colonialism. Elided in Stanivukovic's use of this passage is its origin as a Spanish colonial document, published in Latin nearly fifty years before by the Spanish priest and member of the Council of the Indies, Peter Martyr d'Anghiera, as *De orbe novo* (1530). The speaker who articulates that critique, as the pronouns in the passage indicate, is (as described in Eden's translation) the "eldeste soonne of Kynge *Comogrus*," whose speech is included in one of the documents forwarded to Martyr in his role as secretary of the council and subsequently compiled and published.[9] Richard Eden translated *De orbe novo* in 1555, a historical moment more significant for Anglo-Spanish interactions than Anglo-American. Like many Englishmen of this turbulent period, Eden had to navigate the shift from a Protestant protectorate under Edward VI to a Catholic monarchy under Mary. His translation of Peter Martyr's text, *The Decades of the Newe Worlde or West India*, is part of that political maneuver, as it opens with copious praise for the Spanish and urgent recommendations for England to unite with Spain and follow in its gloriously imperial footsteps. Eden writes: "howe much more [than Alexander and the Romans] then shal we thynke these men [the Spaniards] woorthy just commendations which in theyr mercyfull warres ageynst these naked people have so used themselves towarde them in exchaungynge of benefites for victorie, that greater commoditie hath therof ensewed to the vanquished then the victourers." Despite Stanivukovic's claims, the work is more a part of English colonial promotion than colonial critique.[10]

When complex levels of mediation are lost to brevity, important interpretative material also tends to go missing: this represents one of the major drawbacks to using small bits of a multiplicity of primary sources rather than engaging with fewer sources in greater depth. As a critical practice, such an approach derives in part from historicism, both new and old, but it is also supported by the importation of postcolonial concerns and methodologies into early modern studies, particularly an interest in tropes. Studies that focus upon tropes in the primary literature reveal shared characteristics across a range of English texts that treat foreign lands and peoples, highlighting the governing assumptions of English writers toward Muslims and other foreign peoples as well as the ways in which different discourses are deployed in support of one another. This has often been a very fruitful line of inquiry: works on the intersections of religion and race and of gender and discovery have provided particularly compelling examples of this approach.[11] What is lost, however, in this horizontal structuring—which treats numerous texts in short order to highlight similarities between them—is the understanding of each text's particular social function, i.e., who wrote the story, for whom, and why. Another weakness of this approach is the inability of such studies to consider the impact of domestic pressures and desires on the representations of foreign peoples and places—why certain tropes might be employed or avoided, why certain authors present Muslims in a positive light and why some demonize them, and why some ignore them altogether and focus on Islamic lands and their histories. I concur, therefore, with the insistence of Daniel Vitkus and others that "we cannot analyze pre-imperial English culture using the theoretical paradigms typically employed by first-wave postcolonial studies."[12] I suggest, however, that this applies not only to such theoretical paradigms as orientalism, but also to the formal structuring of our analyses of texts treating Anglo-Islamic interactions in this period.

There have been several excellent examples of full-length treatments of prose texts published recently, demonstrating the possibilities inherent in such a commitment.[13] But one aspect of such texts that haunts the edges of our treatment of them and has yet to be explicitly considered is their truth value.[14] Prose travel accounts and other travel writings are often implicitly (and sometimes explicitly) considered by critics to be more "accurate" or "factual" than other types of writing about foreign peoples, more like "documents" than narratives or stories. It is this unspoken assumption that allows for their use as "historical context."[15] It also puts them at the heart of recent quarrels over "authentic" versus "fictionalized" Muslims in English writings.[16] And while I would certainly second Jonathan Burton's call for English literary critics to expand their purview into reading more Otto-man history so that, in the words of historian David Goffman, we can bet-ter "grapple with the specifics of [our] subjects' Mediterranean objects," I do not think his somewhat contradictory recommendation to "recover the Islam-related imagery and tropes that dominated the early modern social imaginary and pervaded the drama, regardless of their accuracy" is as helpful.[17] Putting aside the knotty question of what might constitute the twenty-first century idea of "accuracy" in archival documents, I would argue that we should be attending quite closely to early modern under-standings of "accurate" ideas about Islam. As Burton himself points out, the perceived truth value of the representations and stories of Islamic lands was obsessively marked by their English readers and audiences. Whether it is Jonson's Peregrine contrasting Sir Politic Would-be's "Adventures," to be "put i' the Book of Voyages" with the story of his gulling, which should be "registered for truth," or John Cartwright dismissing tales "more fitte for a Stage, for the common people to wonder at, then for any mans priuate studies," the credibility of a given representation was of obvious impor-tance to early modern Englishmen and women.[18]

The manner in which such distinctions were made, however, is not as straightforward as the casual and widespread importation of the terms "fictional" and "factual" (or nonfiction) to describe early modern texts might make it seem.[19] These generic markers were deployed quite dif-ferently in the early modern period, and some, like "factual," did not yet exist as such. Yet the contemporary allocation of truth to a given text is an important socio-generic process to consider, for several reasons. As Richmond Barbour reminds us through his idea of cultural logistics, such cultural products as books, pamphlets, and plays do *work* in the world.[20] Asking what this work is, and how it is accomplished, is a way of link-ing the representations of foreign peoples and the development of English identity—the target of many current literary critical studies—with the

broader historical processes of colonization and empire. It is one method
of connecting the "English *mentalité*" to the British Empire.[21] Whether a
given representation of a foreign land is considered to be true or not conditions the kinds of work it accomplishes. Different kinds of texts strive
to convey different kinds of "truths": a sermon or news pamphlet might
seek to convey an essential religious truth about the world, while merchant letters might attempt to communicate a different kind of truth about
that same world. As studies of early modern history writing have demonstrated, the concept of historical truth (which in this period includes
current events) and how to convey that in writing was undergoing serious
revision in this period.[22] If part of the critical goal in studying early modern Anglo-foreign relations is to describe how the foundations for empire
were built, without losing a sense of the radical contingency of historical
development that is so obvious in this period of English interaction with
the diverse peoples of the Mediterranean, then we must attend to the work
done or facilitated by texts considered to be "true." We must also ask why
certain texts that strive for credibility fail in their attempts.

One way to pursue this goal is to attend to the reception of the texts
we study. Mary Fuller's most recent book, *Remembering the Early Modern Voyage*, provides a compelling model for such work; as Fuller notes,
printed texts "allow us to consider more than the interaction between English voyagers and authors and the places and peoples they encountered;
they also provide us with concrete evidence of how these constructions
of a distant experience were, in turn, received by audiences and articulated with other, larger narratives."[23] Another concept useful to uncover-
ing the work accomplished by true tales in this period is that of mediation.
In their collection, *Emissaries in Early Modern Literature and Culture:
Mediation, Transmission, Traffic, 1550–1700*, Brinda Charry and Gitanjali Shahani remind us of the many ways in which information and ideas
of foreign lands are mediated, through travelers and their experiences,
through ambassadors and translators, through the printed text, and ultimately through the medium of language itself.

> Subjecting the role of the emissary to discussion also serves as a reminder
> that cultural knowledge and even material goods are not always simply
> presented and transferred to "other" peoples. The form and meaning they
> assume are a result of complex processes of mediation and negotiation. Cul-
> tures do not simply receive the impressions carried by mediating agents,
> but rather actively engage with them and with each other to create and give
> expression to social meaning, to notions of identity and difference, as well
> as to political and material desires.[24]

One way in which this process of active engagement is made evident is
through genre, and through the physical form the text is given and through

which it interacts with members of society. How does an author choose to impart his or her ideas about foreign lands and peoples? In what form is the text arranged, and how is it printed (or copied) and circulated? How are these choices circumscribed by the author's status in society and the generic moment in which he or she finds him– or herself? If emissaries were "fixed in social categories such as gender . . . as well as class," how is this manifest in the genre and physical form of the text-as-emissary?[25]

As Mikhail Bakhtin reminds us, "we are most inclined to imagine ideological creation as some inner process of understanding, comprehension, and perception" and thus we "do not notice that it in fact unfolds externally, for the eye, the ear, the hand. It is not within us, but between us."[26] The text's form, including its physical instantiation, plays a crucial mediating role in the creation of ideology. Historical formalists such as Stephen Cohen claim that form "mediate[s] between text and social context as well as author and audience by providing a socially produced meaning or function—an ideology of form—to be reproduced, contested, or appropriated by the text." It is the interaction of any given text's ideologies of form and of content that produces a uniquely charged historical product that does particular work in the world. In focusing on form in this way, Cohen supplements new historical practice, which, while it excels at "mapping interdiscursive circulation, documenting the appropriation of materials from other discourses by literary or dramatic texts, it has been less successful at theorizing the *results* of that appropriation, the transformation visited upon extraliterary [and extratextual] materials before they are recirculated by performance or publication to act upon the culture at large." Exploring the ideological charge of a text's form, as well as its content, allows scholars to gauge a text's "eventual ideological effect, transforming social materials as they circulate into and out of the text."[27]

The chapters of this book are crafted with an eye toward this goal, considering in detail the forms of "true" prose narratives about Islamic nations in order to explore how travel writings develop as a "nonfiction" genre, considering their generic predecessors, their material embodiment as marketable objects, their authors, and the various reading communities that consumed these printed works. Focusing on the fifty-year period that begins with England's formal diplomatic and trading agreements with the Ottoman Empire and ends with Charles I's ban on foreign newsprint, this study treats such high-market folio volumes as George Sandys' *Relation of a Journey begun in 1610* and Richard Hakluyt's *The Principal navigations, discoveries and voyages of the English nation* alongside such low-status publications as Thomas Saunders' captivity narrative *A most lamentable Voiage, made latelie to Tripolie in Barbarie*, the miscellaneous collection of popular print publications treating the Sherley brothers, and multiple anonymous news pamphlets. This period represents the first great wave of English publications treating Islamic nations and peoples and is thus a time of great generic experimentation as English authors worked with their readers to develop modes of writing and publication that would consistently be perceived as credible. By examining the formal and social pressures on travel authors as they crafted their tales of Muslims, this study places at the center of its inquiry the question of how knowledge about foreign lands and peoples is produced, vetted, and accepted as true.

"TRAVELERS MAY LIE BY AUTHORITY"

The most prominent aspect of prose narratives that make truth claims is their need for authorial credibility. Unlike dramatic productions, whose primary desideratum is the attraction of a large audience, most true prose descriptions of Muslims have as their defining goal the acceptance of the narrator and/or author as a trustworthy raconteur. While both genres share the need for marketability and an interest in entertainment, only the authors of true narratives bear the added pressure of being adjudicated reliable or credit-worthy by their reading audience based on what they write and how they tell their tales. Authors of travel tales had a wide range of choices in composing their accounts, and few audience expectations to meet. Moreover, if the truth of the narrative was not supported by accepted formal or generic traditions, neither was it buttressed by any social institutions or established vetting processes as in the case of modern newspapers or peer-reviewed academic writing.[28] Instead, the credibility of a given prose travel tale was guaranteed primarily by the reputation of the author prior to his travels, and the way in which those travels were reported upon the return of the author to England.

Credibility in early modern England was, like society, a hierarchical affair. The credence given to various groups of people was codified in court witnessing standards, where the word of a nobleman was considered more trustworthy than that of a commoner, an ecclesiastic's more than a lay person's, and a man's more than a woman's.[29] As historian of science Steven Shapin notes, "the distribution of imputed credit and reliability followed the contours of authority and power."[30] This order matched *ars apodemica* recommendations on who should travel and who should not: Thomas Palmer states flatly in his 1606 *Essay of the Meanes how to make our Travailes, into forraine Countries, the more profitable and honorable* that certain persons are prohibited from travel by virtue of their nature (infants and decrepit persons), their imperfections (fools, madmen, and lunatics), or their sex (women).[31]

The men who traveled spanned the spectrum of English society, and they left England for a wide variety of reasons.[32] In addition to those who, like sailors and traders, made their living from travel, and those who went abroad at the bidding of the crown, such as ambassadors, noblemen increasingly went abroad for pleasure and sent their clients abroad for information. Under Elizabeth, there were many opportunities for battle of various sorts against the Spanish, and wealth to be had from exploration, discovery, and quasi-legal piracy and pillage. Nobility who could prove their worth by leading martial expeditions or their cunning by operating successfully in foreign courts and locales gained status back in England with their patrons and their peers.

The problem with gaining status from travel was that traveling was seen in itself to be a suspicious activity. Far from the watchful eyes of the community, an individual might act in ways unacceptable in a domestic setting. There was no way to prove conclusively one's good behavior, and the strange customs and peoples a traveler was exposed to in the course of his ramblings did not help to assuage the doubts of his neighbors in England that the traveler was no longer one of them. "It hath beene, and yet is, a proverbiall speech amongst us, that *Travellers may lie by authority*," claimed William Parry at the opening of his *A new and large discourse of the Travels of Sir Anthony Sherley, Knight*. Parry's interest is in defending those travelers like himself, who sought honestly to relate the wonders of their journeys. Along the way, however, he acknowledges the common assumption that those who left the bosom of their local communities were received back with suspicion. Furthermore, he describes those liars in some detail: "certaine I am diverse there are (entiteling themselves Travellers for crossing the narrow seas to the neighbour partes of Picardie peradventure, or the lowe countries perhappes) from thence take authoritie to utter lies in England (at their returne) by retaile, which they have coyned there in grosse."[33] The metaphor involving counterfeiting is telling: travelers of all kinds seek to turn their travels into a kind of currency. Those who invent stories of their journeys simply pass off false coins for true, and thereby damage the entire economy of turning foreign "travails" into domestic gold.

Although Parry is speaking in a figurative manner, there was also a literal link between traveling, audience credit of the traveler's story, and the traveler's financial status. Given the relative dearth of small coins in circulation, many financial transactions in early modern England functioned entirely through credit. As Craig Muldrew explains, "apart from wholesaling, most buying and selling was done on trust, or credit, without specific legally binding instruments, in which an individual's creditworthiness in their community was vital."[34] In other words, shopkeepers, merchants, tavern owners, and many others extended their customers lines of credit—a decision based entirely on the reputation of the customer. The high nobility were notorious for contracting massive debts to tradesmen,

who could not refuse such clientele and were often not repaid, except perhaps upon the death of a nobleman, who might have ordered his accounts
to be cleared in his will. In addition, credit instruments such as bills of
exchange and other sorts of promissory notes circulated like cash: each
potential holder of the bill accepted it as money after making a careful
assessment of the reputation of the original debtor by whom the bill was
signed. If this person were deemed trustworthy, the current holder of the
bill would sign it over to the new holder, who could then pass it along further or go to the original debtor and demand payment.[35] A bill written by a
debtor considered untrustworthy would not be accepted in lieu of immediate payment; such a person lacked credit, in both senses of the term.

Those who had traveled abroad were unknown quantities to local creditors. Some travelers returned with extraordinary wealth, creating a sensa-
tion upon their arrival in London, but many also returned considerably
impoverished. Simply making the journey was considered a significant
financial risk, and many travelers made "travel wagers," essentially bet-
ting on whether they would or would not return in an effort to cover the
costs of travel. Generally speaking, if a traveler had acted admirably or
even heroically while abroad, he might receive a warmer welcome among
local shopkeepers than if his actions were unknown or in some way notorious. Giving a good account of oneself was a crucial step in establishing
and/or recovering a good reputation at home, one that would allow the
traveler to reintegrate into the credit economy on a positive footing.

One way to do this was to publish or otherwise circulate a detailed
account of one's travels abroad. Thus travel narratives, although meant
to be entertaining and to generate sales for the bookseller and publisher,
also frequently had the serious purpose of filling in a gap in local knowledge about the whereabouts and behavior of the traveler. Authors recognized the social function of their tales by the emphasis they placed on the
credibility of their stories, usually through the title, dedicatory epistles,
notes to readers, and other paratextual and introductory material. Parry's
acknowledgement of, and separation of himself from, travelers who lie
about their activities abroad is simply one of many strategies deployed by
travel writers in an effort to gain credibility for their tales.

The ways in which authors sought to establish the reliability of their
accounts depended on the nature of the audience targeted. The ethos
crafted by the author, the generic models adopted in telling the story, and
the mode of printing (or manuscript design) all played a role in the reception of a traveler's tale, and thus all differ, often quite radically, depending
on the intended readership. I have therefore divided my study into several
types of printed travel accounts that address themselves to distinctly different audiences. The first three chapters of this book treat three representative sets of travelers: higher-ranking nobility whose travel and writing

improves their position in society, minor nobility on the verge of ruin who journey abroad and write about their voyages without ever successfully reviving the fortunes of the family, and low-ranking authors or translators who sell the stories of others cheaply and in great quantity, seeking a regular customer base by providing reliably true news from abroad. —journalist?

Chapter 1 examines George Sandys' *A Relation of a Journey begun in 1610* (1615), a highly learned humanistic account of the Levant in which classical and Biblical descriptions of the region are used as a historical base against which to measure an experiential present. According to Sandys' *Relation*, the most notable result of the poor governance that marked the Ottoman Empire was ruin and waste: ruin of buildings and waste of agricultural possibilities. This chapter considers the implications of this focus upon ruin and its connections to the debates on legal land use in England and the country's burgeoning colonial projects. I argue that Sandys' focus on the land and its uses is due in part to the authorial ethos Sandys adopts in order to appeal to his intended audience, i.e., the English nobility. Landowners in early modern England launched an intense debate over appropriate land management in this period through their use of legal action to reappropriate lands locally understood to be held in common and dedicated to common use. Given this profound shift in the moral economy and legal understanding of land ownership and use during Sandys' lifetime—not to mention the serious involvement of two of his brothers in such "improving" projects—it would be a mistake to read Sandys' insistent portrayal of Ottoman lands as ruined or "wasted" as not being implicated in these English land use debates. The insights into effective land use displayed in Sandys' treatment of Ottoman governance and agricultural management in the *Relation* position him as an ideal leader of the Virginia Company's shaky new colony in the Americas, as the settlers and their London backers attempted to create an effective structure of governance and a profitable agricultural economy. In this bid for position, Sandys was successful: after a narrowly failed attempt to gain the governorship of the Bermudas in 1619, Sandys was named treasurer of the Jamestown settlement in 1621. In this way, Islamic political and agricultural practices are made to function, by way of humanist learning, as a negative example for English landowners. At the same time, the traveler-author positions himself not as someone who shares an experience of the Levant with its inhabitants, but as someone who, through his travels, has become a more knowledgeable and effective English nobleman; through his *Journey begun in An. Dom. 1610*, Sandys confirms his allegiances to and place within the community of English noble landowners and those seeking to extend their holdings in the territories of the New World.

Not all efforts to turn Levantine journeys into domestic political gain were successful. Chapter 2 considers the many texts published to trumpet the foreign exploits of Sir Anthony Sherley and his brother Robert, both named ambassadors by the Persian Shah Abbas I and sent on his behalf to negotiate military and trading alliances with the nations of Christendom. Unlike Sandys, whose father as Archbishop of York and whose brothers as parliamentary leaders and noble landowners all retained their high-status places in English society, the Sherley family, although noble, suffered a serious blow to its wealth and position at the end of the sixteenth century when the head of the family was convicted of embezzling funds from the queen. The Sherley brothers' peregrinations through Turkey and Persia were therefore undertaken in a search for wealth and patronage, and the texts describing their travels are markedly different in appearance and content than that of the well-positioned Sandys. This chapter explores the variety of published Sherley travel accounts, from lengthy autobiographical narrative to stage play to popular news pamphlet, charting borrowings from multiple generic predecessors as the Sherleys sought to improve their credit in many domestic circles through a carefully crafted presentation of their actions abroad. I argue that the failure of the Sherley family to recover is partly due to the brothers' inability to overcome a basic social dynamic surrounding foreign travel in the period: those who traveled were suspect, not admired, especially when their travels are perceived to have made them in some way more foreign.

Although many of the Sherley materials attempt to map them back into a familiar English social landscape, or to glorify a new, more flexible understanding of national identity, such texts are ultimately unsuccessful at countering the suspicion the brothers garnered when they returned to Europe dressed in Persian garb, representing the Islamic ruler. They were also simply poorly conceived to fit the times. Anthony's efforts to present the Persian ruler as brave and wise, and Persia itself as a promising military alliance for England, were rejected by James, who sought to distance himself from his predecessor's ties with Islamic nations. The Levant Company was similarly unenthused about jeopardizing its privileged trading status with the Ottomans by making deals with its hostile eastern neighbor. The Persian king and his English ambassadors, despite the heroic billing they received in the Sherley texts, were unwelcome in England. Interestingly, the Sherley texts' efforts to draw links between England and Persia and to insist upon the virtues of a binational identity, while rejected by those in a position to allocate patronage to the brothers, struck a chord with London commoners. The popularity of their story and the manner in which they are referenced in other texts indicates that the brothers emerged as a species of folk hero in the early seventeenth century. This fact points to distinct differences in the reading practices and investments in foreign travel made by poorer commoners as opposed to the wealthier merchant classes and noble elite.

Chapter 3 pursues the representations of Islamic lands in the popular press of London, especially in the foreign news reports of the time. It marks the changes that occur in their depictions as the genre of foreign news reporting alters radically across the period 1580–1630, and argues that a unique system of knowledge-building practices developed amidst the London commons through the reading of these reports. This work thus challenges the implicit contention of such authors as Steven Shapin and others writing on the history of knowledge creation in this period that such practices were solely the province of gentlemen.

Anonymous, cheaply printed pamphlets were considered the least reliable source of information about events and peoples in foreign lands. In early printed pamphlets, however, this criteria seemed of little importance to readers, who sought stories that would entertain and morally instruct them by relaying already-established religious and cultural truths through a novel setting. Functioning similarly to exempla in sermons, such stories related the providence of God in the lives of men. As in their parent genre of history writing, these short pamphlets embellished their "brief and true" histories with speeches and details that would render the lesson more obvious rather than the tales more accurate in the modern sense of the word. Representations of Muslims in such publications remained tightly linked to the values of the crusade tradition, in which "Turks" of all kinds are the enemies of Christendom and capable of all kinds of villainy.

As London Protestants became emotionally invested in the religious wars on the Continent, however, reliable or credible information on battles and treaties became a more desired feature of foreign newsprint. The genre changed to accommodate the new market, as the form of newsprint altered dramatically. Gone were the extended, colorful narratives of the older pamphlets; short bits of information, often no more than a sentence long, replaced these earlier stories. Gone too were the Muslims of the Crusades; Turks and Moors from across the Levant came to occupy a place similar to that of Catholics and Protestants in the terse geopolitical reports that characterize later newsprint. The general *un*reliability of these news reports caused both the development of a new perception of Islamic actors as well as a new comparative reading practice, putting pressure on the purveyors of news to justify their credibility through the printing of reports from multiple sources, confirmations across multiple issues, and other techniques for ensuring the reliability of the news they sold. I support my arguments through a careful reading of the negotiations between publishers and their readers printed on the back covers of newsbooks throughout the 1620s, as the editors of these publications responded to alleged reader complaints. Such books mixed accounts from the Ottoman Empire, Morocco, Persia, and Egypt with those from Germany and the

Low Countries, encouraging all readers to evaluate the reliability, rather than the religious truth, of their accounts.

A similar shift in the presentation of Muslim actors is examined in Chapter 4. Instead of tracing the formal features of a series of publications across time, however, I consider what happens to a single story as it moves from a popular print quarto to a short selection in a massive compendium of travel tales. Drawing more heavily upon recent work on historical formalism, this chapter will explore in greater detail how the form of a travel narrative itself carries ideological implications, and some of the ways in which these interact with the ideology embedded in the content of the tale. More than any other, this chapter thus explicitly challenges the tendency in the field to focus solely on the tropes and themes of travel texts without taking into account the formal structures through which such material is communicated and the ways in which those structures interact with the local contexts that produced them. It takes seriously the contentions of such historical formalists as Stephen Cohen, that form

> mediates two of the more vexed relationships in historical criticism, those between author and audience (or intention and reception) and between text and social context. The key to both mediations is the materialist insistence on the status of literary forms as social products shaped by specific historical circumstances to perform specific ideological tasks—on forms not simply as containers for extrinsic ideological content, but as practices with an ideological significance of their own.[36]

These axioms suggest a methodology of textual analysis that accounts both for the implications of a text's formal elements when read as a discrete whole, and also for the ideological ramifications of that text's reworking of received generic forms.

The chapter analyzes the shifts in form that take place in Thomas Saunders' narrative of his captivity in Tripoli as it moves from popular pamphlet (1587) to one of Hakluyt's principal navigations (1589). Its particular focus is the paratextual material surrounding each publication, as this threshold information is critical in guiding the reader's practice in approaching the text and comprehending its meaning in the manner specified by the author and/or printer. In the case of Saunders' account, a contradiction between the plot of the text and its explicit moral allows for two quite different messages regarding England's relationship with Islamic foreigners to emerge from its reading. The pamphlet paratext leads the reader to a conclusion more familiar from early news pamphlets influenced by crusader attitudes toward a religious enemy; Hakluyt's editing of the paratext in his *Principall Navigations*, on the other hand, leads his readers to consider Turks—both the Ottoman Sultan and his subjects in North Africa—as trading partners who are capable of making equitable and just agreements with Englishmen. These disparate modes of reading highlight the ideological goals of each publication in shaping England's diplomatic relations with the Ottoman Empire and the roles played by individual Englishmen within this context. They also demonstrate the necessity of reading travel narratives not just for their thematic content or "facts," but also with careful attention to the form in which they are published, and the communities implicated in the production of such true stories about Islamic lands.

The final chapter considers another set of travel texts that were printed for the first time in Hakluyt's massive collection and claimed as *Principall navigations, voyages and discoveries of the English nation*: the trading company letter. The chapter begins by examining the attribution by nineteenth- and twentieth-century scholars of a particularly high historical truth value to Hakluyt's two editions of the *Navigations*, examining the collections' strong reputation for reliability and factuality, in light of the work done on the history of factuality. It argues that such claims are highly anachronistic, and explores the alternative methods by which Hakluyt's contemporaries might have evaluated the truth value of his collection, or the individual stories within it.

Drawing on work done by historians such as Barbara Shapiro and historians of science such as Steven Shapin and Lorraine Daston, this chapter insists that the small, seemingly fact-like bits of information contained in so many of the *Navigations'* voyages would not have carried the high epistemological status that they do today.[37] Indeed, the word itself did not carry the same meaning, instead denoting "something done, a deed" during the early modern period. Small units of information regarding tides, distances, geographical markers, weather, etc. were merely the "particulars" of a history, and were not included in the voyages to increase their perceived reliability, but precisely because such details were *not* reliable and needed multiple testaments to their existence in order to reach a "probable" conclusion about them. Many of the voyages that include such fact-like material were originally written as reports by trading company factors to their masters back in London, and their inclusion was dictated by the function of these reports: to account for company goods and to provide information on the desirability of continued trade. The perceived truth value of the details they reported back to the company was not ultimately determined by the form of the report, but by the trustworthiness of the reporter. Unlike in modern knowledge regimes, facts did not exist out there, waiting to be observed by anyone in a position to witness them; reports of events were always yoked to the status of the reporter. As Andrea Frisch argues in the *Invention of the Eyewitness*, the credibility of a witness was in earlier centuries always linked to his public character and status, and this regime of what she calls the "ethical eye-witness" continues into the early modern period.[38] As in the case of the other travel writings examined in this book, the perceived truth value of Hakluyt's collection of travel tales was tied to the perceived status of the collection, its editor, and the individual authors within it, whom Hakluyt includes so that each reader may "refer every voyage to his Author, which both in person hath performed, and in writing hath left the same." Not only would Hakluyt's *Navigations* not have been considered factual by its early modern readers, it would only have been as reliable as the editor and authors themselves. In the case of the merchant letters included in Hakluyt's collection, the credit of these authors—or rather, the economic institution of which they were a part—was so high as to render such accounts, and the formal features deployed to communicate agents' experiences abroad, the preferred form of travel account for those in positions of economic and political power in England as the seventeenth century progressed.

Should the gradual triumph of these seemingly "factual" accounts among certain segments of the English populace be seen as part of the history of the modern fact as it emerges in seventeenth-century England? Can we locate the more traditional modes of prose history narrative considered in this book as predecessors of the English novel? The postscript considers the relevance of the work done in this book to the literatures on the history of factuality and the origins of the English novel. It ultimately rejects the clean trajectories drawn by several major figures of these discourses and, in line with the organizational strategy of this book, insists that the evaluation of credible stories and thus the production of knowledge is essentially a local process, and that multiple communities of writers and readers develop differing strategies for generating and evaluating the truth value of written accounts. This point is relevant as well to the literature on English representations of Muslims, as there has been much work done on complexifying "Muslims" and their depictions in this period, but less work done on exactly which "English" writers were creating those representations, for whom, and why.

The question of what constitutes a true tale of foreign lands—involving the construction of a text's formal features, generic models, author and audience expectations, and the print market—will by no means be definitively answered here, nor is that the goal of this short study. What it does do is call attention to often elided forms of mediation in the representation of foreign peoples. It also raises the stakes in the study of travel writings by insisting that the epistemological status of such texts in their domestic market has a profound impact on more than the perception of Muslims and other foreign peoples by English authors and readers; through the relegation of certain kinds of narrative to the status of fiction and the construction and policing of what counts as knowledge, it affects the political, economic, and ideological basis for empire.

I

1

Waste and Empire: George Sandys'
Relation of a Journey begun in 1610 and the
Successful Gentleman Traveler

> To understand [individual texts'] role in and as social practice they must be
> subject to a formal analysis that is also a thoroughly historicized analysis
> of their social origins and functions.[1]

GEORGE SANDYS' *RELATION OF A Journey begun in 1610* is a text that must be
understood in relation to Sandys' identity as an English gentleman. It was
written and published for the English nobility of the early seventeenth century, and it works to confirm Sandys' position within that community, with an
eye toward his preferment. Whatever contributions the *Relation* made toward
English colonial discourses, religious toleration, or a moderate monarchalism,
it did so through a narrative and a physical publication geared toward establishing George Sandys as a capable and trusted member of the gentry.[2]

This chapter will examine both the form of Sandys' *Relation of a*
Journey—its physical appearance, its paratextual framing, its narrative
choices—and its pervasive themes of ruin and poor governance in relation
to the role the text played in Sandys' life as an English gentleman. It will
consider the work done by the author in his efforts to use this text to create
an effect in the world, focusing on the ethos Sandys chooses to adopt when
transforming his lived experiences in the Levant into a prose narration
meant for his peers in the English gentry.[3] In so doing, it will highlight the
function that Turkish Muslims, and the Ottoman state in particular, served
for this author in his historical moment, a function specific to the estate
to which Sandys belonged and the humanist tradition in which he wrote.
Finally, it will explore why the "true" story Sandys tells about the inhabitants and lands of the Ottoman Empire is a successful one; ultimately,
Relation of a Journey extends both the credit and reputation of its author,
helping to create the image of a man faithful to the concerns and expectations of his peers and capable of forwarding their goals in the world.

"MR GEORGE SANDYS WHO INDEED WAS
GENERALLY SO WELL REPUTED OF"

Sometime following his return from the Levant in 1612, Sandys composed *A Relation of a Journey begun in Anno Domine 1610. Foure Bookes.*

Containing a description of the Turkish Empire, of Aegypt, of the Holy Land, of the Remote parts of Italy, and Ilands adjoyning. In 1615, it was printed as an expensive folio volume filled with the additional luxury of many detailed images. The *Relation* was thus published in such a way as to discourage a non-noble audience from purchasing it. In this sense, the orientation of the physical object matches that of its rhetorical composition. The function that such a text was meant to play within this noble community was of course multiform, beginning with simple entertainment. There is no doubt that such a well-composed and learned discourse on what was still a quite exotic locale, ornamented by many maps, vistas and diagrams, would have been powerfully distracting and engaging for the gentry who read it. It also served, however, to establish the character of George Sandys as a man who was learned yet experienced, familiar with the ways of foreign lands yet always ineluctably English. Most importantly, it assured noble readers that the author of this work was English in the manner of the reader himself—in other words, he saw the world through the eyes of an active landowner seeking better to manage his resources.

The ethos established through the *Relation* undoubtedly served as one of the bases for Sandys' good reputation among the men from whom he sought employment a few years after the publication of the account. In 1619, Sandys attempted and nearly attained the position of Governor of the Bermudas (also known as the Summer Islands). The following year a group of gentry, including the Earl of Southampton and Sir Edwin Sandys (George's elder brother), gained ascendancy over the merchants who formerly had the running of the Virginia Company. In 1621, these men appointed Sandys treasurer for the Virginia colony, member of the council of state in Virginia, and member of his majesty's council for Virginia in London. Sandys' reputation was such that both the gentry and the merchants enthusiastically supported his appointment to these positions of power within the company, noting that he "indeed was generally so well reputed of, for his approved fidelity sufficiency and integrity: as they conceaved a fitter man could not be chosen for that place."[4] Note that two out of these three characteristics—fidelity and integrity—have nothing to do with Sandys' expertise and everything to do with his character as evaluated by his peers.

Sandys' experience in the Levant as he presented it in *A Relation* also had a direct relevance to the colonizing project at hand. As Sandys describes the lands of the Ottoman Empire, they have both been inappropriately used and allowed to fall into neglect. Sandys begins his book with a dedication to his royal pupil, Prince Charles, decrying the ruin that the poor governance of the Ottomans has brought across the wide expanse of its dominions, all so rich in history, culture, and natural abundance.

The parts I speake of are the most renowned countries and kingdomes: once the seats of most glorious and triumphant Empires; the theaters of valour and heroicall actions; the soiles enriched with all earthly felicities; the places where Nature hath produced her wonderfull works; where Arts and Sciences have bene invented, and perfited; where wisedome, vertue, policie, and civility have bene planted, have flourished: and lastly where God himselfe did place his owne Commonwealth ... Which countries once so glorious, and famous for their happy estate are now through vice and ingratitude, become the most deplored spectacles of extreme miserie: the wild beasts of mankind having broken in upon them, and rooted out all civilitie; and the pride of a sterne and barbarous Tyrant possessing the thrones of ancient and just dominion. Who aiming onely at the height of greatnesse and sensuality, hath in tract of time reduced so great and so goodly a part of the world, to that lamentable distresse and servitude, under which (to the astonishment of the understanding beholders) it now faints and groneth. Those rich lands at this present remaine wast and over-growne with bushes, receptacles of wild beasts, of theeves and murderers; large territories dispeopled, or thinly inhabited; good cities made desolate; sumptuous buildings become ruines; glorious Temples either subverted, or prostituted to impietie; true religion discountenanced and oppressed; all Nobility extinguished; no light of learning permitted, nor Vertue cherished: violence and rapine insulting over all, and leaving no security save to an abject mind, and unlookt on poverty.[5]

The contrast presented here between a glorious, fruitful, and well-governed past and a rather postapocalyptic present is the basic rhetorical trope of Sandys' *Relation*.[6] Through it, Sandys both depicts the powerful Ottoman Empire as plagued by decrepitude (a common fantasy in seventeenth-century Christendom not necessarily seconded by modern historians), and argues that this state was brought about not by "the pride of a sterne and barbarous *Infidel*" but that of a "sterne and barbarous *Tyrant*." Despite the author's notable Protestant faith and his travel being in the Holy Land, the focus of the work is not so much religious as civic. Unlike many English writings on the Holy Land in this period, this is a work not about perverted religion, but poor governance, a common theme among the humanists of the period, especially those who, like Sandys, were employed as tutors to those destined to rule. Also remarkable about Sandys' text is his literalization of this abstract point. He begins by claiming that the "wild beasts of mankind" (presumably the Ottomans but perhaps the nomadic Arab tribes in the area as well) have "broken in" upon the civilized fields and homes of admired ancient societies; then in the very next sentence he makes the same claim in a literal mode: the "rich lands" of the Levant "at this present remaine wast and overgrowne with bushes, receptacles of wild beasts." The land itself, as visually witnessed by the traveler, is a manifest example of the universal decay brought about by a ruler's improper stewardship of his lands and people.

This "doubled vision" of ancient glory and present ruin, of classical authorities and eye-witness testimony, metaphorical decay and literally "wasted" land, is unique to Sandys' *Relation*. This combination of authorities marks the English author as an expert in humanist learning, in traversing dangerous lands successfully, and in knowing how proper governance can produce healthy, fruitful "commonwealths." It shows him to be a man of learning, a man of action, and a capable governor all at the same time. It is, in other words, the perfect résumé for a man soon to be appointed secretary to the nascent Virginia Company.[7]

This text also links Sandys' writings on the Levant and his colonization activities in America in another way, however, and that is in his depiction of the "wasting" of "rich lands." Sandys' employment of such English legal land-use terminology as "waste" marks him as a part of a landowning family and displays a shift taking place at the time in the nobility's attitude toward their land. In particular, it displays a new understanding of what constituted the moral use of one's land, and gestures toward the case landlords made for appropriating lands traditionally understood as commons for their own discretionary use. In other words, Sandys' account of the Levant is steeped in a model of land use based primarily on economic efficiency and the moral responsibility a ruler has not to "waste" his land's natural resources. It is this model that would be brought to the new English colonies in America, in part by Sandys himself, and eventually used for justifying the appropriation of land known to belong to a whole series of native peoples. Sandys' account of Turkey, Egypt, and the Holy Land thus serves not only to warn a young prince against governance so poor it results in the "wasting" of a land's resources, it also marks Sandys as a man "approved" for his "fidelity, sufficiency and integrity" in carrying out the Virginia Company's desires for high agricultural productivity in its newfound lands.

ABUNDANT WASTE:
GREECE AND EGYPT UNDER OTTOMAN CONTROL

In his initial travels away from Venice and into the eastern Mediterranean, Sandys observes many Greek-populated islands under the control of either Venice or the Ottoman Empire. His commentary is primarily chorographic in nature: he focuses upon the shape of the land, its history and cultivation. He looks upon these countries with the dual eye of a landowner, assessing their agricultural riches and possibilities, and of the humanist, noting the characterizations of the people and their lands in ancient Greek and Roman authorities.

Sandys paints the Greek islands as overflowing with natural abundance. "The whole [island of Corfu is] adorned with groves of Oranges,

Lemonds, Pomegranates, Fig-trees, Olives and the like: enriched with excellent wines and abundance of hony" (3). Cephalonia is "abounding with wheat, honey, currents, Manna, cheese, wooll, Turkies, excellent oile, incomparable (though not long lasting) Muscadines," and is thus fruitful in spite of being "unwatered with rivers, and poore in fountaines" (4–5). Chios is blessed with "the best hony of the world, which intermingled with water, is not much inferiour in relish to the costly Shurbets of Constantinople," and their orchards are "enriched with excellent fruits: amongst the rest . . . Oranges, Lemons, Citrions, Pomgranates" (12, 13). Chios, Sio, and Mar de Marmore are all covered with "incredible numbers of partridges . . . greater then ours, and differing in hue: the beake and feete red, the plume ash-colour" (27, 13). Lesbos boasts "sheepe and cattle . . . here bred and sustained in great plentie: horses, although low of stature, yet strong and couragious" (16). This abundant production is symbolized in the "Lenticke" tree, which gives to Chios

> the greatest renowne and endowment. These grow at the South end of the Iland, and on the leisurely ascending hils that neighbour the shore. In height not much exceeding a man, leaved like a Service, and bearing a red berry, but changing into black as it ripeneth. Of this tree, thus writeth an old Poet: The Lenticke ever greene, and ever great/ With gratefull fruite, three different sorts doth beare,/ Three harvest yeelds, is thrice drest in one yeare. (12)

So fruitful are these islands that one tree bears "three different sorts" of "gratefull fruite" in a single year. Such famous plants were known to the ancients, and according to Sandys' report, still grow on the islands at the time he journeyed by them. Similarly, the studied traveler, familiar with Martial's *Epigrams*, can still taste the "figs, so much esteemed by the Romanes for their tartness: 'The Chian Figs that to me Setia sent/ Taste like old wine: they wine and salt present' [*Mart. l.13. Epig. 23*]" (13).

In addition to possessing abundant wealth in agriculture and livestock, these islands are also endowed with mineral and natural dye products that, when properly mined or harvested from the land, can be very lucrative for the landowner. Cephalonia has a "powder for the dying of Scarlet: This growes like a blister on the leafe of the holy Oke, a litle shrub, yet producing acornes: being gathered, they rub out of it a certaine red dust, that coverteth after a while into wormes, which they kill with wine when they begin to quicken" (4–5). In addition to the Lenticke tree and other virtues, Chios possesses "quarries of excellent marble;" it also has a quantity of "a certaine greene earth, like the rust of brasse, which the Turkes call Terra Chia" (12).

Most impressive in Sandys' eyes was the isle of Zant, which he describes as "unspeakably fruitfull, producing the best oile of the world, and excellent strong wines, both white and red, which they call Ribolla." Yet despite the quality of this olive oil and wine, such products are nevertheless out-shone by the island's chief export, currants. The cultivation of currants, especially for markets in England and Holland, has enriched the island-ers beyond measure, who were once "scarce able to free themselves from importunate famine." They now "(besides their private gettings, amount-ing to 150000 Zecchins) do yearely pay unto S. Marke 48000 Dollars for customes and other duties." Sandys attributes this wealth to proper hus-bandry of the island's natural resources: "it is impossible that so little a portion of earth, so employed, should be more beneficiall: the mountanous part being barren, and the rest comprized within two or three not very ample vallies, but those all over husbanded like an entire garden." It is careful tending of the island's little arable land that allows it to produce beyond measure, bringing riches to all the inhabitants. Paradoxically, the focused monoculture that brought such wealth to Zant also occasionally results in a return to famine. So much of the arable land is given over to currants in place of grain cultivation or pasturing of livestock, that the farmers "sometimes suffer, being ready to starve, when the weather con-tinueth for any season tempestuous: and they cannot fetch their provision, which they have as well of flesh as of corne, from Morea, being ten leagues distant." Sandys describes this decision to plant currents rather than grain as "employing their grounds to better advantage," and makes no further comment upon its practicality or morality (5). His clear admiration of the wealth of the island, however, is close to open approval of the decision made by the landowners in Zant to utilize their land in this way.[8]

At the time that Sandys wrote of it, Zant was an island governed by Venetians and occupied almost entirely by Greeks. Although the island maintained good relations with Turkey and annually sent the sultan a gift of falcons in order to remain unharassed by Turkish galleys, it was independent of the Ottomans and therefore populated almost entirely by Christians (there was also a small population of Jews on Zant). This is in contrast to many of the other Greek and Levantine islands that Sandys visited, which had long since come under direct Turkish rule.

Chios, for example, had fallen to the Turks years before. As described by Sandys, it seemed to have suffered very little by this civic upheaval; it remained a land of great abundance, as noted above. But in describing the social structure on the island, Sandys makes a distinction between its few Turkish overlords and the broad population of Greeks still living there, a distinction that is often repeated throughout the *Relations* as a whole: only the Greek Christians "husband the earth." The Turks merely "lived in command" (14). This division of labor is echoed in Sandys' descrip-tion of the Greek people as a whole. They are "of divers trades in cit-ies," he reports, "and in the country do till the earth (for the European Turkes do little meddle with husbandry) and dresse their vines, by them onely planted" (78). In their status as overlords, the Turks are repeatedly portrayed as neglecting the proper cultivation of the land. Where there remains a substantial Christian population, as in Chios, the land remains well-husbanded and fertile. Where such a native population is lacking, or has been uprooted, the natural abundance of the land falls off, as in Turkish-controlled Thessaly, north of Istanbul along the Bosphorus:

> The European side is bordered almost with continued buildings, the other with fruitfull hils, & orchards, not yeelding (I suppose) in delights to that celebrated Thessalian Tempe, when kept by the more curious Christians, and adorned with their now prostrated pallaces. (42)

When under the "more curious," or attentive and solicitous, care of the Christians, the land along this stretch of river rivaled the famed Tempe valley of classical Greece, renowned for its pastoral beauty and natural abundance. The implication is that this condition no longer pertains, as the area is no longer "kept" by Greek Christians, whose "prostrated" palaces mark their downfall and speak of the neglect and ruin that now mark the land. Sandys can note the "fruitfull hils, & orchards" of the area, but here such fruitfulness only serves as an indicator of former glory and a condemnation of current mismanagement on the part of the Ottomans. This falling off from ancient glory into a state of indifferent neglect or abuse is literalized in the manner in which the Turks utilize the stone ruins found on the plains of Illium. Sandys visits a site that he deems the rebuilt city of Troy after its destruction by the Greeks, claiming "this notable remainder of so noble a Citie was once a small village of the Ilians. For the Ilians after the destruction of that famous Illium, often shifting the seate of the new, here fixt it at last, as is said, by the advice of an Oracle." His own reverence for this ancient city is not matched, however, by the Turkish elite in nearby Istanbul, as "now the ruines beare not altogether that forme, lessened daily by the Turkes, who carried the pillers and stones unto Constantinople to adorne the buildings of the Great Bassas" (22). According to Sandys' account, the Turks literally dismantle the area's classical past, changing the shape of the landscape through their destruction and neglect.

Sandys' description of Istanbul tells a similar story. The great Constantinople, seat of Byzantium and of the Greek Orthodox Church, has faded both from the cityscape and also from the minds of its inhabitants. Sandys, who like most Christians still refers to the city as Constantinople, visited "all the remaines that are left (or all that are by the Christians to be seene, besides the relikes of the Pallace of Constantine, now made a stable for wilde beasts) of so many goodly buildings, and from all parts congested antiquities, wherewith this soveraigne Citie was in times past

so adorned" and is struck by the paucity of such sites. The current configuration of the city does not live up to classical descriptions of the ancient
Greek capitol and its elegant structures. Moreover, the missing Christian
palaces and civic structures are symbolic of a larger erasure of Christian
history; with the disappearance of these architectural remains "are their
memories perished" as well. The Greeks, who might be expected to possess a lively memory of the past greatness of their realm, have retained
no such stories or local memory: "not a Greeke can satisfie the Inquirer
in the history of their owne calamities. So supine negligent are they, or
perhaps so wise, as of passed evils to endeavour a forgetfulnesse" (36).
This is characteristic of the Greeks in general, according to Sandys. They
have not only lost their empire, their capitol city and many of its buildings
and monuments, but also their high culture. Even their language has fallen
from its ancient elegance: "the vulgar Greeke doth not differ so far from
the same, as the Italian from the Latine: corrupted not so much by the mix-
ture of other tongues, as through a supine retchlesnesse [recklessness]"
(81). The Greeks have allowed their language to become corrupted; they
are guilty of a sort of moral and mental inactivity that has caused them to
be negligent of their duty to themselves and their history. The one aspect
of their traditional culture they retain is their "merriness" and its pastoral
expression in drink and dance.

This division between an active Turkish ruling class and the conquered
and "supine" Christians persists throughout the first book of Sandys' travels. Both this dichotomy and the (somewhat contradictory) parallel division Sandys draws between Christian stewardship and Islamic neglect
of the land, however, are interrupted by the author's arrival in Egypt,
which he finds astonishingly fertile despite the country's relative paucity
of Christians. The "fruitfull soile possess[ed] us with wonder; and early
maturity of things, there then as forward as with us in June; who begin
to reape in the ending of March." Sandys paints an idyllic picture of the
English walking along the banks of the Nile, long sugar canes in their
hands that both "served our hands for staves, and feasted our tastes with
their liquor" (118). And indeed, "no place under heaven is better furnished
with graine, flesh, fish, sugar, fruites, roots, &c." despite the fact that the
land is kept primarily by Muslims (116). Here, it would seem, the land has
continued to live up to its ancient reputation of being "the granary of the
world; insomuch as it was not thought possible for the Romane Empire to
subsist, if not assisted by the affluence of Aegypt." Where once the rich
floodplains of the Nile fueled Roman centurions, it now does the same
for the Turkish janissaries, a fact not unrecognized by the sultan himself, who after conquering the country claimed that "Now he had taken a
farme that would feed his Iemoglans" (93). The lists of fruits, trees, and
nuts that Sandys piles up in his descriptions of the orchards surrounding

Cairo enact the overabundance that he claims "is rather to be admired then expressed" (93):

> orenges, lemons, pomegranats, apples of Paradise, Sicamor figs, and others, (whose barks they bore full of holes, the trees being as great as the greates oakes, the fruite not growing amongst the leaves, but out of the bole & branches) Dates, Almonds, Cassia fistula, (leaved like an ash, the fruite hanging down like sausages) Locust, (flat, and of the forme of a cycle) Galls growing upon Tamarix, Apples no bigger then berries, Platains, that have a broad flaggy leafe, growing in clusters, and shaped like cucumbers, the rind like a pescod, solid within, without stones or kernels, to the taste exceeding delicious . . . and many more, not knowne by name, nor seene by me elsewhere: some bearing fruite all the yeare, and almost al of them their leaves. To these adde those whole fields of Palmes (and yet no prejudice to the under-growing corne) of all other most delightfull. (121)

It would seem that perhaps the Muslims, both Egyptians and their Turkish overlords, are not unskilled in the ways of agricultural production after all. The land could hardly have been portrayed as more fertile.

Yet even among such abundance, Sandys returns to his familiar trope of decay from ancient glory, caused at least in part by poor Turkish governance and lack of proper stewardship of the land. Cairo may be "the fairest in Turkie" yet it still "differ[s] from what it was, as from a body being yong and healthfull, doth the same growne old and wasted with diseases" (122). The same disease afflicts Alexandria even more acutely. Ovid is called in to bemoan the famous city, once so great and now so fallen: "such was this Queene of Cities and Metropolis of Africa: but 'Ah how much different is/ That Niobe from this!' [Ovid Meta.] Who now hath nothing left her but ruines; and those ill witnesses of her perished beauties: declaring rather, that townes as well as men, have their ages and destinies" (114). In the case of Egypt's cities, time, rather than Turkish neglect, appears to be the party responsible for their decay. Yet even here, Sandys' descriptions carry an implied critique: Egypt's antiquities have not been kept "healthfull." The Turks have put little effort into "reedifying" these cities—especially Alexandria—so that they might regain something of their youthful beauty. Instead they are allowed to remain in ruin.

Throughout these books is the sense of wasted potential. The constant citation of a more glorious past is a reminder of what was possible for these lands, cities, and peoples. The lands retain much of their natural richness, and they are sometimes properly tended by the local inhabitants, producing a measure of wealth for the land and its people. None of these places, however, are living up to the promise held out by ancient accounts of their greatness, whether it be in agricultural wealth or in architecture.

Sandys cites this explicitly in his economic assessment of Egypt and its place in the empire:

> The revenues of this little country amount . . . to three millions of Shar-iffes. The Great Turke having one (viz. foure hundred thousand disbursed yearly in sugar and rice, and sent to Constantinople; the residue sent over-land with a guard of six hundred souldiers for feare of the Florentine:) another million is spent in payes, and in setting forth the Carvan unto Mec-cha; the third he [the Turkish governor of Egypt] hath for the supportance of his owne estate, and entertainment of his dependents. **But this is litle in regard of that which was raised thereof in the reigne of Auletes, who received seven millions and a halfe of Crownes; much more supposed to have yeelded to the more provident Romanes.** (108, my emphasis)

The Turks are getting less than half of what the country was capable of pro-ducing under other rulers, perhaps even less, considering that Sandys does not attempt to quantify the revenues generated under Roman suzerainty. Despite the unspeakable fruitfulness of Egypt as witnessed by Sandys, he nevertheless insists that it could be yielding much much more.

What was true in Egpyt is also true of the empire as a whole. Sandys paints the Turkish emperor as generating a disproportionately small amount of revenue given the extent of his holdings:

> the yearely revenew which he hath to defray his excessive disbursments, such a world of people depending upon him, amounts not to above fifteene millions of Sultanies, (besides the entertainment for his Timariots) which is no great matter, considering the amplitude of his dominions: being possest of two Empires, above twenty kingdomes, besides divers rich and populous Cities: together with the Red, most of the Mid-land, and Aegean, Euxine, and Proponticke seas (76).

Here Sandys posits a specific reason for such a poor showing in com-parison to ancient profits. This lackluster economic performance "may be imputed to the barbarous wastes of the Turkish conquests: who depopulate whole countries, and never reedifie what they ruine." Unlike the Romans, the Ottomans do not build, or rebuild, the cities or infrastructure that they destroy in the conquering of the country or that time has caused to decay before their arrival. They do not "reedifie" or bring back to health the lands that they govern, instead allowing them to suffer from a careless neglect that causes them to fall further and further from their ancient glory and their present potential. And not only are cities and infrastructure not rebuilt, the sultan allows the populations of the countries to decline as well, "so that a great part of his Empire is but thinly inhabited, (I except the Cities) and that for the most part by Christians: whose poverty is their onely safety and protectresse." Without proper and fair governance, there is no point in building up wealth—in people, in stock, or in agriculture. Only merchants in cities are well enough protected by law and by their ambassadors that they might safely accumulate wealth. Local inhabitants, especially Christians, have no incentive to do so, since such wealth would only attract unwanted and often violent attention from unchecked bandits and even more so from corrupt Turkish officials: "for as in the Sea the greater fishes do feede on the lesse, so do the Great ones here on their inferiours, and he [the Sultan] on them all: being, as aforesaid, the commander of their lives, and generall heire of their substances" (76). The corruption thus comes from the very top, as the sultan gathers all inheritance to himself, allowing no wealth to build up in families. In Sandys' depiction of the empire, tyranny creates uncertainty and prevents the formation of a noble class that might serve to check and to guide the emperor's exercise of power. It also discourages the cultivation of wealth on the local level, depressing the revenues of the empire as a whole. In short, it is a system seemingly designed to "waste" the land and its peoples.

WASTING THE HOLY LAND

No land was more wasted by the sultan than the Holy Land. The word emerges to prominence in Sandys' account almost the moment the author enters the bounds of the Holy Land. While traveling in caravan on the way to Gaza, the group stops to rest "about noone by the Wels of Feare; the earth here looking greene, yet waste, and unhusbanded" (140). The land is green, and could therefore be fertile, yet is unhusbanded and therefore "waste."[9] The trope of lost glory, evidenced through the contrast of classical quotation with descriptions of current ruin, runs absolutely rampant through Book III of Sandys' account, saturating his sentences and structuring his paragraphs. The density of ruin in the Holy Land as Sandys depicts it is astonishing; to take one paragraph as an example, as Sandys' group traveled about to see the wide variety of holy sites in the vicinity of Jerusalem they journeyed through an area Sandys calls Bethania, about two miles outside the city. In traveling through that area, the group

> came to a desolate Chappel, about which divers ruines; the house heretofore of Simon the leper . . . close under which lies Bethania . . . now a tottered village, inhabited by Arabians . . . a little North of Bethania, we came to the ruines of a monastery, now levell with the floore . . . southward of this, and not far off, stood the house of Martha, honoured likewise with a Temple and ruinated alike . . . far from the top, stood Bethfage [sic], whose very foundations are now confounded . . . a great way on this side the river, there stands a ruined Temple, upon the winding of a crooked channell,

forsaken by the streame, (or then not filled but by innundations) where
Christ (as they say) was baptized by John. (197)

Temples and monasteries are ruined, cities have become "tottered" villages, and even the rivers have ceased to run as they should. The density of
disaster here is extraordinary, as the land and everything on it is assessed
as sadly fallen from former glory. The trope of ruin becomes so insistent
that even buildings still erect and functional begin to be described as "yet
unruined" (198) or "not altogether subverted" (201). Ports are "choaked
with sand" (153), temples, "once sumptuous" are "now desolate" (184), the
fountain of Bethesda "a barren spring [that] doth drill from betweene the
stones of the Northward wall and stealeth away almost undiscerned" and
the doors where the ill used to wait for angels to trouble the waters and
bring healing are now bricked up or "halfe choked with rubbidge" (192).
Even Jerusalem itself "lies waste; the old buildings (except some few) all
ruined, the new contemptible . . . Inhabited it is by Christians out of their
devotion; and by Turks for the benefite received by Christians: otherwise
perhaps it would be generally abandoned" (160).

   Although Sandys explicitly exempts cities from his charges of depopu-
lation when discussing the Sultan's poor management of the empire, in this
section of the *Relation* he notes with gloomy (and episcopal) regularity the
lack of inhabitants in formerly populous Levantine cities. "In the time of
the Christians [Lydda] was the seate of a Suffragan, now hardly a village"
(202). "In the time of the Christians [Hevea] was an Episcopall sea, now a
place of no reputation" (209). The Christians apparently knew how to fill
a city and keep it prosperous. Under the Turks nearly all cities, regardless
of situation or past greatness, fall to "thinly populated" decrepitude. The
famous port of Sidon, from whence Dido made good her escape unto the
Libyan shores, used to be a notable city, but predictably, "the towne now
being, is not worth our description; the walls neither faire nor of force; the
haven decayed, when at best but serving for gallies. At the end of the Peir
stands a paltry blockhouse, furnished with suitable artillery. The Mosque,
the Bannia, and Cane for Merchants, the onely buildings of note" (210).
Although unworthy of extensive description Sidon is at least doing better than Acre, which Sandys compares to a corpse: "the carcasse shewes
that the body hath bin strong, double immured, fortified with bulwarks
and towers;" this mode of backhand compliment is about the only way
that Sandys musters any praise for the cities of the Holy Land. And true
to form, the carcass of the great castle now merely looms over a "towne
[where] there are not above two or three hundred inhabitants, who dwell
here and there in the patcht-up ruines" (204–5). It was also "when possest by the Christians . . . an Episcopall Sea" (205). Episcopal sees aside,
even Turkish monuments do not escape the degradation brought about

by Turkish rule: "we passed by a place called Sereth: where by certaine ruines there standeth a pile like a broken tower, engraven with Turkish characters, upon that side which regardeth the way: erected as they say, by an Ottoman Emperour" (201). It's not entirely clear given the syntax whether there was a tower originally erected by an emperor and then later broken, or whether the "pile" that happens to resemble a "broken tower" was erected by an aesthetically challenged emperor, but either way, it carries the same scent of ruin that plagues all civic and religious structures in Sandys' Holy Land.

This decrepitude in the works of men is echoed by the land. The famous purple dyes of Tyre, found in certain local sea snails "is no more to be had: either extinct in kind, or because the places of their frequency are now possest by the barbarous Mahometans" (216). Outside the city, there is "a levell naturally fertil, but now neglected: watered with pleasant springs; heretofore abounding with sugar canes, and all variety of fruite trees" (216). This abundance was formerly augmented and cultivated by the Romans, whose cisterns "in times past conveyed [water] by the Aquaduct into the aforesaid orchards: but now useless and ruined, they shed their waters into the valley below" causing the fields and orchards to fall fallow due to lack of proper irrigation (217). Such carelessness with the precious agricultural resource of water has in some places resulted in its nearly complete loss: the famed fish pool of Siloe "containing not above halfe an acre of ground, [is] now dry in the bottome: and beyond the fountaine that fed it: now no other then a little trench walled in on the sides, full of filthy water: whose upper part is obscured by a building (as I take it, a Mosque) where once florished a Christian Church built by Saint Helena" (188).

The fragrant balsamum plant that used to grow near Jericho, so treasured in ancient times that when there yet "remained two orchards thereof in the dayes of Vespasian . . . a batell was fought" in defense of them, is also now entirely gone. "[The plant was] Of such repute with the Romanes, that Pompey first, and afterwards Titus did present it in their triumphs as an especial glory: now [it is] utterly lost through the barbarous waste and neglect of the Mahometans" (198). The loss of balsamum is not only a shame, it is a significant economic loss for the empire, as the "fragrant and precious tears" distilled from the plant "are onely brought us from India; but they farre worse, and generally sophisticated" (198). Moreover, the plant had other uses that might also have generated revenue; "the bole of this shrub is of least esteeme, the rine of greater, the seed exceeding that, but the licour of greatest: knowne to be right in the curdling of milke, and not staining of garments."

Indeed, in contrast to Egypt and the Greek Isles, Sandys writes the natural landscape of the Levant as one of general decay, matching the man-made structures crumbling within it. The Mount of Olives, "bedect with Olives, Almonds, and Fig-trees, heretofore with Palmes" would indeed be "pleasantly rich when husbanded" but "now upbraid[s] the barbarous with his neglected pregnancy" (199). In the mountains of Judea, the hills show the evidence of former cultivation, where the "levels yet beare the stumps of decayed vines, shadowed not rarely with olives and locusts," which Sandys takes as confirmation of the accounts he has read of the area's past abundance and population: "surely I thinke that all or most of those mountaines hath bin so husbanded, else could this little country have never sustained such a multitude of people" (183). Mount Carmel testifies to the same former fructitude, "rich in olives and vines when husbanded; and abounding with severall sorts of fruites and herbes, both medicinable and fragrant." Lacking the husbandry needed to keep the land cleared and fruitful, however, it is "now much overgrowne with woods and shrubs" (203). As should be evident by now, the conditional clause "when husbanded" is a frequent occurrence in this section of the *Relation*, and contains within its tight phrasing the root of Sandys' critique of Turkish governance. He presents the reader with the potential of the land "when husbanded," using both physical evidence of past cultivation (vine stumps, etc.) and classical and biblical testament; then he implies that these riches are not currently being produced due to the lack of good husbandry on the part of the inhabitants. Like the temples and churches of the Holy Land, the agricultural inheritance of the land is being neglected and is falling to ruin.

Although all of this ruin, both structural and agricultural, is blamed on Turkish mismanagement, a pattern emerges in the language of blame for the two types of ruin. Buildings and cities are either ruined anonymously—they simply "are" ruined, perhaps by time or age, as in the case of Cairo—or a specific account of their destruction is related from ancient and classical history, as in the case of Alexandria or Jerusalem. The Turks may neglect their "reedification," but there is no undue blame laid on the Ottomans for their original destruction. The natural riches of Ottoman-controlled lands, on the other hand, are nearly always ruined due to the "barbarous waste and neglect of the Mahometans." The Ottomans are not necessarily expected to rebuild the endless array of monasteries, temples, churches, castles, etc., but they *are* expected to cultivate the land and harvest its riches. This is made most explicit in Sandys' description of the Holy Land, where the "barbarity" of the agricultural waste perpetrated by the Ottomans is most frequently denounced. Unlike in Egypt or on the Greek isles, the Levant is not an area so naturally abundant that it can tolerate much neglect. Careful husbanding would be essential for the vines, orchards, and groves Sandys has read about in classical and biblical sources to have remained alive and fruitful.

The few exceptions in Sandys' Holy Land descriptions, where the land is depicted as naturally rich and fertile, are highlighted by Sandys for special consideration. He departs from his incessant comparatives of past glory and current ruin and instead notes the bounty of the land and its rich agrarian possibilities. On the way to Jerusalem, outside of Hebron, Sandys relates that the group

> past this day through the most pregnant and pleasant vally that ever eye beheld. On the right hand a ridge of high mountaines, (whereon stands Hebron): on the left hand the Mediterranean sea, bordered with continued hils, beset with variety of fruites: as they are for the most part of this dayes journey. The champion betweene about twenty miles over, full of flowry groves of olives, and other fruites dispersedly adorned.

This reads initially as welcome praise for something in the Holy Land, echoing the luxuriant fructuousness of Egypt or Zant. More so than in his descriptions of these lands, however, Sandys emphasizes the waste of possible agrarian riches by the Levantine inhabitants and their Turkish overlords.

> Yet is this wealthy bottom (as are all the rest) for the most part uninhabited, but onely for a few small and contemptible villages, possessed by barbarous Moores; who till no more then will serve to feede them: the grasse wast-high, unmovwed, uneaten, and uselesly withering.

Like Mount Carmel or the Mount of Olives, this bountiful land reproaches its inhabitants, who have neglected to develop it properly as productive agricultural land. The reason for this, Sandys supposes, is that it is

> infested by the often recourse of armies, or maisterfull Spaheis: who before they go into the field (which is seldome untill the latter end of harvest, least they should starve themselves by destroying of the corne) are billited in these rich pastures for the benefit of their horses, lying in tents besides them: commiting many outrages on the adjoyning townes and distressed passengers. (150–151)

The problem once again is one of proper governance: the standing armies of the ever-militant Ottomans make it impossible for the villagers to farm with any security. This is a local example of the precept noted above, where Sandys remarks how dangerous it is to appear wealthy, as this merely marks one out for more persistent rapine and extortion by various bandits and officials. There is "no part [of that country] so barren, but would prove most proffitable, if planted with vines, and fruites," but the lack of security brought by tyranny makes such planting a pointless enterprise that few attempt with any success (152).

WASTE AND IMPROVEMENT IN ENGLISH AGRARIAN LAW

The inevitable result of such poor governance, as Sandys notes, is "waste." In its modern definition, to waste something denotes a lack of proper use, resources that are not being fully utilized, an unnecessary neglect of possibility. This is particularly true in terms of natural resources, including arable land. It was in the early modern period that this understanding of land use generally and of the term "waste" in particular became current, as the old feudal manorial systems gave way to a more capitalistic use of the land. In her excellent article on English New World colonization, Jess Edwards gives the definition of "waste" inherited from medieval English law: it was "the contravention/abandonment of locally engendered, prescribed and regulated configurations of usage . . . what has wasted away is the customary and therefore legitimate identity of a piece of land, and thereby its capacity to transmit the status quo."[10] It was, in other words, land that had fallen from its original and/or proper use. Note that it was *not* necessarily land that was desert or otherwise incapable of being cultivated; waste land at this time could be quite luxuriant in its growth, like the valley through which Sandys passed outside of Hebron that was lush with overgrown and untended fruits, flowers, grasses, and olive groves. It was being "wasted" because it had clearly fallen from its original and proper use, i.e., the careful cultivation of the fruits and grains still in evidence at the site. As on the Mount of Olives, the groves and orchards were no longer tended, and the fields were no longer carefully cultivated with grain; the land had become "wasted." Even more paradoxically for modern readers, land that was being fully and properly cultivated could also be designated "waste," if that cultivation were not its original and traditional allocated function in the community. A tenant who carefully cultivated wheat on a piece of land traditionally reserved for grazing of the lord's cattle, or simply for his hunting pleasure, could legally be understood as farming "wasted" land because such farming was not the use for which the land was originally intended; its "customary and therefore legitimate identity" had "wasted" away, perhaps by means of that very wheat cultivation.

It is not a coincidence that Sandys often notes that in places where the land has been "wasted" only the small number of oppressed Christians still living in the area attempt to tend and cultivate the land. As in the case of the Greeks who continue to cultivate their traditional crops, orchards, and vines, Sandys not only draws a distinction between current agricultural and labor practices (Christians properly husband the land, while Turks both personally neglect it and also cause its neglect through poor governance), he also emphasizes that land now obviously "wasted" through neglect was once traditionally Christian land, fallen from its legal and understood function. Where orchards and vines once flourished, Christians once ruled and husbanded the land. Legally speaking, the land is now "wasted" because its traditional usage has been contravened and/or abandoned by the occupying Turks. Thus, because of the insistent depiction of Turks as unable properly to engage in agriculture, the transfer of land ownership from Christians to Turks essentially guarantees the "wasting" of the land; the linking of religious/national identity to agricultural practices nullifies the possibility of maintaining the legal status of the land despite a change of ownership. Since in medieval and early modern England the legal status of land was linked not necessarily to an owner's deed of title but to a set of customary rights and understandings regarding land use agreed upon by both the owner and entire community of people living on that land (various kinds of tenants and their families), land use generally remained constant even when the lord of the manor changed (through inheritance, death, ruin, etc.). Thus, according to the logic of English understandings of land ownership and use, it would be perfectly possible for lands formerly in Christian control in the Levant to have maintained their customary and thus legal identity despite being conquered by the Ottomans, provided the new landlords respected the rules governing land use "since time immemorial" preserved in the memory of the local inhabitants. By making an inability to maintain or support traditional agricultural practices a national and religious characteristic, Sandys ensures that the land occupied by the Ottomans will never be anything other than "wasted."

To designate land as "waste" was not simply to engage in legal nicety: land that was "waste" became legally available for "improvement." To once again quote Jess Edwards, "improvement" or "approvement" denoted "an owner's monopolisation and harvesting of benefits from a resource previously 'farmed out' to the use of others . . . A legitimate improvement as these statues defined it could only then be one that took possession of a resource for which the prescribed use had been contravened or abandoned, or for which no prescription had ever been made."[11] In other words, the only land open for improvement was "waste" land—land whose prescribed use had been "contravened or abandoned." The appropriation of resources by a landowner could only be effected if traditional claims on the land had withered away, or the resources were not being used in accordance with those traditional agreements. The most frequent example of this in early modern England was the appropriation and enclosure by landowners of sections of their land whose originally designated purpose had fallen out of memory, often including the land usually known as "common" land. Some common lands were appropriated and enclosed by the landlord for the grazing of sheep used in the wool trade, leading to serious diminution of resources for his tenants who used the commons in multiple important ways in their daily life. Such "improvements" were increasingly favored by landowners and sanctioned by law, as land ownership came to be understood less as a traditional set of moral obligations to a manorial community and more as an individual right to use a defined space as the landowner saw fit. Andrew McRae summarizes this shift in his book *God Speed the Plough*:

> [The discourse of improvement, in] its strict distribution of common and waste land privileges individual interest over communal relations, and thus facilitates the gradual formulation of a modern conception of property, as a right "to exclude others from some use or benefit of something." The notion of the manorial land as a resource over which each member of the community would own a particular "bundle of rights" is confronted by a structure which promotes absolute rights and autonomous action. While it need not spell the end for a manor as a social and economic unit, enclosure inevitably undermines traditional concepts of landholding within a moral economy.[11]

As English ideas of land use shifted to a more capitalistic stance, those in favor of improvement (primarily landowners), began to collapse this specific legal definition of the word onto the modern sense of realizing potential—of land being used in a new way to maximize its economic productivity. As Edwards puts it, "The discourse of improvement [championed and adopted by landlords] works to present efficient use—productivity in yield—as an absolute good whatever social bonds its establishment might break, and to present inefficient use as an unqualified evil whatever bonds its maintenance might sustain."[12] Thus, while landowners still sought to make a moral use of their land, and one that would be approved by society and by God, the definition of what constituted moral use was changing. As McRae elaborates, mid-Tudor descriptions of appropriate stewardship were primarily about the treatment of tenants and others on the land; the Edwardian tract *A Prymmer or boke of private prayer nedeful to be used of al faythfull Chirstianes*, presents a prayer "For Landlordes" that includes a long list of moral and financial duties towards the manorial community:

> The earthe is thyne (O Lorde) and al that is contayned therein, notwythstandynge thou haste geven the possession therof unto the chyldren of men, to passe over the tyme of theyr shorte pylgremage in thys vale of misery: We heartlye pray thee to sende thy holye spirite into the heartes of theym

that possesse the groundes, pastures, and dwellynge places of the earthe, that they remembryng them selves to be thy tenauntes, may not racke and stretche oute the rentes of their houses and landes, nor yet take unreasonable fines and incoms after the maner of covetous worldelynges, but so lette theym oute to other, that the inhabitauntes thereof maye bothe be able to paye the rentes, and also honestly to lyve, to nourishe their familye, and to relief the poore: geve theym grace also to ... be content, with that that is sufficient, and not joyne house to house, nor couple lande to lande, to the impovryshment of other, but so behave them selves in lettinge out theyr tenementes, landes, and pastures, that after thys lyfe they maye be receaved into everlastyng dwellynge places: Through Jesus Christ our Lorde, Amen.[13]

The idea that a landlord might, by means of some abstract right of ownership, act autonomously to dispose of his land in whatever way seemed best to him was emphatically rejected by most participants in the debates over land use that raged throughout the sixteenth century. As one forceful pamphlet author noted, "If ther were no God, then would I think it leafull for men to use their possessions as thei lyste ... But forasmuch as we have a God, and he hath declared unto us by the scripturs, that he hath made the possessioners but Stuardes of his ryches ... I thynke no Christian ears can abyde to heare that more then Turkysh opinion."[14]

By the early decades of the seventeenth century, however, this emphasis had changed its focus from the treatment of tenants to the development of land. As McRae asserts, "the clergyman of the middle of the seventeenth century was just as likely to celebrate the godly improver of the land operating within a dynamic market economy." Quoting from Thomas Fuller's *The Holy State*, he notes the shift in prescribed behavior for "The Good Landlord" that "teaches a lesson of industry and economic stimulus" focusing on the efficient use of land: "He is 'a Gentleman in Ore,' who '*improveth his land to a double value by his good husbandry* ... By marle and limestones burnt he bettereth his ground, and his industry worketh miracles, by turning stones into bread'."[15]

Given this profound shift in the moral economy and legal understanding of land ownership and use during Sandys' lifetime—not to mention the serious involvement of two of his brothers in such "improving" projects[16]—it would be a mistake to read the insistent portrayal of Ottoman lands as "wasted" as not being implicated in these debates. The question then becomes what function the designation of Ottoman territories as generally "wasted" might serve. Why does Sandys see Ottoman-controlled lands in the eastern Mediterranean as "wasted" regardless of their level of natural productivity? The answer, I believe, is one that points toward later English colonization of the Middle East, but does not yet advocate or even contemplate English control of Ottoman lands. The relative power differential between the two nations at the time (or rather, the nation and the empire) was such that any English incursion onto Turkish territory would be unthinkable in a rational geopolitical context. Sandys was interested in delivering a realistic assessment of Ottoman power and military might, not engaging in flights of imperial fancy.

That said, the effective function of designating Ottoman lands as generally "wasted" was to render these lands open for a complete overhaul upon the accession of a new landowner. Locally engendered customs of land use that were continuously maintained had the force of law; customs that were broken through the "wasting" of the land (i.e., the contravention or abandonment of these customs) could legally be ignored, and the lands reallocated or remade in whatever way the landlord saw fit. The driving force behind such an overhaul by a landlord was the desire for "improvement," in the modern sense of an increase in productivity and revenue. Land that could be legally "improved" by the landlord was free to be improved in the capitalistic sense of the word, regardless of the objections of the local inhabitants, who no longer had a say in the allocation or use of the land. Rendering the entire Ottoman Empire "waste" meant that a new owner might exploit its natural resources in any way that he saw fit, regardless of whatever local customs might hold at the time, since they represented contraventions of original use and therefore were not legally binding. It is here that Sandys' humanistic learning is put to use. His ability to see both the land as it currently is and as it was depicted verbally by ancient authors enables him to identify the land as wasted, and its current uses (or lack thereof) as contravening original and customary usage.[17] Sandys can select any number of ancient accounts of the land in order to show the differences between ancient and early modern usages and buttress his claim that this land was "waste." Furthermore, Sandys' habit of emphasizing the negative differences between the ancient and modern (the insistence on "ruin") effectively links him to the discourse of "improvement," where any changes made by a new owner would be seen as an absolute good: just as the Ottoman's neglect of the land's potential (its "ruination") is depicted as immoral, so would the "improving" of the land by Christians be seen as an essentially moral, as well as legal, act.

The ideological links to later British imperial discourse should be fairly clear, however, as stated above, I do not believe Sandys is engaging consciously imperialistic rhetoric in describing the Levant as he does. Instead, I would argue that Sandys is attuned to the agricultural potential and legal status of the lands he sees as a consequence of his social position as a noble lord in England. This choice of focus is part of Sandys' ethos as a traveler witness, adopted as a consequence of his own identity in England and that of his audience. As he notes explicitly in the text, trade is "no part of my skill or profession" and therefore, for the most part, he "forbeare[s] to mention" it (86). What *is* part of his skill and profession as a noble English landowner is the management of agricultural lands and other natural resources. Traders would be little interested in Sandys' incessant discussions of crops and orchards, vineyards and mines, except insofar as they might indicate a possible commodity to import. The land is discussed from the perspective of a landowner and is meant to speak to a readership of landowners, who were themselves deeply engaged in issues of capitalistic productivity and of legal waste and improvement.

THE ETHOS OF A GENTLEMAN

Another way in which Sandys constructs the ethos of a noble landowner and similarly implicates himself in the discourse of improvement back in England is through his choice of images and of grammatical person. One of the major shifts in the representation of the good landowner in English agricultural discourse as presented by McRae is the placement of the lord on his manor. The discourse of moral landownership inherited from medieval manorial tracts portrayed the ideal landlord as "manuring the land with his footsteps," in other words, walking (or riding) frequently across his lands in order personally to supervise their management. By the mid-seventeenth century, the prosperous and right-minded landlord is depicted in his study, surrounded by surveyors' maps of his lands, all carefully cataloged on paper from a bird's-eye view, and possibly even worked into his coat of arms.[18] Like the landlord with his maps, Sandys uses visual images to project the power, knowledge and control of the armchair landlord over the lands he describes while carefully retaining the claim to experiential knowledge as well. Many of the images in the *Relation* are drawn from overhead, and thus position both Sandys and the reader/viewer as in full possession of the land or building in question. At the same time, such depictions deny, or at least de-emphasize Sandys' own firsthand experience of the buildings or lands which he walked, sailed, or rode through—not flew over or viewed from space.

These overhead images are complemented with several cityscapes that *are* portrayed from the perspective of a land- or sea-bound traveler (see fig. 1). The beautiful woodcut of Istanbul/Constantinople, for example, gives, as the caption indicates, a "Prospect of the Grand Signiors Seraglio from Galata" (32).

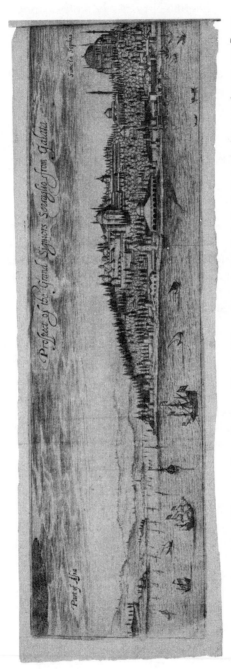

1. "Prospect of the Grand Signior's Seraglio from Galata," from George Sandys' *A relation of a iourney begun an: Dom: 1610* (1615). By permission of the Folger Shakespeare Library.

The viewer is thus placed within the landscape, and is even given a speci-fied location within it, i.e., Galata. Here we are presumably given a sense of what Sandys saw while traveling outside the main part of the city. Yet, while his placement in the story is thus highlighted, it should be noted that the city is still presented from far away, and Sandys is the presumed focalizer of the picture, not its subject. The reader/viewer is reminded of the bank of experience within the author, but the author is not implicated in the foreign scene depicted. Sandys sees the heart of Istanbul just as the reader sees it—as a distant skyline. He is aligned with the reader and not with the foreign city.

This visual alignment of Sandys' knowledge of Mediterranean lands with his noble reader/landlord's increasingly omniscient and passive knowledge of his own land finds its narratological analog in the differ-ence between first and third person narration. Roughly three-quarters of the text is in the third person, and the remaining instances of first person usages are rendered in such a way as to keep the author carefully separate from the foreign places he describes. In accordance with this goal, Sandys rarely depicts himself as an actor in the *Relation*. Instead he draws upon his classical learning to discourse abstractly upon cities and lands, often commenting on places he clearly could not have travelled personally, and interrupting the narrative with pages-long historical accounts of peoples and sites. While Sandys repeatedly claims he is following his "journall" and the lands he discusses do indeed follow the order of his movement through the Mediterranean, he organizes his comments on each land and/ or city more by logical subject groupings than by a paratactic linking of place through his own footsteps across them. In his travels through the Greek Isles, for example, Sandys often (barely) registers his travels from one island to the next by phrases so detached from himself that they are put in the passive voice: "*Val de Compare*, a little beyond presenteth her rockie mountaines" (4). We can assume that she presents her mountains to Sandys' view as he sails toward them, but the traveler himself is thor-oughly occluded in the grammatical presentation of this new land. The furthest he goes in noting his own presence in most scenes of his travels is to record the movement of the ship or caravan using the first person plural: "having past through the Streights that divide this Iland from the next, (vulgarly called *Canale del Zant*) on the second of September we entred the haven of *Zacynthus*, and saluted the Castle with our ordnance" (5). Once within a city, the traveler vanishes altogether as the city's history is recounted, a description of its major architectural features is given, and any other unique details are recounted. Sandys never eats, sleeps, walks, or rides through an urban cityscape. The rare times that direct interactions with Muslims are recorded in the story, they shift into the second person: "What is here sold by the Greeks, you may agree for on a price: but the

Turks will receive your mony, and give you a quantitie for it, according to their owne arbitrement; but truly enough, and rather exceeding, then short of your expectation" (27). Similarly, on certain Islamic holy days "you cannot stirre abroad but you shall be presented by the Dervises and Janizaries, with tulips and trifles, besprinkling you with sweete water; nor ceasse so to do, till they have drawne rewards from you" (57). The implication of this grammatical shift is clear: this would happen to *any* Englishman who visited Istanbul and it is acknowledged to have happened to Sandys only insofar as he is closely identified with "you," the English reader. These interactions therefore serve to reinforce the identification of author with reader, rather than with the foreign places and peoples described. In this telling of the story, Sandys is not set apart by his travels, but is made a representative of his nation, and therefore even more strongly marked as English.

The only way in which Sandys allows himself directly to connect with the foreign is through his eyes. Indeed, the most frequent verb used in conjunction with the first person singular in Sandys' *Relation* is "seen." Sandys seems to use this construction primarily to contradict common wisdom about the Turks, to present something positive about them, or to state something about Turkish behavior or culture that might not quite be credible (these last two categories frequently overlap). He testifies to their generosity to the poor: "they say, they give much in private: and in truth, I have seene but few beggers amongst them" (57); he confutes their reputation for violence (at least toward each other): "during the time that I remained amongst them (it being above three quarters of a yeare) I never saw Mahometan offer violence to a Mahometan" (58). He also claims to have seen that mysterious and tantalizing inner sanctum, the seraglio, in this case one belonging to the empire's most respected "Mufti":

> I oft have bene in this mans Serraglio, which is neither great in receit nor in beautie; yet answerable to his small dependancie, and infrequencie of suters . . . He is not restrained, nor restraineth himselfe from pluralitie of women. His incomes are great, his disbursings little, and consequently his wealth infinite. (61)

Yet while Sandys has "seen" many things about the Turks, and has even visited them in their homes, he is never depicted as exchanging a single word with them, even through a translator. Insofar as Sandys walks through the foreign landscape in his *Relation*, he does so primarily as a disembodied gaze, and not as a man who ate, drank, slept, spoke, or otherwise opened himself to possible intermixing with the foreign.

Given this depiction of himself, it is not surprising that the majority of first person usages in the text do not refer to Sandys' experiences "incountry," but rather to indicate his position as author. He often uses both "I" and what we might term the authorial "we" to order the text, to direct readers, and to explain his logical narrative structure. He begins *A Relation* by stating that "I will forbeare to speake of" France (because that country has so frequently been described) (1) and later, of merchant wares in the Levant (because trade is "no part of my skill or profession") (86). Sandys wishes to present the reader with a text that depicts only less well-known lands, and to do so according to the experience and interests of a gentleman. He uses the first person to refer the reader forward and backward in the text to particular discussion groupings, for example, "(we omit to speake of the Jewes untill we come into Jewry; and now will bend our discourse to the Grecians)" (77), Turkish search and customs procedures "(of which we shall speake in the processe of our Journall)," (26); or the isle of Aex "(whereof we have spoken something already)" (18). As noted here, most of these usages occur in parenthetical comments, thus emphasizing the grammatical separation of Sandys' first person voice from the events and lands described, and aligning him with the reader who is experiencing these lands as a mediated, written text and not in the immediacy of the flesh. Indeed, Sandys emphasizes his closeness to the reader by frequently using verbs that imply an oral conversation rather than an anonymous author/reader connection. One of his favorite constructions is "speaking" in the first person plural: "it remaineth now that we speake of the persons of the Turks" (63), "now next to their wives we may speake of their slaves" (69), "now speake we of their funerals" (71). In his relation of his journeys, Sandys speaks *of* the foreign *with* Englishmen, not with the foreign while abroad. As in the image of the "Grand Signior's Seraglio from Galata," Sandys' experience of the Levant is distanced while his retelling of his experiences is emphasized.

Sandys similarly identifies himself with his audience by using the first person plural to denote things English or Christian. Jesus Christ is mentioned as "*our* Saviour" (11, my emphasis), "the feast of Great Byram" is "observed by them [Muslims] as Easter is with *us*" (56, my emphasis), and one of the "Turkish commandements" is "drawn originally from *our* Saviours" (62, my emphasis). English children and dogs are compared to those Sandys sees in Turkey; English spaniels turn out to be superior in breeding—"in beauty not like unto ours, but of a bastard generation" (76)—but the children don't make out as well, the Turks apparently having "generally the sweetest children that ever I saw" (69). Where "we" English really shine, according to Sandys, is in "our" beverages, as the Turks "preferre our beere above all other drinks" (66) despite the prohibition against alcohol. Sandys claims to have witnessed few Muslims leaving the English ambassador's house "unled" (presumably unable to walk so well on their own). The ambassador serves as a focal point for "our Nation"

(85, 86) in the Ottoman Empire, and his residence is the only place Sandys admits to staying while abroad. Indeed, references to staying with or seeking out English (or "Franke") ambassadors, consuls, or ships make up five of the eight times Sandys uses the first person singular to note his actions while in the Greek Isles and Turkey (i.e., in all of Book I, totaling eighty-six pages). Otherwise, Sandys uses the first person singular to make authorial comments on the text, to give eyewitness testimony (both described above), or politely to express an opinion or clarify his meaning. This final usage is numerically the most frequent and once again emphasizes Sandys' status as a learned gentleman. Such parenthetical niceties punctuate the text as they would a conversation, politely asking the reader for leave to speak with such phrases as "if so I may speake," "if I may so tearme it," or "as I may say" (75, 83, 77).[19]

In fine, Sandys carefully controls the grammatical constructions in his text so that he is consistently aligned with his English readers, and in particular those of a certain social standing (landowners, polite gentlemen). He also makes sure carefully to seal off any undue contact with the foreign places he describes, so that "Sandys the traveler" remains at all times uncorrupted by the places through which he travels.[20] "Sandys the author" reinforces this impression by casting the entire relation as a polite conversation with the reader about the lands of the Ottoman Empire, a conversation in which he is particularly well-informed, but not substantively different from his interlocutor. Both Sandys the author and his reader together experience the Levant in a mediated, textual manner, and it is they who are presented as interacting. Sandys the traveler is merely a character in the book, who doesn't appear in person in more than a quarter of the narrative even while his journals are understood to be governing the order of the story. Like the landowner who is reading Sandys' text, Sandys can discuss the lands he now "knows" while distant from them, through the use of maps, books, and a firm sense of "owning" that knowledge of the land while not in any way being owned by it.

LANDFALL IN VIRGINIA

Sandys reflects the shifting definition of the understanding of waste in England by combining both the medieval and the modern usages of the term: the lands of the Ottoman Empire are wasted both in contravention/ abandonment of traditional usage (as evidenced by all the ruins of various sorts), and in the sense that it is brimming with resources that are not being properly cultivated and utilized. The natural riches of those lands are being left un- or under-utilized because of the misgovernment of these lands. Every agricultural ruin testifies to natural potential in the land that is being wasted, and begs for improvement by a responsible and godly landlord. To bring these lands into their full agricultural potential would be a moral, even a religious, act.

Although differing immensely in their character and history, the lands of the Americas were also legally "waste" lands by the contemporary English definition of the word. Waste was land whose traditional usage had been abandoned or contravened, but it was also land for which traditional, locally agreed-upon usages had never been defined. While the Americas were obviously dense with such understandings between the local native inhabitants, the English were not privy to such traditional agreements and considered the land wasted, and subsequently legally open to improvement.[21] By applying the concept of waste to the Levant, and constantly evaluating the ways in which governance encourages or depresses proper stewardship of the land's resources, Sandys shows himself to be in line with the colonizing project. More specifically, he demonstrated his agreement with the goal of the Virginia Company leadership, which was to bring the waste lands of Virginia into a high state of agricultural cultivation and resource utilization. As would eventually become the case, the American colonies were designed not only to be self-sufficient, but to provide England and its trading companies with raw natural resources for it to sell at home, or to refine and export for resale abroad. The land and its resources were to be brought to a state of maximal yield, a plan that was both godly and lucrative at the same time.

Sandys arrived in Virginia with that vision of agricultural plenty and high-yielding stewardship of natural resources intact. Unfortunately, an assault on the English colonists made shortly after his arrival by Opechancanough (brother and successor to Powhatan) and the several nations under his command rendered such plans impossible unless the safety of the colonists could first be assured—a task made nearly impossible by the company leadership's habit of giving land grants so large as to be quite distant from each other—and thus Sandys' descriptions of his improvement plans for Virginia are all made in the wistful subjunctive.[22] He wrote to his brother Miles, a notorious "improver" and drainer of the fens, that

Vpon this occasion [the attack] wee drew the remainder [of the colonists] Close together, whereby they might haue beene the better gouverned, and haue added to their lyues both comfort and securitie presentlie wee should haue begunne to fortifie Townes, to haue built framed houses, to haue planted hortyards and gardens to haue inclosed ground for our Cattle, and set vpon more reall Comodities, by wch the Collony in short time would haue growne strong, beautiful, pleasant rich and reputable.[23]

This vision of the colony as "strong, beautiful, pleasant, rich and reputable" by means of careful cultivation and care of crops and of stock arises in several of Sandys' letters to friends and family back in England. Writing to Samuel Wrote, Sandys once again lays out this vision for the colony, so hampered by native hostility and company policies:

> Lastlie, whereas it was the onelye benefit *wch wee reapt from the treacherie of the Indians in drawing ourselves into a narrower* Circuite, whereby the people might haue beene better gouℓned, and lived with more Comfort and securitie, publique Charges more easilie defraied, forces raised with lesse difficultie, and hazard to the Remaynder, townes in short time would hayue beene forfeited, framed houses erected, Orchards planted, and ground impailed for the keeping of cattle, staple Comodities the better aduanced, strength, beautie, pleasure, riches and reputaĉon added forthwith to the Collonie.[24]

Sandys' dreams of a community surrounded by "hortyards and gardens," "orchards," "cattle," and "staple Comoditites" was not to be seen during Sandys' time in Virginia, wherein colonists continued to starve for lack of basic sustenance, in part because almost all the colonists—including Sandys—soon abandoned corn and other staples for the more lucrative, if less ethical, crop of tobacco. As Englishmen starved and died, and efforts to produce such lucrative and honest products as silk, glass, and wine faltered, the company leadership became increasingly frustrated with the colonists' abandonment of their georgic ideal in favor of planting the "devil's weed." As historian Edmund Morgan notes, Virginians "would not grow enough corn to feed themselves, but they grew tobacco as though their lives depended on that. As a result, all of [Edwin] Sandys' projects faded away . . . the tenants on both the public lands and the particular plantations scorned the various projects assigned them, so that by 1623 it was reported that 'nothinge is done in anie one of them but all is vanished into smoke (that is to say into Tobaccoe).'"[25]

The tight link between good governance and orderly abundance, sanctioned by God and harmoniously enacted by men, that Sandys puts forth in his descriptions of the Levant clearly represented an abstract ideal that was frustrated by real conditions on the ground in Virginia. The very citation patterns of the *Relation* signal both the intense desire for and the slightly unrealistic nature of such a goal. Although Sandys quotes from many classical sources, passages from Virgil's *Aeneid* and Ovid's *Metamorphosis* occur more frequently than any other work. (Sandys would go on to render the first English translation of the *Metamorphosis* in the years following his trip to the Mediterranean.) The founding of an empire, and the transformations that would need to take place for this to happen (in this case in the land itself), were clearly on Sandys' mind as he journeyed through the Levant, or at least as he was preparing his rhetorical presentation of those travels. Indeed, the former scenario is not unlikely, as Sandys had already been listed on the second Virginia charter when it was granted by James in 1609, indicating his involvement with the company's colonizing projects even before he left for the Levant in 1610. Just as the small selections of the *Metamorphosis* found in the *Relation* served as the basis of Sandys' translation project, accomplished during the quiet nights in Virginia, so the living example of the Ottoman Empire and its Roman predecessor, so often evoked in the *Relation*, provided Sandys, in the form of good and bad exemplars, with a foundation for the imperial governance he would help to establish in Virginia.

The ironic fact that Sandys himself participated in the destruction of his brother's georgic ideal (and reputation) by employing the same unscrupulous and profit-driven land practices as the other major land-owners and councilmen of Virginia did not affect Sandys' standing as a man of "approved fidelity, sufficiency and integrity."[26] Even after the crown reasserted its direct control of the company in 1624, removing Edwin Sandys from his leadership position, George was reappointed to the colony's governing council. Upon his return from Virginia in 1626, he was appointed a gentleman of the privy chamber of Charles I. Beginning in 1631, Sandys served on a royal commission which gave advice on the state of the colony in Virginia, and in 1638 he was appointed to the subcommittee for foreign plantations under the Laud commission.[27] Sandys was clearly seen as a capable and favored advisor on how England should best manage her colonies abroad. His travels and his carefully crafted book describing those travels helped to create that reputation and ensure Sandys' success among England's highest nobility. His judgments on proper land management and his descriptions of the lands under Turkish governance must have been taken seriously enough to justify or at the very least not injure Sandys' bid for positions of trust in the new American colonies. In other words, both Sandys and his depictions of the Levant were given credit. Both his reputation and his means increased through this transformation of travel into words and words into credit.

In the following chapter, I will examine three English gentry who traveled to the Levant and beyond, in an effort to turn travel to credit. Unlike Sandys, however, the Sherley brothers were notably unsuccessful in translating their travels into the kind of reputation that inspires appointments to positions of trust within the government. Indeed, the Sherleys failed so spectacularly in this project that they are generally dismissed in the secondary literature as a species of early modern buffoon, "errant knights" whose "misadventures" provoke more amusement than anything else.[28] Yet the Sherleys were popular enough in their day to command significant audiences and readerships when the tale of their travels was presented to the English public. The generic, social, and rhetorical question of why "true" accounts of travels succeed with some and fail with others will direct my exploration of the Sherley family's fortunes and the written records of their lives.

2

"The Robe of Truth": Fabricating Credit from the Sherley Brothers' Travels to Persia and the Ottoman Empire

LIKE SANDYS' *RELATION OF A Journey*, the corpus of materials detailing the exploits of the three Sherley brothers in Persia and the Levant were almost all composed with the aim of improving the Sherleys' position in English society. Many of them sought to do this by promoting a political and mercantile alliance of England with Persia, a goal of the embassies led in part by Anthony and Robert Sherley on behalf of the Persian Shah, Abbas I.[1] Unlike Sandys, however, who died a well-respected and reasonably affluent nobleman, the Sherley brothers all died stripped of royal favor and virtually penniless. Despite three attempts, the embassy's mission was never carried out, the Sherley family lands passed into other hands within their lifetime, and that branch of the family essentially died out with their deaths. The rather awkward question that the Sherley literature thus poses for the literary critic is, what to do when language fails?

As scholars who study language we tend deeply to believe in its efficacy in the world, and whole sections of our discipline have been devoted to identifying and tracking the deployment of particular linguistic configurations—tropes, for example—believed in some fundamental way to have shaped history. But what happens when a rhetorically crafted discourse meant to do some work in the world fails utterly to achieve its goals? These "failed" texts are still perfectly amenable to the analytic methods we usually deploy. It is still possible to perform a compelling reading detailing how well the published works are crafted to perform their particular tasks. From there, it is easy to assume the success of the literature from the quality of its craftsmanship, and then project praise and acceptance of the piece onto a largely inaccessible historical audience.

Unfortunately, when that audience finds a way to speak, what it says can be rather disconcerting because it doesn't always agree with our polished readings and breezy conclusions about the persuasiveness of particular texts. Although it is logical to expect that not all readers will be impressed

or convinced by a particular text, we lack the methodological language to
account for this, because, while we routinely examine in depth how a text
works internally, we largely ignore the specifics of how it works in the
world, often skipping from individual passages to broad national or period-
specific discourses.[2] But how can critics begin to address the rhetorical
effectiveness of a text in its own time? To use the evaluative language of
generations past, none of the Sherley materials are literary masterpieces.
To say that they are badly written, however, merely replaces with later
aesthetic judgments the essential question posed by these texts. After all,
lots of "bad" literature is extremely popular when first published.[3] So why
do these texts fail to do their work in the communities for which they
were written? Some might argue that this is a question for historians, but
I would argue that such situations result in part from failures in rhetorical
judgment—of audience, of authorial ethos, of the management of generic
expectations—and are therefore appropriate subjects of study for literary
critics as well. Addressing such areas is particularly important when the
texts in question make truth claims about their content. Why do some
claims gain the status of an accepted truth and others become something
less: just a good story or even a dismisssable lie?

The first question to ask when approaching such materials is thus "by
whom and for whom were these 'failed' texts composed?" In the case of
the Sherley materials, one intended audience was certainly the royal circles of power in which the Sherleys once moved and to which they desired
to return. The other may have been more local—shop owners, investors,
and other creditors to whom the Sherleys owed money and who routinely
threatened to throw them in prison if the debts were not paid. And while
the fate of the Sherley family speaks to how profoundly they failed to
impress the first group, their popular legacy as heroic travelers of the early
modern era, like Drake or Cavendish, registers their success with the latter. Samuel Purchas fittingly ranks them among the best of his *Pilgrims*,
claiming that "[a]mongst our English Travellers, I know not whether any
have merited more respect than the Honourable, I had almost said Heroike
Gentlemen, Sir Anthony & Sir Robert Sherley."[4]

This chapter will explore the limits of the Sherleys' discourse and consider why it succeeds with one large section of English society, and why
it fails so profoundly in another. It will take on part of what Anthony
Parr calls the Sherley paradox: "that their exploits and endeavours were
for the most part entirely abortive, and unpopular with people of influence in England, yet they attracted in the period a considerable literature, much of which is dedicated to enrolling them in the pantheon of
the nation's worthies."[5] Unlike Parr, however, I will not be passing over
the "circumstantial" details of each text's context of production; the ways
in which each true account of the brothers' activities was produced and

published, and the generic and rhetorical choices made by each author will play a central role in my story. For it seems to me that an examination of the pressures that helped shape the composition of each account and affected its presentation of the Muslims each brother met and engaged in their journeys is the right place to begin when attempting to paint larger pictures about cultural discourses that shaped communities and national histories. It is particularly important in the case of the Sherleys because their mixed success with readers points to a shift taking place in English society regarding England's place in the world and the role of England's gentry within it, and the epistemological rift that was beginning to occur between stories that catered to those who chose to retain their traditional beliefs, and to those who sought to change them.

THE SHERLEY (MIS)FORTUNES AND THE NEED FOR CREDIT

In 1585, the Sherley family looked to be as firmly footed as that of Sandys, if somewhat lesser in scale. Sir Thomas Sherley the elder was a successful courtier to Elizabeth's favorite, the Earl of Leicester, and would soon reap the fruits of the earl's affection in the form of lucrative government posts. When Leicester was sent to the Netherlands to assist the Dutch in their war against Spain, Sherley accompanied him; when Leicester incurred the queen's anger for accepting the governorship of the Low Countries, it was Sherley who was sent back to England to try to placate her. Sir Thomas was appointed Treasurer at War and was also allowed to maintain a company, the latter being the most lucrative position one could hold in the army. He was soon estimated to be making, through legitimate means and dishonest embezzlement, nearly £20,000, an astonishing sum at that time. It seemed that the Sherley fortunes were on the rise.

The queen soon became suspicious of the vast sums continually demanded by her officials in the Netherlands, however, and eventually peremptorily declared that she would send no further funds until she had an honest accounting of where the money went. Moreover, Burghley wrote, the queen wished for "a good declaration made in particular how Sir Thomas Sherley hath paid such great sums as (she saith) he hath had."[6] Despite royal scrutiny, supported by his patron Leicester's encouragement and his own acumen, Sir Thomas remained Treasurer at War and continued to embezzle the queen's money until 1597, well after Leicester's death and over a decade after he first received the post.[7] When the queen finally called Sir Thomas to account, his books were so enigmatic that ultimately no one—least of all Sir Thomas— could produce the clear account demanded by the queen. It was clear to those charged with investigating the matter, however, that Sir Thomas owed the crown a staggering sum of money. The crown postmaster, who served as an informer to Sir Robert Sidney, noted in 1597 that Sir Thomas "accepts no bills of exchange, keeps his house and can hold up his credit no longer." Soon the good gentleman was completely "broken"; as the postmaster wrote, "Now I may boldly write unto you that he is fallen . . . Sir Thomas Sherley's suit is that Her Majesty may suffer him to sell his lands for her satisfaction . . . and seems resolute that his debt to the queen is small; but the world thinks otherwise."[8] The queen thought otherwise too, rendering Sir Thomas and his heirs—Thomas, Anthony, and Robert Sherley—both "fallen" and deeply in debt to the Crown.

One of the central problems of the "fallen" courtier was the completeness of his collapse. Once it was clear that a previously powerful and wealthy gentleman had incurred the wrath of his sovereign, no one could risk being associated with that person in any way. No one could speak in his favor; no one could work to his relief. The process was highly ritualistic, characterized by speed and the absoluteness of the ruin:

> the instantaneity of the fall results . . . from everybody dropping the courtier who seems to be losing the favor of the prince . . . Once the prince has decided to drop somebody, nobody could save the victim without joining him in his ruin. The widespread withdrawal of support from the falling courtier fit the interest of the prince by speeding up the courtier's expulsion."[9]

In Sir Thomas' case, the shock of losing his good name and all his support and position at court was compounded by the heavy debt penalties laid upon him by the queen's ministers. It was found that Sherley owed the queen £23,000, and while it was also concluded that he himself was owed £18,000 by a partner he had hired to manage his affairs, that man was unable to pay, and so both sat in the Fleet prison for some time. Ultimately, Elizabeth released Sir Thomas, but required that his lands be placed in the hands of trustees until the income they generated could pay back the sums he owed. This left Sherley and his family very little on which to live, and they were a very poor family indeed for many years, eventually losing the family lands at Wiston permanently.

Gentlemen who, like Sir Thomas, lacked ready money had several modes of credit available to them, the simplest being that extended by tradesmen who agreed to supply food and goods to their noble customers, trusting that they would honorably pay their debts once money became available. As Lawrence Stone notes, however, this method of borrowing "is regulated by the basic financial resources of the debtor. Those whose need is greatest are least likely to find their tradesmen obliging."[10] Unless tradesmen had faith in the honor and ultimate financial solidity of the debtor, they were unlikely to be obliging in extending credit. Similarly, one could pay for goods and services by paper documents, such as promissory notes or bills of exchange. Such paper credit instruments often circulated as money at a time when coinage was scarce; the one who held the note would endorse it and make it over to someone else, who could collect from the note's original debtor whenever they chose. Such a circulation of notes extended credit over longer periods of time, but it ultimately relied on the buyer's trust that the original debtor would indeed repay the money when asked. Bad notes—those whose debtor was thought to be unreliable—circulated like hot potatoes, with the last person aware of the debtor's poor reputation left holding the worthless note.[11] Promissory notes and bills of exchange "required a great deal of trust and confidence to be functional, and therefore they could only circulate within close-knit groups."[12] The reason for this lay in the need for each new holder of the note or bill to have solid information about the honor and finances of the original debtor; without such knowledge, one risked buying a bad bill.

It is in this way that reputation played a crucial role in securing credit. A fallen courtier like Sherley, who had just lost his reputation and all of his support at court (and thus any hope of regaining his position there), was not likely to be extended much credit either by local tradesmen or the unofficial moneylenders of Elizabethan England: the rich merchants, tradesmen, and lower court officials. All of these people would be aware of Sherley's position, and skeptical of his ability to repay loans. The fact that he had lost his reputation and position due to financial mismanagement and lay in heavy debt to the queen could also hardly have helped inspire much enthusiasm for dealing with Sir Thomas or his family. In order to change this situation, the Sherleys would have to regain their reputation for honor and for favor among the nation's great. To gain financial credit, they would need reputational credit.

The search for credit led all three of Sir Thomas's sons—Thomas, Anthony, and Robert—to take to the seas. In doing so, they followed the advice of successful world traveler Francis Drake, who in 1583 had written a poem commending such a course to aspiring gentlemen:

> Who seekes, by worthie deedes, to gaine renowme for hire:
> Whose hart, whose head, whose purse is prest, to purchase his desire;
> If anie such there bee, that thirsteth after Fame:
> Lo, heere a meane, to winne himselfe an everlasting name.
> Who seekes, by gaine and wealth, t'advaunce his house and blood:
> Whose care is great, whose toile no lesse, whose hope, is all for good
> If anie one there bee, that covettes such a trade:
> Lo, heere the plot for common wealth, and private gaine is made.[13]

The Sherley brothers clearly shared Drake's view of the possibilities that traveling offered one who sought to gain renown and fill his purse. Thomas the younger launched a series of privateering voyages, primarily

to the Mediterranean, with an eye toward Turkish shipping. Anthony and
Robert journeyed as far as Persia, only to return to Europe as ambassadors from the Persian shah in a bid to unite Persia with Christendom in a
league against the Ottomans. Each of them sponsored a series of publications detailing their exploits in Islamic lands, seeking to turn their travels
abroad into credit at home. For their stories to work in this way, however,
they needed to be regarded as true, and not just travelers' lies. They also
needed to portray the Sherleys' actions, whatever they might be, as heroic
and worthy of great esteem. Fortunately, these requirements dovetailed
nicely with the fiscal goals the printer had for each pamphlet, as the story
of heroic English actors promoting England's fame in an exotic land might
expect to sell extremely well. In the pursuit of these joint goals, the details
of the Sherleys' voyages, as well as the rationale for those journeys, were
often altered. More importantly, the nature of the foreign lands described,
and Persia in particular, underwent all kinds of alteration and editorial
manipulation. As discussed earlier, such changes in the particulars of the
story did not necessarily undermine a given publication's claims to be
true, although the Sherley pamphlets certainly stretched this generic flexi-
bility to its limit in relation to Persian identity. Painted as ignorant pagans,
pseudo-Turkish skeptics, Zoroastrians, Christ-haters, sectarian Shiites,
politic secularists, enemies of our Turkish enemies and thus friends, enemies of our Turkish enemies and thus useful . . . the Sherley publications
wrest Persian national and religious identity in every direction in order to
achieve their rhetorical goals.

The remainder of this chapter will explore the ways in which the Sherleys sought to use their travels in Islamic lands to regain credit in England,
and the writings they used in the course of that project. I will examine
several of these publications in detail, to see the ways in which they sought
to convince readers and spectators that their story was true and their protagonists worthy of esteem. Drawing on the conventions of popular news
pamphlets, stage plays, court panegyrics, and prose travel narrations, the
authors of the Sherley corpus used every generic resource at their dis-
posal to please their patrons and their customers alike in a bid to generate
money and social credit out of the labor of travel.

1600–1601: THE PERSIAN EMBASSY ARRIVES IN EUROPE

In 1598, Anthony Sherley and his brother Robert left England bound for
Italy with a large party of soldiers with whom Anthony and his patron, the
Earl of Essex, hoped to intervene in the succession dispute in the duchy
of Ferrara. The dispute was resolved by the time they arrived, and so
Anthony continued on to Venice, where he ruminated for several months

over how to deploy Essex's men and money to achieve the glory he had fruitlessly sought in Ferrara. He settled on a journey to Persia, for reasons that changed with each audience or reader and remain somewhat obscure today. After a stay of less than six months at the court of the Persian Shah Abbas I, Anthony departed that land as one of the shah's ambassadors, leaving his brother Robert behind as surety for his successful return. He returned to Europe in the summer of 1600, leaving the Russian port of Archangel in one of the Muscovy Company's many ships and landing in the city of Stade at the mouth of the Elbe River.

Anthony had left England without the queen's license, and was aware that he had likely incurred her displeasure. He was also aware of the oddity he presented in returning to Europe as ambassador from an Islamic prince. He would need the queen's permission to enter the country, and he would need to prove his status as an official representative of the shah in order to have any opportunity to transmit the shah's proposals to Elizabeth. He would also have to overcome the objections of the Levant Company, which had spent years developing England's relationship with Turkey in tandem with the queen; the merchants would hardly appreciate an Englishman bringing proposals for a military alliance against the Ottomans. It was customary for a ruler to send an escort out to meet the arriving foreign ambassador, to arrange lodgings for the ambassador and his suite near the court, and to provide him with a stipend while in residence. These preparations took advanced notice, and the ruler's reply to such notice would indicate the level of favor with which the ambassador would be received. Fortunately, Anthony had several destinations on his route through Europe, and thus plenty of time to try to smooth his passage to England before putting the matter to the proof. He began by sending his traveling companion, William Parry, back to England in an effort both to drum up publicity for his eventual arrival in the country, and to lay the groundwork for his claims to legitimacy. Parry transferred from Anthony's ship to a passing merchant vessel off the coast of Holland, and arrived in London at about the same time that the embassy began its journey across the Continent. Shortly thereafter, an anonymous news pamphlet was printed by J. Jaggard and R. Blower with a title that emphasized Anthony's official status as ambassador and highlighted the profit his journey had yielded to English merchants: *A True Report of Sir Anthony Shierlies* [sic] *Iourney . . . his Letters of Credence to the Christian Princes: and the Priviledg obtained of the great Sophie, for the quiet passage and trafique of all Christian Marchants, throughout his whole Dominions.*

The pamphlet is a conglomeration of small pieces. There are several sections of news summarizing Anthony's journeys, one "oration" reported verbatim to us in Anthony's voice, and two copies of important

ambassadorial documents. The latter are entitled "Coppie of Sir Anthony
Shirlies letters of Credence from the great Sophie, to the Christian Princes"
and "Coppie of the free Priviledges obned [sic] by Sir Anthony Shierlie,
of the great Sophie, for all Christians to trade and trafique into Persia." By
printing his "verbatim" speech, the pamphlet evoked the classical histories that sought to glorify the deeds of great men; by printing the letters
of credence, the pamphlet used the formal features of a letter to bolster
Anthony's credibility, relying on the mixed nature of news reports, their
frequent epistolary origins, and their habit of printing official government
documents after the narrative report to guarantee the legitimacy of the
printed "letter." The *True Report* thus employed the conventions of both
history writing and foreign newsprint in its efforts proactively to legitimate Anthony's status as ambassador.

The presence of the speech and the letters at the end of the pamphlet
marks a pointed shift from what is a standard mix of descriptive narration of events and traditional reported speeches by the hero of the tale to a
more modern, documentary approach to credibility, one made famous by
Richard Hakluyt in his 1589 *Principall Navigations* in the sections entitled "Ambassages, Treatises, Priviledges, Letters and other observations
depending upon the Voyages." As Barbara Shapiro notes in her discussion
of evidence in both early modern law and history, documents, "long part
of the lawyer's domain,"

> increasingly became a part of the historian's. In some kinds of historical
> investigation documentary analysis and interpretation would become more
> important than first-hand witnessing. Lawyers and historians examined
> charters, deeds, and legislation, acquiring the philological learning neces-
> sary to authenticate, date, and interpret these "testimonies" often in order
> to determine current rights and settle current disputes.[14]

The increasing appearance of printed letters or other documents in popular histories (like those included in news reports) indicates that presenting
information in the form of a "true Coppie of a letter" was also becoming increasingly well-regarded by these printers and readers. Frequently
printed at the end of narrative sections detailing current events, these
documents repeated information imparted in the first half of the pamphlet
in different form, and with different rhetorical expectations. Such documents were presented as beyond editorial interference, printed wholesale
as received from "reliable sources."

Caught between two separate conventions of historical truth, these documents acted in two contradictory manners. First, they hearkened back to
the primacy of the firsthand participant of perfect history, borrowing from
the status and credibility associated with that form of history writing. First
person verbatim statements made by "the great Sophie" reproduced in

miniature the greatness of the perfect history author writing about current events of great magnitude in which he himself participated. When
Anthony Sherley is paired with the sophie through a similarly "verbatim"
reply, he shares in the prestige of that position. Yet paradoxically, such
documents also moved further from the traditional conceptions of historical truth exemplified in the perfect history. Within that traditional form,
the author's greatness acts as a buttress to already agreed-upon cultural
truths, which in turn stand as proof of the author's distinction by virtue
of his understanding of and participation in deeds that exemplify these
truths. That circle is interrupted when such authorship is excerpted into
bits of letters and declarations in which the author's status is made to stand
witness to previously stated events, which are themselves under question.
In such pamphlets, truth lies not in the moral of the history and the great
man's role in the divine pageant of history, but rather in its *authenticity*;
the epistemological question has shifted from how an understood truth
has worked itself out in the world in the events described, to whether the
events described ever "really" occurred. Unedited documents and the status of their authors are made to stand witness to this latter query, improving the credibility of the previously given report of events.

One of the documents in the anonymous Sherley pamphlet has an additional rhetorical twist. The first printed document is itself a letter of credence. This doubling of the function of documents in a history such as that
of the Sherley pamphlet has the effect of both magnifying questions of
credence and answering them emphatically in the affirmative. The shah's
letter of credence for Anthony touches upon several things that must have
puzzled Englishmen who heard of Sherley's travels: why did he and his
brother Robert go to Persia in the first place, how could they have gained
so much trust and favor in Persia so quickly, and why would England wish
to form to alliance with Persia? Indeed, when Anthony's autobiographical
account of his journey was printed thirteen years later, it was prefaced by
a note to readers that referenced exactly such questions:

> Many have beene desirous to understand on what hopes, helpes, and
> grounds, Sir Anthony Sherley, with his brother Sir Robert Sherley, and
> many other friends and followers, of our Nation, could not onely be
> induced to undertake to travell into a Kingdome so farre remote, and to
> live amongst a people so farre different in Religion, Language, and Man-
> ners, as that of Persia is from ours: but also be supplied of all necessaries
> for life, in a plenteous and magnificent manner; and so highly endeare his
> service and industry to that King and State, as to bee esteemed and called a
> Mirza, or Prince of Persia, and to bee employed, within few monthes after
> his comming thither, as Embassador from so great a Potentate, in a matter
> of such maine consequence and trust, to many of the greatest Princes and
> States of Christendome.[15]

The letter of credence in the 1600 pamphlet does not offer to answer the questions, but to attack directly the uncertainty at the root of such queries. The shah claims repeatedly that Sherley came to Persia "of his owne free will out of Europe" implying that Sherley came on purpose to "remove the vaile that was between us and you [Christian Princes]." This task might have been accomplished long ago except that there "was none that came to make the way." The "great Sophie" presents Anthony as the human link between his country and those in Europe, binding them together and making "Friendship betweene you and me." The alliance with Persia is thus presented as *a fait accompli*—Sherley the Englishman speaks with the voice of the Persian king and "you shall Credite him in whatsoever you shall demaunde, or he shal say, as mine owne Person."[16]

It is with this statement that the function of the letter shifts from a single function as witness to the truth of previous reports to a double role of witness and speech act. If the letter is indeed the printed representation of the ruler's word, then it renders Sherley's voice into that of the shah whenever the document is read. This speech act simultaneously lends a powerful boost to the credibility of the "True Report" and establishes the absolute credibility of Sherley's embassy in Europe. With these words, Anthony is shown to be trusted implicitly in Persia and must be so in Europe, at least in his status as Persian ambassador. The statement repeatedly enacts the living link between England and Persia through the medium of Anthony's body, a body that could then be metaphorically figured into the corps of a joint Anglo-Persian army, standing in vital opposition against the common enemy, the Ottomans. Printing a letter of credence in a pamphlet meant to promote the embassy and to confirm or boost Sherley's credibility before his arrival in England elevates the function of documentary evidence in this short history; evoked as a witness to the accuracy of reported events, this letter *makes witnesses of its readers* to an embassy already metaphorically accomplished through the living link of Sherley himself.

This publication and that of William Parry, who printed his own autobiographical account of the journey in 1601, were in many ways successful in arousing the enthusiasm of the Londoners who read them or heard about the journey by their means. [17] By the time the embassy began to break up in the summer of 1601 in Rome, references to the Sherleys had begun showing up in the popular writings of the day, reflecting relatively widespread knowledge of the brothers' exploits. They even occur in the Shakespearean oeuvre: *Twelfth Night*, performed in February 1602 and possibly as early as January 6 (Twelfth Night), 1601, contains two references to Englishmen in the service of the King of Persia. In Act Two, Scene Five, Fabian watches with delight the duped Malvolio ruminate on his upcoming greatness, and exclaims "I will not give my part of this sport for a pension of thousands to be paid from the sophy." Later in the play the sophy returns once again as Sir Toby attempts to frighten Sir Andrew with elaborate lies about Cesario/Viola's fencing prowess: "Why, man, he's a very devil. I have not seen such a firago. I had a pass with him, rapier, scabbard, and all, and he gives me the stuck-in with such a mortal motion that it is inevitable; and on the answer, he pays you as surely as your feet hit the ground they step on. They say he has been fencer to the sophy." [18] Both the vast wealth the sophy was believed to have, and the generous gifts he had lavished on the Englishmen, Anthony and Robert Sherley, were clearly points of great interest; equally so was Anthony and (especially) Robert's rumored military assistance to the shah. Robert's participation in several of Abbas I's campaigns spawned elaborate rumors of the Sherleys' impact on Persian military history, which survived unchallenged in English histories of the region for hundreds of years. Unfortunately, the advance publications and messengers sent by Anthony were less successful in fascinating the queen, whose fury at the meddling minor nobleman continued unabated. She refused to allow Anthony back into the kingdom, ambassador or not, leaving him stranded when the embassy dissolved in Italy, unable to return to his homeland and unwilling to return to Persia after failing to secure any results for the shah.[19] The Sherleys' first attempt to translate their travels in Islamic lands into credit in their own with the assistance of the popular press had failed decisively.

SUMMER, 1607: SIR THOMAS SHERLEY'S CRUSADE AGAINST THE TURKISH TRADE

After spending three years in a Turkish prison, Sir Thomas Sherley the younger returned from his last privateering expedition in December 1606 to find the family finances in the same precarious position as when he had left four years before. Thomas' own activities had not improved matters. Having scraped up enough credit and investors to float and man three ships destined for lucrative privateering ventures off the coast of Spain and North Africa, Thomas had lost all three ships and returned with nothing but his memories of ignominious capture in a small Greek coastal village.[20] The trip had gone poorly almost from the start. After having been abandoned by his other two ships, which had become impatient with the fruitless voyage (and presumably with Sherley's command), Thomas weathered a minor rebellion on his own vessel, placating the mutinous crew by promising to attack the next possible target, whether legal or not.[21] Poor weather drove them into a port on the Ottoman-controlled island of Zea, which was populated largely by Greeks. In January of 1603, Sherley landed and attacked one of the villages near the port, seeking booty enough to satiate the rumblings of the crew. Unfortunately for them, the villagers had been warned of their coming and had fled with all of their valuables into the nearby hills. There was nothing of value left in the town. While the crew was still searching the town, the villagers returned armed and in greater numbers; the marauders turned and fled. Most of the crew made it safely back to the ship; Sherley and two other men, however, were taken prisoner.[22] After suffering three very uncomfortable years in a series of Turkish prisons, Thomas was released upon the direct intervention of King James. He returned home by way of Italy, spending considerable time at both Venice and Florence and making many close friends there.

Upon his return, Thomas immediately sought to parlay his experiences in the Mediterranean into an improved financial position at home. Despite the spectacular failure of his privateering expeditions, Thomas presented himself as a highly knowledgeable and capable actor in the region's affairs. His first project was to act as an intermediary between King James and a community of Levantine Jews who sought to settle in England, or barring that, in Ireland. Thomas argued to James that while allowing the Jews the freedom to settle and practice their religion in England might be distasteful, the community was largely made up of merchants. Once these merchants had set up their businesses, they might be an excellent source of (forced) loans to the state; such a practice had been followed by many Christian sovereigns in the past, and had been highly lucrative. Thomas, as agent for the wealthy Jewish community, could hope for a good commission from them if his petition to the king were successful. He also sought to make himself the permanent intermediary between the crown and the Jews should they settle there, noting that "at the first they [the Jewish immigrants] must be tenderly used for there is great difference in alluring birds and handling them when they are caught; and your agent that treats with them must be a man of credit and acquaintance amongst them who must know how to manage them, because they are very subtile people."[23] Painting himself as a man of credit among the Levantine Jews was a means for Thomas to gain a possibly lucrative position managing crown affairs, and thereby to make himself a man of greater credit among his English compatriots.

Another way that Thomas sought to present himself as a man of honor with great experience in Mediterranean affairs was to sponsor two popular representations of himself and his brothers—a pamphlet composed by the hack writer Anthony Nixon and a stage play collaboratively written by John Day, William Rowley, and George Wilkins.[24] The pamphlet was registered on June 8, 1607 and the play was performed at the Curtain Theatre sometime that same summer, roughly six months after Thomas' return to England. At the time, Thomas was not only in pursuit of the Jewish resettlement project, but was also seeking by various means to disrupt the English trade in Turkey and thereby divert those resources to

Venice and Florence, England's main competitors in the region. Thomas would be arrested and imprisoned that fall for "overbusying himself with the traffic of Constantinople, to have brought it into Venice and to the Florentine territories," according to one contemporary.[25] During the spring and summer of 1607, however, he pursued his project unaware of the official scrutiny being given to his correspondence and with good hope of gaining his object, along with much wealth and reputation by way of a grateful James and his many friends in Italy. The primary way in which he hoped to effect his plan was to bring to the attention of royal officials the fact that Levant Company merchants routinely sold arms to the Turks, causing a general hatred of the English by other Christians in the region and insulting the King's dignity and reputation as a pious Christian ruler. Thomas noted that his time in Turkey had made him aware that "all Christians there did exclaim against the English for furnishing the Turks with powder, shot, musket barrels, brimstone, cordage, and other kinds of munitions, and because our English rovers did make their rendezvous in Turkish harbors, selling both the goods and persons of Christians to the infidels." As he later reminded the government ministers who questioned him on the matter, upon returning home he attempted to "tell your Lordships of certain abuses (as I took it) offered to His Majesty by the English merchants in Turkey, whereof some Your Lordships condemned in the merchants, some you regarded not."[26] Thomas hoped that such zealous care for the reputation and spiritual well-being of his sovereign would be looked upon with favor, and secretly expected generous thanks from his friends abroad as well. It was at this uncertain time, with two projects set to enrich his status and coffers, that Thomas commissioned the two popular representations of his exploits in the Ottoman Empire and his brothers' journeys in Persia.

Both the pamphlet and the play can be described as having two main goals: to present the Sherleys in a heroic light and to do so by highlighting their joint efforts to weaken the Turkish enemy. The latter is a plausible link between the brothers' disparate activities in the region, and also fits in well with traditional understandings of heroism, developed during the Crusades and kept alive in sermons, popular pamphlets, and stage plays. Furthermore, it worked beautifully as a solution to the problem of how to represent the Sherleys' exploits—so easily described as a long series of spectacular failures—as the work of admirable men.

While the pamphlet could take this rhetorical tack and run with it, the playwrights had a slightly more difficult task. The play needed to work as a play, and yet, for it to serve the goals of its patron, Thomas, it also needed to be regarded by its audience as a relatively honest account of the Sherleys' activities abroad. The playwrights therefore make strong claims for the "truth" of their story, maintaining, like all the authors in this study, that their tale has a truth value superior to that of the overtly poetic representations of Muslims that had previously walked the stage, such as *The Jew of Malta, King Cambyses,* or *The Merchant of Venice.* The authors of *The Travels of the Three English Brothers,* however, were also working within a generic tradition that included such so-called "chronicle" plays as *The Battle of Alcazar* or *Sir Thomas Stukeley* that depicted recent events or starred still-living Englishmen, like Stukeley. So, by 1607, there were recognized generic conventions in place—both for stage plays performed at this time in London and for chronicle plays in particular—that Day, Rowley, and Wilkins could follow when writing, and that the audience could expect to see. In this sense, *The Three English Brothers* is unique in my study, as the rest of the single-pamphlet travel and news reports I examine belong to genres that were extremely irregular and unstable in their conventions. Day, Rowley, and Wilkins had several accounts of the Sherleys' activities in Persia and the Levant on hand,[27] but they had the delicate task of balancing theatrical convention against the details presented in their sources, meshing drama with prose history. Generally speaking, the authors more often sided with Philip Sidney in choosing to present a "golden" history of a more perfect Sherley than was included in their sources, than to mar their tale with all the gory details.[28] The specifics most manipulated were those dealing with the Sherleys' and the Persians' respective identities. Both of these areas of uncertainty were beautifully controlled to match the requirements of the genre, creating an entertaining piece of drama that must have simultaneously pleased the playwrights' patrons.

In order to achieve the desired presentation of the Sherleys and their story while remaining within the bounds of dramatic expectation, the authors played heavily on their audience's ignorance of Persian geography and religious beliefs. For example, in the very first scene of the play, Sir Anthony Sherley is advised by the Persian governor of Qasvin to set off his ship's cannons in greeting to the newly arrived Persian shah, or sophy, as the English mistakenly named the Persian ruler.[29] This traditional honor would be all the more impressive in Persia, given that the thundering of such "high tongues of war . . . ne'er was heard in Persia/ Till you [Anthony] gave voice to them at Qasvin first."[30] Anthony gracefully assents, sending his younger brother Robert off to supervise the firing of the guns. This courtly scene is plucked from the middle of the story of Anthony and Robert Sherley's journey to Persia and sets the stage for the martial themes dominating *The Three English Brothers.* Dramatically, it is a well-chosen beginning, given that the play centers on the brothers' relationship with the Persian ruler and their subsequent military activities on his behalf. Had contemporary readers or audiences been familiar with Persian geography and history either through earlier Sherley pamphlets or other sources, however, they would immediately have caught two rather large mistakes: namely, that the Sherleys arrived by ship—or that it would even be possible for them to arrive by ship—and that the Persians were unfamiliar with large artillery pieces.

Qasvin was (and remains) a landlocked city many miles south of the Caspian Sea. The Sherleys, by their own account and that of others, traveled overland through Turkish territory, beginning at Aleppo and passing through Baghdad before arriving via caravan in Persia. Indeed, when coming from Venice there was no other practicable route than sailing around the Cape of Good Hope and up into the Persian Gulf, before once again switching to overland travel. In fairness, the same ignorance of Persian geography extended to the audience might be attributed to the playwrights as well; yet it is difficult to offer the same excuse for the change in route taken by the Sherleys into Persia. Nixon's pamphlet, as well as other pamphlet accounts previously published in 1600 and 1601, are perfectly clear as to the overland route followed by the Sherleys. It seems certain that the change in the play was deliberate.

As to the erroneous account of the Persians' military expertise, what begins as a small inaccuracy about the use of heavy artillery in the region soon blossoms into downright exaggeration, as the sophy's court overreacts with comic naïveté to the firing of the guns. "Mahomet! It thunders," cries a courtier. "Sure this is a god," murmurs the great sophy in awe:

> First teach me how to call thee ere I speak.
> I more and more doubt thy mortality.
> Those tongues do imitate the voice of heaven
> When the gods speak in thunder; your honours
> And your qualities of war more than human.
> If thou hast godhead, and disguised art come
> To teach us unknown rudiments of war,
> Tell us thy precepts and we'll adore thee.[31]

Neither the modern nor the early modern audience could miss the echoes of reported New World encounters, as Pagan King offers to worship Seafaring European because of the vast military powers displayed by the latter. Sherley's military prowess is only enhanced by this echo; Persian cultural identity, however, suffers as it is reduced to that of the "uncivilized" natives of the Americas.[32]

The authors made a conscious decision significantly to alter the Sherley story as they knew it, a *modus operandi* that they justified in the opening chorus of the play. It begins with an immediate interrogation of the "truth" of the "historie" about to be presented, spoken by the Chorus "attired like Fame." Fame justifies the liberties taken by the playwrights with an extended culinary metaphor worth quoting in full:

Our scene is mantled in the robe of truth;
Yet must we crave, by law of poesy,
To give our history an ornament
But equalling this definition thus:
Who gives a fowl unto his cook to dress
Likewise expects to have a fowl again.
Though in the cook's laborious workmanship
Much may be diminished, somewhat added—
The loss of feathers and the gain of sauce—
Yet in the back surrender of this dish
It is, and may truly be called, the same.
Such are our acts. Should our tedious muse
Pace the particulars of our travellers,
Five days would break the limits of our scenes
But to express the shadows. Therefore we
(Leaving the feathers and some needless stuff)
Present you with the fairest of our feast,
Clothing our truth within an argument
Fitting the stage and your attention.
Yet not so hid but that she may appear
To be herself, even truth.[33]

The distinguishing feature of the genre of history, "particulars," clashes here with the practical requirements of drama, and clearly the playwrights see themselves as operating within both realms, although primarily in the latter. Should they attempt to represent every moment of the Sherleys' journey, the play would last nearly as long as the journey itself did. Severe abridgment of the history is called for, and various "ornaments" are allowed to help weave the pieces together. The adaptation of a history into the medium of "poesy" compels the playwrights to alter the material of the story as they have received it. The choices they make are thematically significant, but the problem is at root a generic one. But so too, according to the playwrights, is the solution. For implied in such lines as "Clothing our truth within an argument" is the assumption that the "truth" of the Sherley history lies outside an allegiance to detail or "argument" that here signifies the subject matter or themes of the play. The "truth" is made manifest through her clothing in such subjects or thematic matter, but she exists independently of these particular trappings. This may be an early case of poetic license ("the law of poesy") altering the facts in order to produce a more artistically graceful presentation of the moral/philosophical/religious truth contained within the tale, but it is assisted by a parallel assumption regarding the nature of the travel history that they are importing onto the stage. The dramatists can change the "particulars" of the story without sacrificing its "truth" value because the notion of truth in history need not be coterminous with the "accuracy" of its "factual" description. As in medieval histories, or the single-publication news pamphlets that will be treated in the next two chapters, a Renaissance history, conservatively read, can be "truthful" regardless of the configuration of the details.[34] The law of poesy approves the same laxity in detail as traditional history writing: both allow manipulation of particulars as long as the essential "truth" of the story is maintained. These two generic allowances meet in the history play *The Three English Brothers*. The playwrights are presenting in the Prologue a slightly defensive and folksy metaphor meant to invoke this conservative and entrenched understanding of the genre of history, which, when combined with the license given to poets, more than permits them to alter the details of the Sherley story in writing their play. The "truth" of the Sherley story will be unimpeded by their literary plucking and basting of the history's particulars because the particulars were never the keepers of truth, only its vehicle.

This appeal to the more traditional understanding of truth in history is a significant statement on behalf of the playwrights as to the manner in which they saw their presentation of a foreign culture functioning in English society. The authors clearly invited—and expected—their audiences to reconfirm their belief in traditional English understandings of the matter presented in the play. As expressed in the prologue of the piece, John Day, John Rowley and George Wilkins conceived of their work as a confirmation of certain truths already known and accepted within their culture, not as a challenge to them. What, exactly, constituted that "truth" in *The Three English Brothers* remains to be considered.

Certainly one of its primary truths was the continuance of Christian heroism, in the shape of Thomas, Anthony and Robert Sherley, "worthy subjects" inspiring the very "idea and shape of honour." The printed play's dedication reads "To Honour's favourites, and the entire friends to the family of the Sherleys, health," and later "to all well-willers to those worthy subjects of our worthless pens, we dedicate this idea and shape of honour."[35] Presenting three heroes engaged in honourable deeds in three separate locations was not an easy task, artistically speaking, however, and it stretched to their limits the structural possibilities of the short dramatic piece.[36] Nor were the Sherleys being overly helpful in the creation of their roles as English heroes. To wit, Thomas the elder was still embroiled in the scandal of his financial mismanagement of the late queen's money; Thomas the younger's activities have already been summarized above; Anthony had been actively pursuing an anti-Turkish alliance contrary to England's trade interests and was currently working for the King of Spain, having already converted to Roman Catholicism; and Robert was still resident in Persia, having taken a "Persian" wife, and was rumored also to have converted to Catholicism.[37]

Yet, once molded to fit familiar dramatic conventions, the Sherley brothers were an easily acceptable trio of heroes, bound together by their anti-Turkish activities: Thomas as defiant Turkish captive, Robert as Persian captain, and Anthony as fighter and ambassador. The opening scene of the Sherleys' shipboard military salute to the approaching sophy is followed by a mock demonstration of the manner of Persian and Christian styles of battle, with Anthony and Robert fighting against one another for the sophy's pleasure.[38] Even before this joint display of military technology and personal prowess, the sophy seems overwhelmed by the two brothers, wondering "What powers do wrap me in amazement thus?/ Methinks this Christian's more than mortal./ Sure he conceals himself! Within my thoughts/ Never was man so deeply registered. But God or Christian, or whate'er he be,/ I wish to be no other but as he."[39] The martial demonstrations that follow serve to confirm the admiration of the sophy, who is plunged into ecstasy at their offer of military service. The playwrights present the Sherleys' heroism as military glory achieved while fighting for the Christian faith; it is this decision that necessitates the shifts in plot detail analyzed above. The sophy's recognition of the English brothers as highly worthy fighters and noblemen is given a rationale in the cannon fire and military display that follow. It is these examples of their worth that set the stage for their appointment as Persian generals and their glory-filled battles against the Turkish enemy. Clearly an example of the poets' plucking and basting of the Sherley story in order that it might fit comfortably on the stage, the playwrights substitute a stock character motif for the set of perplexing questions that often recur in relation to the Sherleys: why did Anthony and Robert go to Persia in the first place? Why would anonymous English travellers be placed in positions of trust and power in the shah's army? And who were the Persians anyway?

The popular confusion surrounding this last question, especially as it related to the Persians' religion, was emphatically dispelled by the playwrights' treatment of the issue. Turks and Sherley antagonists are Muslim; the Persians, therefore, are not. Hostile Persian characters are made to exclaim "By Mahomet!" in order to emphasise their similarities to the archenemy Turks; the king and his loyal supporters worship the elements and not the Prophet. An explicit discussion of religious difference between the pagan Persians (later to be revealed as hostile characters sympathetic to Islam) and the Christian Anthony Sherley takes place in the lengthy Scene Two, won (as you might expect) by the Christian, although not through theological acumen. Sir Anthony rather abruptly ends the debate by declaring that he will leave Persia rather than hear Christ's name abused and threatens to withdraw his offer of military assistance to the king in his wars against the Ottomans: "You then, that scourge my Saviour with your words,/ My sword hath no assistance for; nor this arm/ A growing strength to bear in your defense." This proves too much for the sophy, who begs

Anthony, "worthy Englishman, and worthy Christian," to stay, claiming that he "cannot lose a mould of so much worth."[40]

Thus the Persians are presented as pagans (something that only one other Sherley account does) in order clearly to demarcate the heroes from the enemies: the Sherleys are soldiers fighting for the glory of Christ against an expansionist Turkish Islamic enemy, and those who oppose the Sherleys within the Persian court are constantly allied with these enemies through references to Islam. Those who, like the sophy, admire and support the brothers are presented as allies ripe for conversion, a process that will be accomplished through the brilliant example of the Sherleys' military might. The sophy eventually promises to preside over the christening of Robert's child and gives religious freedom, including the right to build churches to all Christians; however his "pre-conversion" status is apparent from the first scene as he wishes that "God or Christian, or whate'er he [Anthony] be,/ I wish to be no other but as he."[41] The presentation of Persian identity is modified to fit neatly into the play's function as hero worship, simultaneously answering the question as to why the Persian ruler might favor two random English strangers who stumbled into his land.

The reason that the play gives for the Sherleys' presence in Persia is also provided by the traditions of their genre. As noted above, the reason for the Sherleys' journey is rather unclear; the seven different published accounts list or imply nearly as many possible reasons. The answer provided by the play is therefore as logical as any: Anthony speaks as an unemployed soldier, complaining of the recent cessation of war in England following the peace made between James I and the Spanish.

> All princes league with us, which causeth us
> That wont to write our honours down in blood,
> Cold and unactive. To seek for employment
> Hither am I come, renownéd Persian.
> My force and power is yours, say but the word,
> So against Christians I may draw no sword.[42]

While anachronistic in the Sherleys' case, this was not an uncommon sentiment on the stage in the early years of James's reign, and fit nicely as an explanation for the Sherleys' journey to Persia. As Nabil Matar has noted, many inactive English soldiers were presented in the drama of this period as pursuing or considering employment in Islamic armies in Morocco and elsewhere.[43] This was a reflection of a very real social problem, a problem not unlike that faced by the Sherley family during Elizabeth's reign: what should those traditionally employed as soldiers do in a time of peace to maintain themselves and their families, or in the case of the nobility, their wealth and status? Anthony Sherley's explanation for his presence in

Persia as stated in this play would not then be unfamiliar to his audience, and would place him in the growing ranks of English stage heroes who fought on foreign soil, displaying the glory and might of English Christian soldiery. The popularity of such a hero would be unquestionable, as would the integrity and religious inviolability of the man himself. The playwrights' decision to cast the Sherleys as Christian warriors battling for the glory of Christ against an acknowledged enemy not only made the story generically recognizable to a playgoing audience, it accomplished the goal demanded by the play's patrons—to glorify the Sherley family.

In order to effect this basic understanding of the relative position of the three main groups of characters (Turks, Persians, and Sherleys), details could be eliminated, added, or manipulated. The history-within-the-play could have its plot entirely remade, its speeches fabricated, and its geography altered, and still remain a legitimate history. The play-of-the-history could make legitimizing claims about the "truth" of its presentation, borrowing status from its more respected generic half, and expect support from the living breathing Sherleys to whom it was dedicated. Difficult questions surrounding the Sherleys' actions—such as why they might go to Persia in the first place, why this foreign king might accept and honor the English brothers, and why the Persians should not be viewed as religious enemies unworthy of any association—all dissolved before the powerful image of the crusading Christian knight. Fighting on the side of right against the forces of evil is the traditional requirement of such heroes, thus simplifying the cast of characters in the long and complicated Sherley tale. The Turks were the obvious villains, both of the stage and of the culture in general, and were known to be enemies of the Persians. In the world of the play, the Sherleys' actions on behalf of the Persians were easily rationalized by this moral simplification, just as the Persians' acceptance of the foreign Sherleys into their most trusted counsels was justified by the brothers' prowess. Similarly neutralized were the suspicions usually attached to those who voluntarily spent long periods of time outside of England, especially in Islamic countries.[44] The play thus functioned as an effective dramatic panegyric on the Sherley brothers, raising their status among the populace, even if it was unsuccessful at appeasing the hostility of the Levant Company merchants or paying off the Sherley family's many debts.

Ironically, the only serious disadvantage to the tack taken by the playwrights in presenting the Sherley history as a heroic tale is that it undermines the very project that gained the Sherleys so much fame: Anthony and Robert's embassy on behalf of the shah. The artistic advantages of presenting the Sherleys as militarily superior to the Persian ruler are discussed above; yet who would want an ally astonished and frightened to the point of worship at the mere sound of a cannon? The sophy is a likable and courageous character who supports both the heroes and their Christian ways almost throughout the play; yet he is necessarily always inferior to his honored English generals, both culturally and militarily. The very thing that makes the Sherleys heroes in the play renders their political goals on behalf of the shah seem less practically desirable in their home country.

The reason this depiction is acceptable, I believe, lies in the timing of the production. Anthony's embassy was well over by 1607 and news of Robert's arrival would not reach Europe until 1609. As far as anyone in England knew, the Persian embassy was dead and the proposed military alliance with the shah highly unlikely. The two Sherleys involved in sponsoring the play, Sir Thomas the elder and the younger, were not invested in promoting the shah's affairs. They merely sought to raise the family honor and reputation for expertise in Levantine matters. Thomas the younger did likely have more specific goals for this publicity onslaught that related to the projects he proposed to King James, but Persia played no role in these.

What Thomas sought to do was disrupt English merchant trade with the Ottoman Empire, and he had both pecuniary and personal motivations for doing so. The means by which he hoped to achieve his goal, however,—revealing to King James and his noble advisors that Levant Company merchants carried on an active arms trade with the Turks— points to a further dynamic at play in this plot, one that both *The Three English Brothers* and the pamphlet by the same name reinforce in their treatment of the Sherleys. Namely, a world in which providing weapons to such religious enemies as the Turks was acceptable for financial reasons was not a world in which traditional aristocratic values inherited from previous centuries could survive. Despite repeated calls for crusade in the early modern period, the time when the nobility gained honor by fighting the infidel in the Holy Land was over, and an era of domination through overseas trade had begun. Minor noblemen like the Sherleys lived in a time of shifting values regarding Anglo-Islamic relations, one in which traditional religious and aristocratic values sat alongside a new nationalism built on mercantile wealth.

So while the Sherleys needed wealth, they sought it in ways that highlighted their devotion to age-old aristocratic ideals of honor. As Anthony wrote of his decision to journey to Persia in the first place, he was anxious "to do some good and extraordinary thing before I returned back," which would bring him "all sorts of reputation" and honor.[45] The way in which the nobility usually gained such honor was on the battlefield, but there were precious few such battlefields under the peaceful rule of James I. Under Elizabeth, gentlemen seeking glory could assist the Protestants in the Netherlands in their war for independence from Spain, or they could attack the Spanish directly by assaulting their vessels and New World settlements and, in the case of Cadiz, their mainland cities. The privateering licenses obtained by Thomas in 1602 were given with a naval assault against Spanish and Portuguese towns and vessels in mind. Under James, those "wont to write our honours down in blood, [are rendered] Cold and unactive" since "all princes league with us."[46] One prince that James had inherited a firm alliance with, however, was the Turkish sultan, and the league did not please him in the least. The author of a lengthy poem celebrating the Christian victory over Turkish naval forces at Lepanto,[47] James was not as comfortable as Elizabeth was with England allying itself with Islamic nations, despite a thriving trade that brought revenue to the crown. News that his subjects had joined in battle against Turkish expansionism would likely receive tacit approval from the new English monarch. James might not have been inclined to lend English troops to the Holy Roman Emperor in his fight against the Turks in the east, but he admired those who, like the Christian knights at Lepanto ("Three thousand venturers brave/ All voluntaries of conscience mov'd"), sought to break the infidel armies.[48] Fighting the Turks, therefore, was an acceptable field in which to obtain glory if you were an Englishman lusting after fame and reputation, and the funds that came with it. What was unlikely to be as acceptable to the English king was news that his own merchants had been providing the Turks with munitions that they would then use in battle against Christian forces in Eastern Europe. Thomas Sherley knew this, and sought to promote the traditional aristocratic valuation of martial prowess against an implacable religious enemy at the expense of the merchants who sought peaceful trade with that same nation.

The tack taken by both the playwrights and Anthony Nixon, the pamphlet writer, show a keen awareness of this dynamic. In promoting the Sherleys' actions abroad, the authors paint the Turks in the darkest possible light, while obscuring, changing, or "leaving aside" the Persians' religious beliefs. They were assisted in the latter goal by the fact that the religious practices in nations east of Turkey were probably more or less a blank for the popular audiences and pamphlet readership of the early seventeenth century. The idea repeatedly affirmed in popular drama and prose was that the Turks were inveterate enemies of Christ and thus of England, an impression that was likely confirmed by the increasingly bold and northerly raids conducted by Mediterranean pirates on English ships and villages.[49] Thus it is unsurprising that the tactic used by Day, Rowley, and Wilkins to identify protagonists and antagonists at the Persian court—i.e., rendering the antagonists more blatantly Islamic and the protagonists open to Christian conversion—was not unique to *The Three English Brothers*. This method of defining allies simply by making them enemies of the Turks (or Turkish/Islamic-identified characters), however, meant that the religious identities of these allies were often quite murky.

The depiction of the country's religion, and the shah's beliefs in particular, clearly show this dynamic at work. There had been two pieces published detailing the Sherleys' adventures in Persia and Anthony's role as ambassador from the "sophy" before Nixon's pamphlet was published and the play performed in 1607. In 1600, a news pamphlet was printed describing Anthony's arrival in Persia and his embassy to Christendom. Except for the fact that the shah's letters are repeatedly addressed to "all you Princes that beleeve in Jesus Christ," his religion is not mentioned at all in this pamphlet. In William Parry's longer 1601 publication, the Persians are correctly described as largely Muslims and the Shi'a/ Sunni split between Turkey and Persia explained, but the topic is obviously one among many and not in any way prioritized in the account, especially as Parry spends only a sentence or two on the issue: "Their devotion, as the Turkes, but somewhat different in religion. As the Persian praieth only to Mahomet, and Mortus Ally, the Turke to those two, and to three other that were Mahomets servants. Against which three the Persian still inveighs."[50] Parry does make it extremely clear, however, that Persian conversion to Christianity is not likely to occur any time soon: "Theyr conceit of Christ is, that hee was a very great Prophet, and a most holy and religious man, but no way comparable to Mahomet: for Mahomet (say they) was that finall prophet, by whom all things were, and are to be perfected and consummated. They further say, that because God had never wife, therefore Christ cannot possibly be his sonne."[51] The shah is understood to be Muslim, although some of his generals and counselors are Georgian Christians.

In Nixon's 1607 pamphlet, Parry's clear description is essentially quoted in describing the Persian's religious beliefs; the reader is then quickly recommended to "leave their religion to themselves, and their conversion to his divine power that hath their hearts in his disposing."[52] The Turks, on the other hand, come in for pages of opprobrium, laced with religious slurs and outrage on behalf of Christians living within Ottoman domains: [the Turks]

> are, & have beene ever the most inhumane of all other Barbarians. Their manner of living is for the most part uncivill, and vitious. For their vices, they are all Pagans, and Infidels, Sodomites, and Liars . . . Their Renega-does are for the most part Roagues, and the skum of the people, which being villaines and Atheists, unable to live in Christendome, are fled to the Turkes for succour, and releefe . . . His chiefest forces by land consist of Janizaries: these Janizaries are al made of the sonnes of Christians, that are taken from their Parents, when they are very young, and are called Tribute children . . . The Turkes are beyond all measure, a most insolent,

superbous, and insulting people, everprest to offer outrage to any Christian, if he bee not well guarded with Janisaries . . . They will not permit a Christian to come within their Churches, for they hold their prophane and irreligious Sanctuaries defiled thereby. They have no use of belles, but some Priest three times in the day mounts to the top of their Church, and with a lowd voice cries out, & invocates Mahomet to come in haste, for they have long expected his second comming.[53]

In contradistinction to the sultan, the shah, in Nixon's account, had not only permitted significant religious freedom to Christians but had stood as witness to the baptism of Robert Sherley's child.[54] He allowed Robert to establish a church (the fact that this church was Roman Catholic is not mentioned), and to raise a handful of children in his house, apart from their native language and religion, so that they might in time learn to speak English and become Christians. Robert, moreover, "labours the King very much to christianisme, to which (it is said) he lends such attentive eare, that he doubteth not, but by Gods assistance and his good perswasions, he may in time bee brought to become a Christian."[55]

The 1607 play echoes this predisposition to conversion on the part of the shah, whose admiration of the Sherley brothers causes him to wish himself like them in all respects. His idolatry of the Sherleys early on causes his Persian generals to insist that "ye Persian gods, look on:/ The Sophy will profane your deities,/ And make an idol of a fugitive." The plural here points to a severe alteration that has taken place in the previous Sherley pamphlet depictions of the Persians: they are no longer Shiite, or even Muslim, but pagans. They worship: the "sun,/ The silver moon and those her countless eyes/ That like so many servants wait on her."[56] Given the perceived "convertability" of pagans in the New World, to whom he is likened, when the pagan sophy agrees to stand as godfather for the baby soon to be born to Robert and his "Niece" at the end of the play, his conversion seems that much more imminent. When Robert is promised churches and special houses within Persia where children may be raised as Christians, the audience can be sure that England's ally against the Turks is very likely to join with them in their religion too.[57]

Thus in both of the pieces commissioned by Sir Thomas Sherley in 1607, the Turks are made metonymically to stand in for all Muslims, understood as the enemies of Christ and Christendom. The Islamism of the Persians is downplayed, altered, or represented as on the verge of Christian conversion. This allows for the presentation of the Sherleys as noble English knights, fighting for honor and glory against a traditional enemy, and it reinforces these aristocratic values at the expense of a worldview in which the Turks are a nation with which England might carry on a peaceable trade in an increasingly interconnected world of nation states defined by their own financial and political interests rather than their participation in a wider European Christendom. Furthermore, both the play and the pamphlet accomplish their rhetorical aims through claiming a high truth value for their story—they are peddling a well-recognized truth, one known to be such from centuries of retellings in various garbs. The Sherleys are merely the latest robe in which this truth is clothed.

Unfortunately for Thomas Sherley the younger, James's ministers were entirely unimpressed by either the Sherleys' exploits or the "truth" they sought to promote through *The Three English Brothers*, pamphlet or play. During the first week of September 1607, Thomas was arrested and imprisoned in the Tower, where he was questioned by the Earl of Salisbury's agents regarding his contacts in Italy and his efforts to undermine the Levant Company merchants. Thomas admitted having written a letter to a friend, who also happened to be nephew to the Venetian ambassador in Constantinople, in which he boasted that he made "no doubt but to shake the foundation of the trade of the English in those parts." He hoped to accomplish this by using "all the forcible arguments [he] could to distaste the State here from continuing the used trade with the Turk . . . plainly declaring the manifold abuses and indignities daily offered to his Majesty's imperial diadem and dignity by the English in those Eastern parts . . . so vehemently did my desires burn to see a disposition in his Majesty to break with the Turks."[58] Thomas might be forgiven for harboring some significant ill will toward the Turks after his imprisonment, and given James' known distaste for dealing with the Islamic sultan, the arguments that Thomas deployed in his own statements on the matter and within the publication and play he commissioned might have expected better success in royal circles. He insisted that while he hoped for some financial recompense from Venetian friends for bringing these matters to the attention of the king and thereby effecting a break in the English trade at Constantinople and Aleppo, his project was an honest one, and that God would better favor his efforts to stop the trade with the Turks than the merchants' efforts to arm them for mere profit. These arguments met with enough success that Thomas was released sometime in the winter or spring of 1608. By 1611, he was back in prison, this time for debt, something which he would now struggle with for the rest of his life.

1609: The Persian Embassy Returns

In February 1608, Robert Sherley left Persia to pick up the work of the embassy that his brother had abandoned several years before. Despite sending numerous ambassadors—often overlapping each other on the way—the shah had yet to establish the military and trade alliances that he desired with multiple Christian nations. Robert journeyed up the Volga River to Moscow, and from there went overland to Poland, where he was well received by the Polish court at Cracow in the fall of that same year. Like his brother, Robert had several destinations in Europe, but he hoped eventually to be received in England, by James, for whom he had advantageous trading proposals. He therefore sent a gentleman named Master Moore from Cracow to London in order to announce his coming. Master Moore took with him some commendatory verses that had been written upon Robert's arrival in Poland, and arranged to have them translated out of Latin and published, so as to boost Sherley's reputation before his return to his home country. The Latin pamphlet, "Encomia Nominis & Negocii D. Roberti Sherlaeii," was written by Andraeas Loeaechius, a Polish scholar who hailed originally from Melrose, Scotland, where he was known as Andrew Leech. [59] The enlarged English version of the pamphlet was composed by the playwright and hack writer Thomas Middleton, and published in 1609 as "Sir Robert Sherley, Sent Ambassador in the Name of the King of Persia, to Sigismond the third, King of Poland and Swecia, and to other Princes of Europe. His Royall entertainement into Cracovia, the chife Citie of Poland, with his pretended Comming into England. Also, The Honourable praises of the same Sir Robert Sherley, given unto him in that Kingdome, are here likewise inserted." This eighteen-page pamphlet is comprised of the following sections: a one-page letter dedicatory from Thomas Middleton to Thomas Sherley the younger; a three-page instruction, "To the Reader;" three pages of "Newes from Persia and Poland, touching Sir Robert;" eight pages of what may best be described as creative panegyric broken into small paragraph-long sections; a closing two-page section featuring the brief anthropological description of the customs of Persia (lifted from the fifteenth book of Strabo's *Geography*); and a closing commendatory poem left in the original Latin.

Middleton's pamphlet adopts many of the same rhetorical tactics used by Nixon and the playwrights in 1607, emphasizing Turkish Islamism, downplaying or altering the same religion in Persia, and cheering the Sherleys' military prowess against the evil Turks. Middleton carries the shah's imminent conversion to Christianity a step further, however, by blithely announcing in an offhanded parenthesis that "the Persian himselfe confess[es] and worship[s] Christ."[60] Indeed, the mission of the embassy itself is described as seeking a "Royall Embassage of honorable, and Christian conferacie against Mahomet & his Adherents." Any nagging doubts about the alliance of powers and religions here are quickly addressed by a description of the Persians, beginning with their religious practices and beliefs:

for their Religion which they have observed of old, doing worship and reverence in their upright zeale to the Sunne, Moone, Venus, Fire, Earth,

Water, and Winds, erecting neythere Altars nor Statues, but in open fields offring their sacrifices, which Sacrifices were superstitious, and full of idle Ceremonies too tedious to be here rehersed.[61]

As G. B. Shand has proven, this description of the Persians and the following cultural information the pamphlet includes is taken from Strabo's *Geography*, a classical work widely available in English translation at the time.[62]

With the release of the Persians from any shade of Islamism, Middleton is free to emphasize Robert's military activities on behalf of the shah. In the context of the renewed embassy, however, his martial prowess does more than merely promote the aristocratic honor of a noble English gentleman. Robert Sherley, as a skilled English warrior fighting alongside Persian allies, is in the course of the pamphlet rendered emblematic of the proposed alliance between Persia and the powers of Christendom. The embassy, it implies, is (once again) made a kind of *fait accompli* through the independent actions of the Sherley brothers, who through their intrepidity in travel, negotiation, and/or war have already achieved a sort of alliance between England and Persia. This is a reasonable argument, given the early modern practice of ascribing the actions of all international actors to their national governments, regardless of whether those individuals were acting on behalf of, or even with the approval of, their rulers. It in part explains why the Sherleys' actions were so irritating to those in power; although they acted without the approbation or guidance of London, as Englishmen they still managed to "queer the pitch of English foreign policy."[63]

Middleton's 1609 pamphlet accomplishes this rhetorical alliance between England and Persia in part by making a virtue of Robert's dual nature as native-born Englishman and (now) honored Persian guest. This is an unusual move. Those who spent significant time abroad, especially in lands as different as Persia, were often viewed with suspicion upon their return to England. The arrival in England of Master Moore, dressed in full Persian regalia, highlighted this cultural issue, which was ultimately to cause some difficulty for Robert in England and therefore for his embassy as well: how could one trust an English-born gentleman who had voluntarily left his homeland, and for over a decade lived in the service of a (very) foreign king? As a piece meant to serve as advance publicity for Sherley's upcoming embassy in the country, the pamphlet might be expected to address this problem, and indeed Middleton's translations and addenda hover persistently about this question, trying from all sides to dampen suspicion and provide a framework within which one could safely place (and praise) Robert Sherley. The questions that sprang up wherever the Sherleys pursued their Persian activities—Why did they go to Persia? Who are the Persians and why should a Christian nation ally with them?—are in Middleton's pamphlet routed through the central problematic of dual identity and allegiance.

As with the play, the answer to these questions was at base fairly simple: Robert was a hero. Indeed, the anagram of his name proclaimed it: "Servus, ast Hero Liber."[64] Here, the martial heroism so admired by the sophy in *The Three English Brothers* is supplemented by other kinds of hero worship: "It is the beauty of thy minde wherewith our eyes are inchanted," the "whole body of the Polish Court" exclaims, or more specifically, Robert's "being able to speake and to answere so many severall nations, in their owne proper languages."[65] Sherley's extraordinariness lies in his status as experienced traveler or "Freeman of all the Cities of the world." His dual national identity is what makes Robert unique and admirable. In a clever rhetorical move, Middleton attempts to convert a possible liability by confronting it directly and describing it as a positive strength.

The fact that the bulk of the pamphlet falls into the genre of encomium allows Middleton to deal with the issue in a more direct manner than a travel history bound in some part to the narration of events. When, for example, "England" is made to complain to Persia "for her Sherley," she can wrestle directly with the fact that Sherley is now an "English-Persian" (one of the earliest examples of hyphenation?):

> O Persia! thou glorious kingdome, thou chiefe of Empires . . . with griefe dost thou inforce me to tell thee, that against all Law of Nations, thou robbest me of my subject. Why should the right of another bee thine? It is Justice for every one to keepe their owne. But thou makest up thy gaine by my losse. Is this Equitie? Is this tolerable? Cease to doe it: and send home (O Persia) that sonne of mine to me that am his mother: for to me onely is he due. But (aye me) the honors of his owne Country, and the palaces of my Kingdome, are by him (belike) neglected and seeme not worth the looking on; And though to the eye of the world I may perhaps appeare beautifull and great, yet in his eye, I shew no bigger then a small corner of the world. I doe envy thee therefore (O Persia) onely for him: yet sithence I cannot enjoy him, Fare thou well, O thou my darling, and with that farewell beare along with thee, the Praises which I give thee. I rob Persia, Persia robs not me: My losse is to mee more honour: for the Persian Empire, borrowes her brightnes from the beames of one of the Sonnes of England.[66]

With this dramatic monologue, Sherley's sojourn abroad and actions on behalf of the Persian king are naturalized into the familiar dynamics of family relations: the son must eventually leave the nest to seek his fortune, but his valiant deeds reflect glory upon the family name regardless of how (and where) they are achieved. Cultural identity is not chosen any more than one's relations: the accident of birth decides both. "England's" final chiastic declaration cements Robert's identity as essentially English:

England's son brings glory to England through deeds that Persians might otherwise achieve. Being a decade in the service of Persia had not succeeded in cutting the tie that rendered Robert's actions a tribute to England (indeed nothing could) and thus he remains inalterably English, regardless of his dress, language abilities, or previous travels. Sherley in some sense belongs to both nations; as the previous encomium summarized, "Let rich Persia enjoy thy presence, and reckon thee in the number of her Citizens, & bee proud in the possession of a man, so worthy: Let England glorie that shee alone, is happy in thy Birth, and that she beares the honor of giving thee thy name." Sherley must not be "quarreled" over but "shared."[67]

It is this international relationship, embodied in the "shared" Robert, that both makes the man praiseworthy and his embassy wise. Several times throughout the pamphlet Robert is praised "as well for his Wisedome and experience, as for his knowledge and understanding of many Tongues."[68] His "Semyter" had been raised often against the Turks; in this embassy he has turned his linguistic and rhetorical skills against the "general enemy." A formal agreement of alliance between England and Persia would merely cement what has been already been rhetorically achieved in this pamphlet: the joining together of "the Dignitie and Luster of two renowned kingdomes."[69] Travel, "the chaine that at first tyed kingdomes together," called to Robert, causing "desire of glorie still more and more [to] burn within him" until he voyaged to Persia and then back again. He was destined to become that chain that would tie kingdoms together and bind all Christian nations against the Turk. The only question that remained was whether England would turn her back on her native son, deny the heroic link that travel had so naturally formed between herself and Persia, and refuse "to give him now a welcome home."[70]

The answer was in fact a quite emphatic refusal in many influential circles in English society. Merchant distrust of the Sherleys had only grown over the years, and merchants had steadily gained wealth and power in English society across the twenty years of the Sherleys' travels. Robert arrived with extremely advantageous trading proposals, which the shah supported in order to divert trade from Turkish middlemen and drain the coffers of his Ottoman neighbor. The King and several of the high nobility thought favorably of this offer, and joined Sherley in purchasing and outfitting a ship to engage in the proffered trade to Persia. Merchants already well established in the Levant, however, reacted with immediate hostility to this development. Those in the East India Company regarded it as an infringement on their charter, which allowed them sole trading rights in the East. In short, the English merchant establishment did not look at all kindly upon the king and his noblemen meddling in established trade, and they were suspicious of the likely success of that offered by Sherley on the shah's behalf. During the second of Robert's two embassies to England, the merchants produced their own counter-ambassador (one of many sent in overlapping fashion by the shah to Europe), who denied Robert's legitimacy as ambassador. They refused the king's orders to help accommodate Sherley, resisted carrying him back to Persia with a representative to check the claims of the rival ambassadors, and generally evaded or outright refused to follow the Privy Council's attempts to clear up the question of Sherley's legitimacy. By the 1620s, London's merchants had gained enough experience and resources abroad and enough credibility at home to be able, if not to claim a monopoly on the truth of events happening abroad, at least to muddy the waters enough to stymie the efforts of the last of the Sherley brothers to gain honor and influence through his travels.

This merchant-led conclusion to the Sherleys' efforts to unite England with Persia—militarily, economically, and textually—reminds us that the Sherleys' success was highly determined by the audience to which they addressed themselves. Pieces detailing the Sherleys' travels were sporadically published in London for over two decades, beginning with the anonymous news pamphlet of 1600 and concluding with Samuel Purchas's treatment of Robert in the 1625 edition of *Purchas his Pilgrims*. As the many popular references to the Sherleys during this time attest, they were quite popular among the London populace reading the accounts of their journeys or watching them on the stage. Their subsequent legacy confirms this. Where the Sherleys failed was at court and among the merchant communities who might have embraced their cultural expertise and/or trade proposals from the shah. The only time a Sherley succeeded at court was when Robert brought trade proposals with no strings attached, which attracted the personal interest of the monarch through the promise of wealth.

I would argue that this discrepancy is due to the increasingly unsettled understanding in England of what constituted aristocratic culture. The Sherley materials very strongly promote an understanding of nobility that is rooted in older definitions of aristocratic behavior: they distinguished themselves through prowess on the battlefield and in statecraft, not through the petty tasks of money making, which was left to commoners who were looked down upon for their venality. This understanding of the distinction between noble and merchant held true for most overseas expeditions as well. As Theodore Rabb has shown, the nobility participated and invested in voyages that promised military glory or an extension of the English state into new territory (colonization); voyages seen as safe money makers were routinely shunned by higher-status investors. Such easy and lucrative trading ventures were supported almost entirely by merchant commoners.[71]

The need for ready money, however, to support a lifestyle that conspicuous consumption demanded by an increasingly absolutist court drove the nobility to push the boundaries of traditional noble activities, as witnessed by King James' interest in the Persian silk trade.[72] The wealth of the merchants was obviously desirable, and the money they brought to England was recognized by the Privy Council and the monarch as extremely important sources of revenue for the state and for the country as a whole. Both Anthony's and Thomas' activities threatened the safety of the Levant Company trade in the Ottoman Empire and were accordingly met with great suspicion by those in power. Robert received a slightly better welcome because he proposed including the court in a lucrative trade that would supplement and possibly rival already-established merchant trading lines in the region.

Thus when the Sherley materials treated the brothers' activities as heroic because they fought against a traditional "infidel enemy," they pitted an older aristocratic identity against the emerging power of wealth brought by overseas trade. They also pitted, against the violent fractiousness of the post-Reformation political landscape, an older pan-European Christendom in which religious unity against Islamic nations mattered more than internal divisions. Purchas's praise for the Sherleys registers this dynamic, calling them "Heroike Gentlemen . . . And if the Argonauts of old, and Graecian Worthies, were worthily reputed Heroicall for Europaean exploits in Asia: what may wee thinke of the Sherley-Brethren, which not from the neerer Graecian shoares, but from beyond the Europaean World . . . have not coasted a little way (as did those) but pierced the very bowells of the Asian Seas and Lands, unto the Persian centre."[73] Although the Sherley depiction of aristocratic martial prowess and religious piety had not yet reached the point of nostalgia, they were clearly marked as traditional. This familiar and well-loved depiction of errant knighthood obviously appealed to the portions of the English populace who did not have to deal with the realities of European political alliances and the desperate need for ready money, which could not be gotten from traditional land revenues. Those who could afford to revel in tales of English heroism on far-off battlefields and in courts, where the infidel Turks were fought and the princes of Christendom allied together with a new Eastern ally (of uncertain religious affiliation) to oppose his terrifying expansion across the globe, did so. These audiences loved the Sherley tales. It is due to their popularity with those groups that the Sherleys are enrolled in the annals of such Renaissance adventurers as Drake and Raleigh. Those in power were clearly aggravated by the Sherleys' activities, and found their arguments impracticable in the world in which they now found themselves. By the time the Turks had become settled trading partners and important sources of revenue, it was not only indulgent but dangerous to hearken back to earlier crusading paradigms of aristocratic honor. Time had sailed on in the culture of the English aristocracy, and the Sherleys' insistence upon recognition for their anti-Turkish activities only showed that they had missed the boat.

This shift in attitude toward the Turks was not limited to aristocratic culture. Other areas of English life were affected by the political and religious realignment brought about by the Reformation in ways that can be tracked through evolutions in the genres promising "true" stories of the world outside England's borders. Foreign newsprint was one of the genres most obviously affected by these shifts in the political landscape, as the general London populace sought true news on events happening on the Continent and beyond. Across the fifty-year period of this study, the genre of popular newsprint changed dramatically as readers sought to gain "truth" from published reports of foreign events, and the truth they sought shifted along with the form of the news itself. In the following chapter, I will examine these changes in foreign newsprint and the truth that they communicated to readers about Islamic lands, exploring the most widespread and accessible means for Englishmen and women to receive true stories about foreign peoples and cultures.

3

True News from the Islamic World

THE PREVIOUS TWO CHAPTERS ANALYZED TEXTS WRITTEN to promote particular individuals and their skills as diplomats, governors, soldiers, or courtiers. Their efforts involved a careful consideration of the character of their readers in order most convincingly to create an ethos that readers would consider credible. The truth of the tales they told about Islamic lands was wrapped up in their efforts to establish their own credibility and advance their place in English society.

In this chapter, we turn to a genre of prose narrative that was both anonymously written and seriously lacking in social credibility: newsprint. News publications, although extremely popular, were regarded as one of the least reliable ways of obtaining information about foreign events or locales. For those who had neither the connections nor the money to maintain a network of correspondents abroad or to travel themselves, however, newsprint was one of the primary ways in which they received word of the world outside England's borders. And as the acquisition of this information became more important to English readers, they became more heavily involved in the crafting of the genre, communicating their needs and desires to news editors and printers, and developing strategies for vetting the credibility of given bits of news in order to obtain the most reliable story possible.

This chapter will explore the changes in form that occurred in English newsprint across the late sixteenth and early seventeenth centuries, looking at the ways in which those formal shifts were driven by readers and the kinds of "truth" they sought about foreign lands, and about Muslims in particular. The need for credibility was just as prevalent in this anonymous form of prose account as it was for Sandys or the Sherleys, but because of its eventually serial nature, that credibility could be developed in dialogue with the readers who purchased such publications. As in the previous two chapters, I will argue that the financial side of the "credit" authors sought for their accounts of foreign lands put pressure on the form of the tale they told as well as the "truth" they presented about far-off lands. But whereas the noble travelers treated above sought their rewards within the patronage system of noble "friendship," for the producers of news, establishing credibility was an openly commercial imperative. Although the understanding of "truth in reporting" changed across the period, news always needed to be true in order to be sold.

THE NATURE OF NEWS

Newsprint is rarely studied by literary critics, largely because of its ephemeral nature. Most of the prose that styled itself "newes" was not considered worthy of keeping even by contemporaries, and so scholars are left with a relatively small number of extant sources in comparison to what was printed. Furthermore, none of these were ever thought to have had much literary worth and, indeed, their authors had few if any pretensions to such an accolade. It may therefore be useful to take a moment to describe what will likely be a fairly unfamiliar genre to most readers, even those well versed in the literature of the period.

We should begin by acknowledging and then putting aside the vast amount of private newsletters as well as the oral gossip sent and brought back from abroad. Oral news is as old as antiquity, and stories contained in private letters have a similarly ancient pedigree. There has been considerable recent scholarship discussing the intersections of printed, handwritten and oral news; the point that these three sources are intimately intertwined is well taken. Different writer-reader relations and social structures were implied in each method of transmission, diverse levels of credibility were expected and extended, and the coinage paid for the news in each format varied. Therefore, while keeping in mind the cautions given by scholars such as Ian Atherton and Richard Cust, our quarry here will be the printed news publications that arose nearly coeval with the press itself, and insofar as it is possible to separate printed material from letters (which is not very far) we will attempt to do so.[1]

The genre of news in early modern England accommodated extraordinary variations in form. In fact, throughout the period under discussion, news appeared cloaked in formats sufficiently different and numerous that as a genre it is difficult to classify; most were short, cheaply printed pamphlets styling themselves "news," "reports," "histories," or "discourses."[2] Almost all of them advertised on the title page that the ware they were selling was "true," and frequently also "certain," "credible," or "trustworthy."[3] Protestations of the truth or credibility of the stories printed in these news pamphlets were the most salient features of news reports and, indeed, one of the only relatively consistent things about early modern news reports, especially in the sixteenth century. Thus, for my purposes, the definition of "newes" is anything that described itself as a "true" tale of contemporary events. This definition makes room for the full variety of printing styles, lengths, formatting, and content that characterize such material; it also eliminates a few modes of popular printing that functioned in ways similar to news.[4]

In buying this "true, credible and certain newes," sixteenth- and early seventeenth-century news readers bought printed pamphlets of two to forty pages in length, of which the information contained within might be any-where from weeks to months to even years old (the "current" in "current events" needs to be somewhat flexible here). Indeed, printers often repub-lished particularly popular news stories of years past, merely changing a few titles, names, or details; the story of one John Fox (1579), originally printed as a pamphlet in 1579, reprinted in Hakluyt's *Principall Naviga-tions* in 1589, and then reprinted again in 1608 under the name of John Reynard is typical of this practice.[5] Most current news came excerpted from private letters, or from material compiled by postmasters and passed along with each shipment in the newly organized Continental postal sys-tem. The best news printers were those with access to regular letters from private correspondents abroad; post material was more widely available, as were oral reports brought back to London by travelers, merchants, and sailors. Since the printing of domestic news was banned in England at this time, news pamphlets dealt only with foreign news, peddling stories from the Continent, Africa, the Mediterranean, the Levant, and occasionally the New World.

In 1622, the previously open market for newsprint shifted somewhat when James I granted a royal monopoly for the printing of foreign news to five members of the Stationers' Company: Nathaniel But-ter, Nicholas Bourne, Thomas Sheffard, Bartholomew Downes, and Thomas Archer. The group did not long stay together: Archer left after two years to start up a rival news series, by which time Sheffard and Downes had also left. Butter and Bourne continued on, and in 1625 began also using the alias *Mercurius Britannicus* instead of specifying which of them had published any given piece, or who had printed it for them. As Butter and Bourne are the only continuous actors in this group (ceasing to publish only with the royal ban on foreign news in 1632) I will for simplicity's sake be referring to all of their news pub-lications as those of "Butter and Bourne," even when the other three printers were involved. From the years 1618–1632, Butter and Bourne produced a regular series of news publications eventually called "The Continuation of our Weekly Newes." The "Continuation" was routinely printed in a quarto size of roughly eight to twenty-four pages and came to be known as a news "book."[6]

Although often hailed by historians as the true beginning of English newsprint, this serial publication was neither very regular (gaps in publi-cation ranged from a few days to a few months) nor much of a monopoly in that others continued to print the kind of occasional news pamphlets that had been sold at booksellers since as early as the 1530s.[7] There is a definite shift, however, in both the volume and relative proportion of the type of news printed after Butter and Bourne begin printing in 1618. In the decade and a half following the advent of serial newsbooks, the

amount of news printed grew remarkably. In the form of serial newsbooks, Butter and Bourne and their competitors were able to produce
news more quickly and in far greater bulk than had previously been published. The occasional printing of news pamphlets in the style of those
sold in the sixteenth century and through the first two decades of the
seventeenth continued, but was far outstripped in volume and speed by
the serial newsbooks that had overtaken their pamphlet predecessors in
terms of popularity as well.

The effect of this shift from a heterogeneous mix of news pamphlets
to a series of newsbooks was to regularize the previously chaotic collection of formats available to those printing news. The type of organization
chosen by newsbook publishers was one that I will be calling "coranto-
style." This style of news printing initially became extremely prevalent in
the staunchly Protestant free Dutch Netherlands in the early seventeenth
century; the earliest English versions of such "corantos" were translations
of Dutch prints, and the earliest printers of English coranto-style news
were closely linked by family, trade, and religion to Amsterdam printers.[8]
The short "coranto" was thus one of many formatting choices available
to news publishers in the late sixteenth and early seventeenth centuries.
Once adopted by Butter and Bourne around 1618, these one- or two-page
sheets of news tidbits quickly gave way to longer versions of the same—
the newsbooks of the 1620s.

Coranto-style news differed from many other early modern news
formats in several important ways, the most noticeable of which is the
lack of one continuous narrative. Where most news pamphlets told one
or possibly two related news stories, with accompanying documents
and prayers, coranto-style news presented small chunks of information
organized by country of origin and date only. Any attempt to collate
such information into a linear narrative was left up to the reader. The
domination of the news market by the coranto-style newsbook in the
1620s thus implies a significant shift in the reading practices of the London news-reading public, and a shift in the function of news in London
society. It is this shift that I wish to pursue in this chapter, in order to
ferret out how authors constructed and readers read their "true" news,
and the effect that this changing "truth" had on the presentation of Muslims in the English press.

HISTORY IN SIPPET: SINGLE-STORY
NEWS PAMPHLETS AND EXPANSIONIST TURKS

In 1644, the poet and satirist John Cleveland published an attack on
the newsprint of the time, calling news "a puny Chronicle, scarce pin

feather'd with the wings of time: It is an History in Sippets; the English Iliads in a Nut-shell . . . onely of the younger House, like a Shrimp to a Lobster."[9] In the process of deriding news for its lack of length and complexity, Cleveland highlights the generic origins of news in history writing and therein points toward both its formal roots and its social function. Most early news pamphlets presented one continuous narrative about a particularly important or dramatic foreign event, such as a battle. Like classical histories, these stories were discrete, composed of a recognizable beginning, middle, and end; they had a clear narrative arc and featured a fairly stable cast of characters.[10] They were tiny "Iliads" insofar as they resembled many other short prose narratives that today we would call "fictional," following a clear plotline in chronological order and doing so in the most dramatic and exciting way possible. Similar to histories and to sermons, news pamphlets were also meant to provide moral instruction and move the reader to virtuous action: according to Thomas Blundeville's *The true order and Methode of wryting and reading Hystories* (1574), such true and credible reports are written "first that we may learne therby to acknowledge the providence of God, whereby all things are governed and directed. Secondly, that by the examples of the wise, we may learne wisedom wisely to behave our selves in all our actions, as well private as publique, both in time of peace and warre. Thirdly, that we maye be stirred by example of the good to follow the good, and by example of evill to flee the evill."[11] Like its older cousin history, news sought to provide readers with examples of the providence of God at work in the world and to stir its Christian readers to good action, usually prayer.

These moral goals are evident in the way in which news pamphlets were written and printed. Structurally, news pamphlets began with a brief summary of the story, often on the title page itself and then reiterated in the first paragraph. The events would then be recounted in further detail over the course of several pages. Many pamphlets concluded with a prayer to God for the enactment of a particular event in the future. Usually these prayers were woven into the conclusion of the news story itself, but sometimes they were included under a separate heading following the main news, along with other relevant letters, proclamations, or treaties. The 1571 pamphlet "Letters sent from Venice," which delivers the news of a Christian victory over the Turks, is supplemented with an open letter from "The French King to the Bishop of Paris, with expresse commandement for Publike thankes to be given to God for the happie successe of the Christians againste the Turke."[12] Similarly, long editorial harangues entitled something like "To the Christian Reader" were occasionally printed at the end of news pamphlets, making explicit the function of the included prayers as well as the exhortatory and moralistic language that appeared throughout the body of such publications.[13]

Almost all single-story news pamphlets were larded with this type of explicitly moralistic commentary meant to guide the reader in his interpretation of the news story. News stories were meant to function as exempla: living proofs of the providential nature of worldly events. This exemplarity is typical of the way in which many texts functioned for early modern English readers; as Eugene Kintgen writes in *Reading in Tudor England*, "reading occurs against a background always already known; the fundamental interpretive question to be asked of any passage is not 'what does it mean?' or 'what is it?' but rather 'what is it an example of?'"[14] In the case of news pamphlets treating Turks or other Muslims, such stories are examples of accepted truths about the cruelty and lust of Turkish rulers, the tyranny of their rule, and their desire to extend that rule across Christendom. Commonly accepted explanations for why the Christian God has permitted this to occur are also confirmed: namely, that Christians are being punished for their sins, particularly for the continuing lack of unity in the ecclesiastic and temporal leadership of Europe when faced with Turkish expansion. (Hence the frequent exhortations to repent and pray for forgiveness in order that God might be moved to release his erring children from the terror of the Ottoman "scourge.") Those Christians who struggled against this long-standing foe are uniformly praised for their heroism and are shown to receive great rewards on earth (usually in the form of booty) as well as glory in Heaven.

As these stories functioned to confirm things already known and accepted among readers, news pamphlet titles primarily serve to identify what kind of already familiar story could be found within the covers of a given publication. For example, in John Wolfe's 1595 pamphlet, "A true discourse wherein is set downe the wonderfull mercy of God, shewed towards the Christians, on the two and twenty of Iune. 1591 against the Turke, before Sysek in Croatia. Truly translated out of the high Dutch Coppie," readers could expect to find an example of the Christian God's relenting toward the sins of his people, and displaying his mercy to them by giving them victory over their enemies. This pattern would be familiar to anyone aware of the travails of the Old Testament Israelites whose sinning caused frequent rifts with God, and whose repentance often resulted in divine forgiveness displayed through a great military victory. Such biblical parallels are occasionally made explicit, as when one author expresses his confidence that "the almightie, gratious, and mercifull God . . . will undoubtedly take pitie and compassion on his poore Christians and breake the stout stomacke and pride of this enemie (as he did Pharao in the red sea) overthrowing him to the ground with all his might, and to keepe and release Christendome from his yoke."[15] The religious link was further emphasized by the frequent use of the black letter print commonly used when printing the Bible.

The woodcuts that sometimes appeared (and reappeared) on the covers of news pamphlets similarly functioned to emphasize visually the contents of the pamphlet, portraying ships in battle, one sporting the cross and the other the crescent, or distinctly medieval-looking combatants (no doubt invoking crusades of past centuries), singly or en masse, flying similarly designed flags. Woodcuts, especially on cheap print-like news pamphlets, were not usually meant to be strictly representational; they were used repeatedly by printers on all kinds of publications as a broad indicator of the topic of the publication. Occasionally, however, the images were more closely keyed to the news advertised in the title. A large and detailed example of this can be found on the cover of "A Great and Glorious victorie obtained by the Emperour Rodolph the second against the Turke, and the great Cam of Tartarie this Sommer last past 1595. &c. And of the taking of the mightie Towne and strong fortresse of Simblet in Moldavia and Hungarie, &c. and of the tyrannie of Mahomet now raigning: who caused his 19. brethren to be put to death, and his owne Mother to be cast into the sea and drowned." In the center top of the woodcut, a large man wearing a turban and carrying a scepter is seated in a royal tent. All around him are soldiers wearing pointed caps carrying a variety of weapons. The solider to the sultan's left is tossing a woman, bound, into the sea. At his feet two bound men (wearing turbans similar to the sultan's) are being strangled with ropes, while one lies already dead on the ground. Below the drowning woman is a soldier with a scimitar preparing to strike off the head of a kneeling man, who is also bound and also wearing a turban (this is a high official who supported the mother in trying to raise a different sultan to the throne). With the exception of the official, who is only described in the body of the pamphlet, the rest of the figures can be identified by reading the title of the pamphlet, thus emphasizing with visuals the horror of the slaughter described in the title.

These cover designs point to the reasons why such pamphlets were likely purchased, and the way in which they were read. With the basic lesson of the story already well known from other, usually biblical, sources (on which the news report was patterned), the interest of the pamphlet lay in "*How* Sultan Amurath the third, Emperor of Turks, deceased at Constantinople. . . . and his eldest sonne Mahomet . . . caused his 19. Brethren to be put to death, and his Mother to be cast into the sea and drowned" (my emphasis). The appeal of news pamphlets lay in the colorful way in which the news was presented, with pictures, dramatic language, and emotional appeal. The death of Amurath the third, for example, reiterates in miniature the tale of God's redemption of his people through the defeat of the sultan's expansionist plans. The pamphlet begins by recounting the treaties broken and castles taken by Amurath, increasing the sense of menace and the triumph of treachery as the list of his victories stretches on. Once the list seems overwhelming, the author revives his fearful audience with the long-expected word: "But"

> as the abovenamed Turkish Emperour, pretended this yeere to imploy all his might against Hungaria, and further against Vienaa, and all Austria, yea against other places in Christendome, to bring the same under his tyrannous yoke (for which pretence there was a great preparation both by water and land:) the mightie hand of God came over him, and was greeved with a paine in his side, and so extremely, that finally he died thereof, the third of Januarie past 1595. in the 50. yeere of his age, and 20. of his raigne, whereby his raging was ended.[16]

Most news pamphlets treating the Ottoman Empire followed the basic emotional pattern of generating fear with the terribleness of the enemy and then releasing it through victories by Christian forces or, as in this case, by acts of God that assaulted the empire directly. Depending on the news the pamphlet had to report, it ended with an exhortation to give thanks to God for victories achieved, or fearfully but faithfully to pray for protection from the Islamic enemy. In "A Great and Glorious victorie," the death of the terrible Amurath is followed by the succession of his son Mahomet, who promptly murders most of his family in an attempt to secure his position on the throne. The pamphlet writer uses this news to confirm Christian fears of the new sultan, and to remind Christian readers of the lesson they should draw from this story, as well as the actions they should subsequently undertake:

> Now may we Christians by these examples easily perceived what goodnes is to be looked for at his hands, for if he shewed no mercie to his owne brethren, what pitie or compassion will he shew Christians: shall we not feare it ten times more in him, who hath such an inhumane beginning? Therefore seeing then, that this new tyrannous Turkish emperour, such a one fully resolved to proceede more stronger [sic] and tyrannously against the Christians, with the wars which his father began: it is very needfull, that all Christians with one accord do call to the almightie God in true repentance and sinceritie and with earnest praier falling downe before him, beseeching him from the bottom of their harts, to defend and destroy such an enimie.[17]

The use of the first person plural—"we Christians"—is ubiquitous in these pamphlets and serves as a grammatical shorthand for the function the pamphlet is meant to serve. Like prayers or hymns in which the congregants collectively pray and sing to God, reading news pamphlets about Turks was an activity calculated to reinvigorate a religious collective and remind them of their common goals, desires, and fears.

News pamphlets like "A Great and Glorious victorie" thus clearly served to reinforce the status quo both in terms of what people knew about the Turks and the function that reading news should serve in society. Borrowing some elements of its prose style from the tradition of popular preaching, its typeset from German Bible printing, and its basic storylines from the bible (especially the Old Testament), news—especially that which treated Turkey—was a religiously charged genre. It called upon readers to reconfirm their participation in the Christian community by reacting to the news in the manner specified as proper, and joining with other Christians to pray for a particular turn of events. Its liberal use of the first person plural served to wrap readers into the Christian fold, and to consolidate the knowledge and attitudes of that community toward the Ottoman Empire and "Turks" in general.

SHIFTS IN FORM AND FUNCTION: THE RISE OF THE NEWSBOOK AND ITS CRITICAL READERS

If single-story news pamphlets worked as moralistic consolidators of the status quo, they also worked as sheer entertainment. They were essentially familiar stories embellished with new details and told in an exciting way. Notably, neither of these social functions required accuracy in the details of reported events. Reader skepticism of the "truth, credibility and certainty" of the news contained within the pamphlet did not stop the story from being entertaining, or from elaborating in a new form the accepted beliefs about the world and its peoples. Written in the same tradition as classical histories, which included fabricated "verbatim" speeches to make their point, news pamphlets often manipulated the details of their reports to make the tales more dramatic, or to serve larger pedagogical goals. If there was any "truth" to news reports from abroad, it lay in the confirmation of the eternal truths of Christianity— such as the just punishment of sinners, God's use of infidel Islamic armies to express his anger with European infighting and sin, or the vindication of all those who fought such armies, living and dying for their Savior. As Blundeville explains, "we seeke by reading Hystories, to make our selves more wyse, aswell to direct our owne actions, as also to counsell others, to sturre them to vertue, and to withdrawe them from vice, and to beautyfie our owne speache with grave examples, when we discourse of anye matters, that therby it may have the more aucthoritie, waight, and credite."[18] The acquisition of greater wisdom, virtue, and rhetorical force is the goal of the serious reader of such histories in sippet; the pleasure that comes with hearing a good story was a less lofty but also significant desire recognized and catered to by news writers, printers, and sellers. It is significant that Blundeville mentions nothing about finding out "what really happened" in the past; the only "truth" of past events of interest to readers was that which led to wisdom and virtue, i.e., a kind of moral or eternal truth.

The form of newsprint shifted when that form of truth formerly considered irrelevant or beside the point—"what really happened"— became the paramount concern of news readers. This happened when readers became desperate for swift and reliable news of events occurring on the Continent during the brutal religious conflict known as the Thirty Years' War.[19] Frederick, Elector of the Palatinate, and husband to James I's daughter, Elizabeth, was at the center of this conflict's tangled beginnings; the sides were drawn clearly along religious lines. Both the religious implications of this Catholic-Protestant conflict and English national interest in Elizabeth and her husband meant that readers became deeply invested in the news from the Continent. With this new and more intimate relation to the foreign news, the goals of news readers seemed to change. They wanted their news fast, and they wanted it to be accurate. In order to accommodate these new reader desires and to take advantage of the new market opening up for more frequent news publications, printers shifted from printing primarily single-story news pamphlets like those described above, to mainly producing what had previously been a fairly infrequent offering: coranto-style newsprint. With this new form came a new ideology, and one that readers took an active part in shaping.

So-called "coranto" news sheets were printed in English in the free Dutch Netherlands, and had been sold in modified form in London at least since the turn of the seventeenth century.[20] However, with the start of the conflict in 1618, such coranto-style prints began flooding the English market. Protestants Nathaniel Butter and Nicholas Bourne soon took over domestic production of coranto-style newsbooks, and quickly learned that nothing could keep pace with their readers' appetite for news. In addition to the usual private correspondence networks, the publishers made good use of the hundreds of corantos pumped out by the Protestant Dutch and the Catholic Antwerp presses; these Continental news pamphlets were regularly digested and translated for domestic English consumption. In order to handle the volume of news coming from the Continent and demanded by their readers, at some point in 1619 or 1620 Butter and Bourne employed the services of one Thomas Gainsford, a well-traveled soldier and writer of history. Gainsford compiled, translated, wrote, and edited all of the news received by letter or imported as foreign publications from the Continent, preparing each week's dose of news for print. Like the coranto writers in the Netherlands, and in sympathy with his employer Nathaniel Butter, Gainsford's political and religious allegiance lay with the Calvinist reformers. Significantly, the likely synchrony between Gainsford's politics and those of the majority of his readers did not result in reader approval of his work. On the contrary, readers constantly accused the news editor of printing false reports, neglecting to indicate where the compiled information had originated, and printing only news biased in favor of the Protestant cause. The series' later editor, the Reverend William Watts, met with similar skepticism and complaints from his readers.[21] The editors responded to these complaints in short paragraphs printed on the back of newsbook front covers, thereby recording the tenor of reader dissatisfaction in print. These notes provide us with a rare glimpse into the reading practices and reactions of the early modern popular print audience, and the picture they paint is not one of a unified community of Christian subjects, but a fractious, opinionated, and outspoken group of people often critical of crown decisions.[22]

Combined with the radical differences in format from single-story pamphlets, newsbook reader complaints point to a significant break in the social function of news. News stories that previously bore a generic resemblance to histories were told in continuous narration and concluded with prayers and other exhortations to virtuous thought and action; in newsbooks, news became short bits of comparatively value-neutral information imparted in no particular order apart from a heading indicating its geographic origin. A glance at a page from "A true discourse vvherin is set downe the wonderfull mercy of God" (1593) and "The Continuation of our weekly Newes" (1624) (see figs 2 and 3) makes vividly clear the differences in format between single-story news pamphlets and the coranto-style newsbooks.

Newsbooks did not offer to create wiser, more virtuous Christians; they offered no advice on how to react to the news morally, encouraged no repentance or prayers, and indeed, did not even tell a full story. Newsbooks instead offered readers small bits of information that they could sort through and make sense of on their own. The practice of keeping a news diary was one of the ways that early modern readers made order out of the chaotic offerings of the coranto-style newsbooks.

The newly popular coranto-style format of newsprint thus put the interpretive burden of the news on readers themselves, who appear to

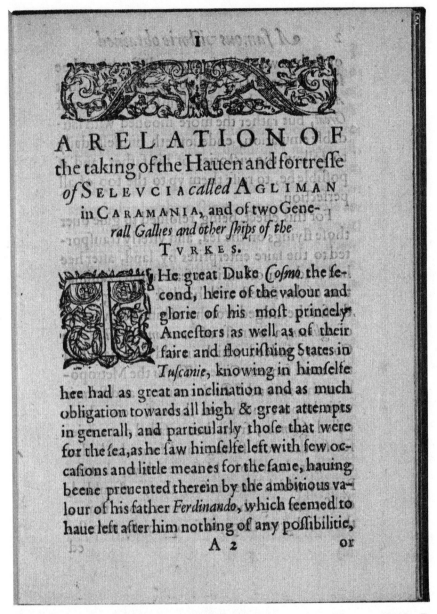

have picked it up with relish. As readers received the latest information about battles fought between Catholics and Protestants on German territory, they debated over the implications of every outcome and developed strong opinions about the role England should play in the conflict.

(55)

Venice the one and twentieth of September,
or first of October.

DOn *Francisco di Melo* with the Spanish army
intended to passe the river of Poneor Villa-
gio, to make an invasion into Montferrat :
but the French and Savoy troupes lay in waite for
them in an advantagious place, and gave them such
entertainement that they were forced to retyre and
leave their bridge behind them.

The Gallies of Malta have met with six Turkish
Gallies of Rhodes, sunke foure of them, and taken
two ; but two of the Maltaza Gallies were sunke
likewise in the fight.

Basill the two and twentieth of September
or second of October.

DVke *Bernard* of Saxon Weymar causeth the
Labourers to worke hard about the circum-
vallation before Brisacke, and hath cut
downe a great part of the wood on this side the
Rhine ; and to secure the bridge he hath raised neer
unto it two Ravelins, and likewise a royall sconce.

E 3   The

3. A page from the newsbook *An abstract of some speciall forreigne occurrences, brought down to the weekly newes* (1638). By permission of the Folger Shakespeare Library.

King James I issued a proclamation reminding his subjects that foreign policy was not an appropriate topic of conversation (or thought) for the common people, indicating just how prevalent such conversations had become. James' 1620 proclamation specifically warned his subjects "every one of them, from the highest to the lowest, to take heede, how they intermeddle by Penne, or Speech, with causes of State and secrets of Empire, either at home, or abroad."[23] This proclamation was repeated in 1621, 1623, and again in 1624. The repetition of this royal command implies that despite the explicit wishes of England's monarch, "vulgar persons" continued to debate the nation's foreign and domestic policy, aided by the new information provided every week by the newsbooks. Far from consolidating the status quo, news had become a genre that aided in sedition, a role it was to keep straight through the early decades of the seventeenth century and into the Civil War.

With this new role came new questions about credibility. Readers needed reliable information in order to form their opinions on the nature and progress of the war abroad, and did not appreciate the frequent mistakes, delays, and complete fabrications that marred their newsprint. Newsbooks that were considered unreliable made fewer sales, and thus publishers had a vested interest in the credibility of the news they purveyed. Discerning "what *really* happened" abroad became the goal of both printers and readers, and as newsbook printing became more established, readers and editors engaged in a lively discussion over how best to ensure the credibility of their news, and how the product should be shaped.

The most prominent complaint voiced by readers through these editorial replies was the inadequacy of the amount of news being printed. Desperate for new information on the progress of the war, readers badgered newsbook editors for more and more frequent reports, and the editors replied by trying to divert the readers' attention to whatever news they had at hand:

> This Weeke you shall heare of no fighting, nor further trouble, then you know already: yet the dayly Letters affoord matter sufficient both of pleasure and varietie, all which are translated for thy contentment, being most of them in Dutch . . . But whereas you expect, and that with great longing, the Businesse of the Palatinate: in this time of cessation, you must not looke for fighting every day, nor taking of Townes; but as they happened, you shall know. In the meane while, take this in good part: For as I conceive, it will afford you much pleasure, and in the publication content the Reader, if he be not too too curious.[24]

Unfortunately for the beleaguered editor, his readers were all too often "too too curious," judging by the frequency with which he felt the need to deflect their demands in print. At the height of the war, more polite attempts to reroute readers' clamor devolved into simple editorial orders to "leave me alone."[25]

Readers had other complaints besides the frustrating pace of news publication. Some complained of the new printing format, expressing a wish for older styles of news presentation; these were no sooner tried by the editor than they were rejected once again by a frustrated readership that was no longer satisfied to sit back and receive instruction on the proper interpretation of the news from an editor. Editors often expressed confusion and frustration over the readers' unpredictable reactions to all their publications, as in Gainsford's exasperated comments here:

> Gentle Readers, for I am sure that you would faine be known by that Character, how comes it then to passe that nothing can please you? For either custome is so predominant with you, or corruption of nature caries such a mastering hand, that you must be finding fault, though you have no cause. If we afford you plaine stuffe, you complaine of the phrase, and peradventure cry out, it is Nonsense; if we adde some exoneration, then you are curious to examine the method and coherence, and are forward in saying the sentences are not well adapted; if the newes be forcible against the Emperour, you breake forth, it is impossible, and all is invention; if it tend to the dejection of the Country, you seeme to commiserate and wonder at the misfortune; if we talke of novelty indeed, you make a doubt of the verity; if wee onely tell you what we know, you throw away the booke, and breake out, there is nothing in it, or else it is but a repetition of the former weekes newes: In a word, what ever we endeavor is wrested by the scrue of passion, and whether good or bad, is fashioned to strange formes by the violence of humor and over-swaying of opinion.[26]

In this quote, Gainsford paints a picture of a reader who is constantly dissatisfied with the pace, credibility, tone, format, and content of the information presented in the newsbooks. If the editor obtained new information and placed it in the insatiable maw of public demand, it was met with doubt as to the "verity;" seemingly repetitive news was cast away in disgust. If the news was good for the Protestant cause (news "forcible against the Emperor") it was met with fretful skepticism; if it reported of Catholic victories, readers fell immediately into a gloomy "commiseration" at the Protestants' misfortune. If the editor merely translated passages directly onto the page with no further comment, giving his readers "plaine stuff," they objected; if he added some "exoneration," the news was met with equal dissatisfaction.[27] In effect, Gainsford accuses news readers of reading unfairly, that is, with inconsistent and unreasonable expectations, and thus breaking an implicit understanding between news presenters and news consumers.

These comments, especially those treating the form and style of the news, highlight some of the generic change and confusion occurring in news at the time. Newsbook editors made small effort to organize, sort, or collate their material in any way that might speed reader comprehension of the situation in any given place. The jumble of information that this format presented to the reader ensured that she would have to do considerable work to put together the history of a conflict occurring in any one place, with contradictory and incomplete reports abounding. The task of making a narrative had moved from the news editor/author to the reader herself. It is perhaps unsurprising then that Gainsford's readers complained that "plaine stuff" was poorly phrased and accused it of being nonsense. The "sense" of story had collapsed into a pile of relatively unconnected sentences.

Readers seemed confused, however, in their reaction to this new interpretative task. On the one hand, they guarded it jealously, jumping upon editors they suspected of infringing upon their interpretative privileges by presenting too much, too little, or too biased news. The besieged Watts seemed particularly apt at crossing his readers' sensibilities in this matter. They obviously also tired of making sense out of tiny bits of information scattered throughout the news from week to week. The alternative to sequential literal translations of received newsletters and foreign news publications, however, was of course the "exoneration" Gainsford describes, which had been the stock and trade of singular news pamphlets for decades. With the open intent of guiding readers' reactions to news, author/editors had for years organized the received material in such a way as to present a coherent story, one that would support the interpretations and recommendations they planned to make. But readers seemed unhappy with this version of news as well. Gainsford, who had apparently given "exoneration" a try, complained that the readers minutely critiqued the interpretation he put forward of events by examining his "method" and "coherence," and concluding primly that his prose style was "not well adapted." Readers seem to have demanded some rhetorically sophisticated interpretative work on the part of the newsbook editors, if only that they might destroy and dismiss it later. Thus, interpretative narrative made by the editor was generally unacceptable to readers, but so also were newsbooks printed without any organization at all. Gainsford might well ask his readers how it had come "to passe that nothing can please you?"

This frenzy of critique and complaint on the part of newsbook readers (the editorial counter-complaints quoted here are only a tiny percentage of what was printed) highlights the main problem with which the genre was wrestling as older narrative formats were being replaced by the coranto-style format. Should news just be "plain stuffe" taken down as clearly and impartially as possible and then passed along by a chain of letter writers and printers unvarnished, straight to the reader's ears (or eyes)? Was it even possible to do so? Should there be an intermediary who would organize the material into a coherent story from which the reader was meant to derive meaning for himself, either as an Englishman or a Protestant? Who should interpret the news, and how should readers deal with varying interpretations, not to mention differing reports? These were questions that struck at the heart of the problem of credibility, highlighting the inter-linked nature of form and witness testimony (who attested to the truth of the news).

Newsbook readers appear to have addressed these questions by means of several different critiques. One was to question the religious leanings of those who wrote, translated, and/or transmitted the news to them. In a strongly Protestant London, one might expect the bulk (if not the entirety) of these complaints to be against possible Catholic sympathizers. Editors replied not only to accusations of printing news with a pro-Catholic bias, however, but of too-frequent Protestant bias as well:

> [H]itherto I have published for the Readers satisfaction divers letters both written and printed in the Dutch Tongue, and so by way of connexion pro-posed the affayres of Europe, especially Germany; . . . I finde some that would as it were pull me back by the sleeve for running too fast away with the newes, as if the Dutch-men were partiall on their owne side.

The way in which this editor proposed to compensate for his previous habit of printing only Dutch copy was to publish in addition several let-ters, "some in Latin, some in Spanish, and most in Italian, from which I have extracted the whole occurrences of the last Moneth."[28] In effect, readers demanded news from *both* sides of the conflict, and became con-cerned if printed news "ran too fast away" with the "partiall" views of only one side.

This determination to print news as reported from Catholic as well as Protestant sources is striking given the virulently anti-Catholic mood of the London populace in the 1620s. Nor was this an anomalous occurrence. Readers continually pulled editors back by the sleeve in the interests of more credible reporting, insisting upon a multitude of sources, and the proper attribution of those sources—a goal often supported and promoted by the editors themselves:

> Gentle Reader, we must advertise you that in our Newes we delivered some things in severall places as wee get the tiding in severall parts to shew you how the parties agree in their relations, seeing it is knowne that many write partially, and the one addes some circumstances more then the other: and hereafter we will put down very exactly from whence every thing com-meth. For you must conceive we set downe some things as we receive them from The High Dutch Copies, and some from the Low Dutch, printed at Antwerpe, which peradventure may speake partially, which I desire you to take notice of, and to judge accordingly.[29]

With anonymous newsprint, readers could not base their assessment of the news on the credibility of known individuals, but they could transfer this standard practice to locations and groups, all of whom were understood to be "partiall on their owne side." Such a practice was profitable for the producers of news, since all available news could then be printed and sold, rather than simply news gathered from Protestant sources. For these reasons, despite the advantages offered by an editorial synopsis of the news—the elimination of news not validated by multiple reports, a more complete and seamless narrative of events—both editors and readers clearly considered the public attribution of each bit of news to its proper source more important (not to mention less work-intensive for the editor). The editor above had previously adopted the practice of printing particular bits of news several times within the same pamphlet in order to show where "parties agree in their relations" and therefore eliminate partisan bias. Usually the place of origin of a pamphlet would be enough to indicate to readers the likely bias of a report: Antwerp and other "Low Dutch" presses would lean on the side of the Catholic emperor while the "High Dutch" Netherlands would cast their narrative equally strongly in favor of the Protestants.[30] In promising strictly to label each relation with its source, the editor coaches the readers to balance the writings of one "partiall" author against another. One editor, however, reminded his readers who was to bear the main burden of interpretation when reading the news, claiming that "I translate onely the Newes verbatim out of the Tongues or Languages in which they are written, and having no skill in Prognostication, leave therefore the judgement to the Reader, & that especially when there are tidings which contradict one another."[31]

When editors neglected to print the details of a source, readers protested vigorously, provoking quite acerbic responses from some staunchly Protestant editors:

> To the indifferent Reader. May it please you to understand, that whereas we have hetherto printed (for the most part) the Occurrances which have come to our hands, from the Protestants side, which some have excepted against: wherefore to give them content, we purpose to publish (as they com now to our hands) such Relations as are printed at Antwerp, Utopia, or other such like places, that they may from time to time have somewhat to build their miraculous faith upon: and to feede them with Milke from their owne dame, and this we do not for profit, but to free our selves from partiallity, and to make a destinction t'wixt each relation let the Readers judge, of the verity by the event. So we give you one for a taste.[32]

Despite their withering scorn, the editors of this news pamphlet did indeed follow through on their promise to print more Catholic pamphlets, faithfully translating a pro-Catholic piece out of Antwerp in the very next issue. While the editors seem to imply they were responding to a Catholic readership that demanded equal time, put alongside the above claims about partiality and numerous others like them, it seems just as likely that a readership accustomed to sifting out the probability of reported events from multiple sources simply protested the univocal nature of the material. If it was accepted by the English readership that "many write partially," and that this "many" included those whose religious leanings matched their own, it seems likely that a process of comparative reading had sprung up in an effort to cut down on the unreliability of reported news. Even the editors quoted directly above felt the need to free themselves of any accusations of partiality by printing the Catholic pamphlets, despite their clear disdain for that creed. Moreover, these editors evidently expected the greater reliability of the Protestant pamphlets they more frequently printed to be proven through this comparison with Catholic accounts; readers were invited to "make a distinction t'wixt each relation" by noting which had contained more "verity" once later reports made clear which version of events had actually occurred.

Of the two known editors of Butter and Bourne's weekly newsbooks, the Reverend William Watts seems a likely candidate to use his editorial position in order to consolidate a religious/political group, as was frequently done with news in the past. Yet even Watts often seemed grumpily at pains to prove his own impartiality in the transmission of news, grumbling that readers had accused him of a Protestant bias in his reports. Watt's identity as Protestant clergy must have been well known, which made him more susceptible to such accusations and often provoked quite snippy responses from him in reply. In the fall of 1631, for example, the actions of the imperial general Tilly were much in the news and caused at least two clashes between Watts and his readers. In the 2 September 1631 issue of Butter & Bourne's newsbook, Watts addresses the "Impartiall Reader," complaining that news of Tilly's numerous defeats were "published by us without addition or subtraction, & might have given some credit to the same, and deserued a more favorable construction from the most malevolently affected, yet from some it could receive no better approbation, than that all was lyes."[33] After being vindicated by newly arrived letters from the Continent, Watts triumphantly published the confirmations "against which, let the most barking curre open his mouth and say as formerly." He wraps up his editorial notice with a final tart salvo: "God grant him [the Protestant King of Sweden] the multiplication of the like victories and good successe untill all his Enemies be vanquished, and a generall Peace setled in all the parts of Germany, Amen." Although this bit of news was published "by us" and concludes with a prayer for the success of the Protestant forces, this passage bears no further resemblance to the single news pamphlets discussed above. The prayer is clearly not an invitation for the reader to join Watts' pious conclusions—it doesn't even bother to use the first person—but, rather is a defiant if somewhat paradoxical move on the part of an editor who feels wrongly accused of spreading Protestant "lies" in transmitting the news.

The second clash between Watts and his readers occurred a mere month or so later. Printed in the 20 October 1631 issue of Butter & Bourne's newsbook is another editorial address to the "Indifferent Reader," protesting that the report of Tilly's death contained in the previous edition was indeed true, despite rumors to the contrary coming from Antwerp.[34] The reader is invited to

> balance each [report against the] other, and accordingly beleeve: onely wee will propose one question unto all gaine-sayers, let them demonstrate where Tilly is and that great formidable Army which he hath since raised, and we will be of that Catholike faith.

The sarcastic tag on the end of this open invitation to compare sources is characteristic of Watts, and once more indicative of an embattled editor insisting that his news is reported truthfully, its accuracy untinged by religious partiality.[35]

Clearly, a paramount concern of both news readers and the editors who catered to them was reliability. Indeed, it was the complaint most often leveled at news publications by readers and against competing publications by printers. The inside covers of newsbooks were frequently peppered with protestations of innocence and good will on the part of their editors, who hoped their "gentle readers" would "justify [their] simplicity or innocency" since they printed "nothing but what is extracted out of true and credible Originals; that is to say, either Letters of justifiable information, or Corantos published in other Countries."[36] Some editors appear to have waited for further news to justify their publications with a confirmation of events; they would then print these later reports, accompanied by a self-righteous announcement of their vindication.

The emotions exhibited by editors in their replies to accusations of inaccuracy or outright lying demonstrate how much this matter struck to the heart of both the business of news and the personal credibility of the editor. Credibility ensured both sales and personal credit with merchants and others; a lack thereof gave away customers to competitors and made the editor's financial situation that much more difficult. News was only as reliable as the person who provided it; publishers with trustworthy correspondents possessed a significant advantage over those who could only reprint foreign publications. Similarly, those who could find editors able to translate many different foreign pamphlets could boast the variety of sources needed for readers to judge the likelihood of reported events given the "partiality" with which each report was written. Printers who proved themselves poor sources of news were roundly scorned by readers and other editors alike, who claimed a high standard for their emerging genre of newsprint. The small battles that must frequently have occurred between London news printers over particular twists and turns of the war have left their marks in these publications; editors gloated over their victories, demanding of their readers "where are your dreaming Gazettes, and corantos now?" and then clucking their rhetorical tongues and wondering at

> the shamlesse reports of strange men, and weake Certificates by Corantes from Foraine parts, especially to have them Printed, to talke of so many Thousands slaine, the Prince kill'd, Sigismond defeated, and the whole Army put to flight, when yet as I said, there was never any such matter, nor any set Battaile fought.[37]

The competition that is in evidence here goes to demonstrate the climate in which publishers were making choices about how to print their news. This chapter has so far traced a broad shift in the format of newsprint over a fifty-year period in London, and some of the implications of this shift for the community of author/editors, printers, and readers of news. But, these "generic" decisions were not taken in a literary vacuum; they were market calculations on the part of both vendors and consumers. Both publishers and readers sought the most accurate news possible, but met with frequent failures, even in reporting such large and significant events as whether battles were fought or whether kings had died. The conditions of early modern communications, especially in a countryside wracked by long-term warfare, were not good enough for any guarantees of accuracy. Readers sought *probability* by comparing Protestant against Catholic news, one news publication against another; most of all, they sought the volume of news that would allow for the greatest comparisons.

These reader demands affected decisions made by business-savvy printers. Although one should not reduce printers' motivations to the purely venal, news printing was first and foremost a bid for profit.[38] It was undoubtedly less laborious and time-consuming simply to translate material coming from abroad than to organize it into any coherent narrative. News could be more quickly and voluminously printed without the work of collation and narration. Moreover, finding an editor who could not only translate French, Italian, Latin, High and Low Dutch, High and Low German, and Spanish but who also possessed some literary skills would surely have been a difficult, if not impossible, quest. It seems likely that these logistical considerations made the generic shift to all coranto-style news printing sweeter to printers like Butter and Bourne, tipping the scales heavily in its direction.

I emphasize the idea of choice here because it is far too easy to forget that there was no natural "progress" toward a version of news printing that would someday find approval with later generations. The two means of gathering news—the private letter and the public post letters—remained open throughout the period and beyond. Those wishing to compile and publish an account of this news were confronted with the same kind of material, although in varying volume, throughout the period under discussion. Gainsford cautions his readers "neither to expect an order from Prioritie of date, nor any such exactness as men are tyed to in a continued Story. For in plaine tearmes, for anything I see they that writ these letters had them by snatches."[39] But such letters had arrived from the Continent for decades, and letters told in a more continuous narrative style still regularly arrived in London during Gainsford's editorship. In other words, it was not the advent of a new method of news transmission that spurred the changes in format under discussion, or any particular technological advance. More and more, publishers *chose* to print serial "snatches" of news rather than longer discreet narrations of particular events, dedicating their resources almost entirely to the former, rather than the latter format, sometimes in the face of reader complaints.

Another factor weighing in that choice would surely have been the stance taken by the crown toward news printers. Elizabeth I, James I, and Charles I all at times used printed news to promote their own agendas, with crown representatives paying printers for the publication of certain supportive news pamphlets. But they just as often sought to suppress news unfavorable to those agendas. Cyndia Susan Clegg has successfully argued that early modern preprint censorship was more a matter of local and selective persecution than a tight blanket of oppression thrown over London's printers; yet news printers could still easily find themselves unhappily selected for just such an official campaign.[40] Butter and Bourne fell afoul of the authorities early on when, in 1622, they printed a scandalous account of the state of Count Mansfield's military camps abroad. They subsequently printed a full retraction, blaming the original printing on someone slipping in the material "without the Licencers knowledge" and noting anxiously "that whosoever hath or shall ob[trude], or put any thing more then hath beene judiciously examined and approved, is liable to be severely punished: therefore expect no such bold attempt from any of us hereafter."[41] Although here it was the content of a bit of news that attracted official censure, one was even more likely to cross the royal will by printing politico-religious speculation or interpretation. Especially as James' and Charles' pro-Catholic policies became manifest and manifestly unpopular with their subjects, providing commentary on the many skirmishes and battles in the war on the Continent was tantamount to risking either one's business or one's neck, and sometimes both. This had not been the case during Elizabeth's reign, or even during the very early years of

James', when one could assume a mild Protestant-Christian group identity and deride Spain, the Pope, and all non-Christians with a fair amount of impunity.[42] The ability of news pamphlets to contribute to Christian and national community building through their reporting must have become more limited and more dangerous as the religious tensions increased and the population became more radicalized. Thus, as the coranto-style format had *always* eschewed interpretation and generalizations, it was a good choice of format for those seeking to avoid crown persecution.

There was of course an alternative to printing inoffensive coranto-style news for a voracious readership seeking word of the religious wars on the Continent. News was also read purely for entertainment, and publishers could capitalize on this aspect of news reading as well. This type of printing was less pressured, as speed was not necessarily required when merely passing along a good story. Single-story news pamphlets continued to be printed throughout the 1620s, alongside coranto-style newsbooks, and clearly remained profitable enough to keep on booksellers' stalls, despite the growing dominance of the newsbook within the realm of newsprint. Reports of wonderful escapes from Mediterranean slavery or pirate attack, battles of Christians against Ottoman forces in Eastern Europe, occasional bits of news from the New World: all of these made for good stories to tell, and to sell. Readers could continue to relate to these pamphlets in the way that they had to news in the sixteenth century, seeking the moral truth in the story and reading the news report largely as an exemplar of that accepted truth about the world. When Charles I banned all foreign newsprint in 1632, due to the domestic turmoil it was causing, these pamphlets continued to be published. Newsbooks, at whom the ban was largely aimed, ceased to be printed, but one-off news pamphlets merely changed their titles from "news" to "report," "tale," "historie," or some other acceptable substitute. In this way, older modes of news reporting ceased to claim the title "news" and instead bequeathed it to the type of publication that suffered a total ban on printing based on its identification as such: the coranto-style newsbook.

MUSLIMS IN THE NEWSBOOKS

The emergence of the newsbook as the most popular form of newsprint sold in London and the reading practices that developed alongside it had significant repercussions for the way in which Muslims were represented in English newsprint. Single-story news pamphlets consolidated readers as members of a Christian community by rehearsing accepted truths about the nature of Turks and their relations with Christendom and coaching them to react to the news in a manner specified as proper to Christians;

coranto-style newsbooks did no such thing. This is perhaps most tellingly indicated by the fate of the first person plural so ubiquitous in single-story printings. In newsbooks, the use of "we" (Christian writers and readers) was evacuated of its religious content, and instead referred primarily to the market transaction between "we" writer-editors/printers/booksellers and "you" readers.[43] Although the relationship between the producers and consumers of news had always been a commercial one, it now dominated the news as writers and readers wrestled over the form such publications would take. The sale and reading of news about Turks and other foreign actors had ceased to function as a community-building activity; no longer a venue for moral and religious instruction, it became instead a product that readers ardently desired and writers and printers were more than happy to supply in the manner that would most satisfy their customers.

Once the news readers addressed as docile Christians in single-story pamphlets forcefully altered their role in news production, the way in which news about Turks and other Muslims was written changed along with the rest of the news. Furthermore, readers trained by the new printing format to exercise skepticism and the evaluation of partiality in news reports were unlikely simply to revert to older forms of news reading when the topic shifted from Christian-Christian clashes in Western Europe to Christian-Muslim clashes in Eastern Europe or in the Mediterranean, even when reading the single-story pamphlets that were still being printed (albeit in fewer numbers than before). Thus, although there is no reason to think that English readers changed their opinion about the Turks being the enemies of Christendom, it would be naïve to think that shifts in the form of news, and thus the ideology embedded in that form, did not cause a shift in the way that English readers read news about the Ottomans. The form of the coranto-style newbooks—piecemeal bits of information and the lack of moral instruction—opened up a space for the portrayal of Islamic peoples less heavily laden with religious angst. There was space, in other words, to distance Muslims from hyperbolic calls for a new crusade, or from the cruel and lustful depictions of Muslims frequently found in single-story news publications. That space lay in the very disjointedness of newsbook information, its habit of indiscriminately mixing together bits of news from across the known world, and its refusal to morally evaluate the news it presented.

A comparison of the 1566 pamphlet "Newes from Vienna" and Butter and Bourne's 1622 coranto-style newsbook publication entitled "Briefe Abstracts Out of Diverse Letters of Trust" makes this space obvious. The full title of the 1566 pamphlet reads "Newes from Vienna the 5. Day of August 1566 of the strong towne and castell of Tula in Hungary, xi. miles beyond the river Danubus, which was cruelly assaulted by the great Turke, but nowe by Gods mighty working relieved, & the sayd Turks marveylouslye discomfited and overthrowen." It is accompanied by a detailed woodcut of soldiers battling each other with pikes, clubs, and swords. Butter and Bourne's 1622 newsbook is entitled, at prodigious length: "Novemb. 28. Numb. 9. Briefe Abstracts out of Diverse Letters of Trust. Relating the newes of this present Weeke, out of Persia, Egypt, Babylon, Barbary, Turkey, Italy, Spaine, Germanie, Silesia, France, and the Low Countries, with divers passages from Sea [sic]. Wherein are remembred the Troubles in the Turkish Empire, the Strength of the Pyrates of Argier, with a touch of the giving up of the Towne of Glatz, and the holding out of Frankendale. With the Victories of Count Mansfield in the Land of Embden, and the flight of the Count of that Countrey; And the going of the Prince of Orange towards Lingen. Together with the Sea Businesses of the Spanish and Hollandish Fleetes. In the end is added something of the French Affaires, with some other Occurrences." The Turks are merely one group among many that are treated in the twenty-page pamphlet, and are labeled as such. There is no reference to God as an actor on the scene; no coranto-style newsbooks posit any such divine causal agents or broader significance of events. Even the derogatory adjectives that accompany the mention of the (evil/cruel) Turks in almost every other printed forum are absent in newsbooks. This includes the less evaluative opening section of "Newes from Vienna," in which the author reports the events of the battle at Tula Castle, where he cannot refrain from labeling the Turks "cruel" and the assaulted Christians "poore." In the section of the newsbook that treats the Ottoman Empire, "From Constantinople, Octob. 3," the political events under discussion there are reported in the same straightforward tone as the events "From Rome" on the page before. The section contains several descriptions of civil unrest on the border of the Ottoman Empire and Persia (near Babylon); this unrest could lend itself easily to the conclusion that God was giving the Christians time to regroup by fomenting conflict between the two Islamic nations. Indeed, a traveler in the region, John Cartwright, made just such a conclusion in 1611, noting with favor that those indomitable English soldiers of fortune, the Sherley brothers, had effectively "stir[red] up the Persian king to take up armes against the great Turke, and to draw by degrees the whole warre upon his owne necke, therby to free and give a time of breathing to the champions of Jesus Christ."[44] The newsbook treatment of this conflict between Persia and Turkey, however, is treated in a resolutely matter-of-fact tone:

the Natives and Subjects of Babylon had before made their Bashaw to disobey the Great Turkes Commaunds . . . And when hee since seemed willing to obey his Lord and Master, the Babylonians have taken and burnt their Bashaw and Mufti (the Mufti being their chiefe Priest or Pope of the Mahometan Religion) and have since chosen to themselves new Governours . . . This is also confirmed by other Letters, which came by the way of Venice: which affirme also, That the Rebellion in Babylon is most certaine.[45]

The only conclusion drawn regarding this rebellion on the part of the sultan's subjects is a tactical political and military one for the Persian shah: "And thus you see the distractions of this huge and vaste Turkish Empire; which begins to change their Obedience, with the Murther of their former Prince: Which Seditions in the people, no doubt will be eagerly apprehended by the King of Persia, who could willingly see every one of the Bashawes (like the Captaines after Alexanders death) catch a share for himselfe, that so hee might be too strong for any one of them single; and at last, whilest they fight with him severally, hee might overcome them all generally."[46]

Far from being irreconcilable "others," the Turks and Persians are easily assimilated to a "Western" understanding of the politics of empire through the classical allusion to Alexander the Great. Thus it is not that Muslims are shown in a favorable light by coranto-style newsbooks; merely, their political, social, and military affairs are included along with those of every other nation outside of England.

Even the Turkish news that might directly affect the affairs of some readers in London was reported without much embellishment. The sea-worthiness of the *al-ghuzat* fleet based in Algiers was a matter of much concern to Christian merchants, as they routinely lost ships, crews, and merchandise to the activities of the multinational pirate fleets based in North African ports.[47] The news "From Rome" on "Octob. 18" briefly notes a large prize taken by these "Turkish Pyrates" and draws a gloomy conclusion about the prevalence of such threats to Christian merchant vessels:

> By the way of Rome also the newes comes from Algiers, that the Turk-ish Pyrates there have lately taken a ship, comming from *Nova Hispania*, wherein were to the value of 20000. Crownes, and 200. men which were found aboard of her, were all made slaves. Thus you heare, that though *Ward* and *Sampson*, be dead, yet the Turkes have Pyrates and Rovers enough to trouble all the Merchants that trade that way.[48]

Given the losses described here, one might expect considerable rejoic-ing at the news printed on September 4, 1622, that such a fleet had been temporarily grounded. As the cause of this could easily be attributable directly to divine intervention (the onset of disease), such jubilation would, if printed in a single-story news pamphlet, inevitably be accompanied by an insistence that readers give thanks to God for smiting such a powerful enemy to Christian interests. The newsbook "Newes from Sundry Places" prints the report as follows:

> They were informed here [Civita Vecchia], that this yeere the Turkish Gal-leys of *Biserta* were not able to set forth, all their slaves and great store of

their soldiers being dead, whole *Barbarie* being likewise mightily invaded
with the plague: And seeing the Turks were not to bring any Navy this
yeere at Sea, it should not bee necessary to send any from *Sicilia*.[49]

No further information or comment is included. The newsbook merely
leaves a blank space and then moves on to its next entry, "Here is arrived
the *Persian* Ambassador comming lately from Spaine."

Muslims do not feature as frequently in newsbooks as Continental actors, but this is due to the fact that fewer "letters of trust" arrived
from Constantinople than from Venice, Vienna, or Amsterdam. Indeed,
the majority of the news treating Turkey, Persia, and Morocco comes by
way of other European cities, printed under headings like "From Rome."
Letters from Constantinople or other Islamic-controlled cities are rare.
Regardless of the origin of the news, the differences between single-story
news printings and newsbook stories are striking. Where, in the pamphlets, religious differences were heavily emphasized, in newsbooks they
are not mentioned, except in certain explanatory asides. Where pamphlets
glorified Christian victories over the Ottomans and chastised Christian
leaders for their sectarian infighting when yet more of Eastern Europe
was lost to the Turks, newsbooks reported the fact of a battle, in the early
modern understanding of that word, i.e., "an action, a deed." Determining
whether this was a "true fact" or a "false fact" was left up to the reader.[50]
Analysis occurred only in the mode of "policy," and never in that of the-
ology. The black letter type so frequently used in single-story pamphlets
is never used in the printing of newsbooks. The effect of the shift from
single-story news pamphlet and its conventions to those of the coranto-
style newsbook thus had consequences for more than just London news
printers and readers. The changes brought to the representation of such
Islamic nations as the Ottoman Empire, Persia and Morocco, although
merely collateral, were nevertheless real. Newsbook reporting broke the
insistence on the crusade mentality that had dominated earlier news print
and other popular genres. The chance of an actual holy war against Turkey
may have been long past any possibility of actualization,[51] and acceptance
of the Ottomans as trading partners and the empire as a destination for
exotic travel may have been growing in practice, but the representation of
the Turks as the "raging" enemies of Christendom was still widespread in
the publications of the day, especially those meant for common readers.
The format of newsbooks helped to forward the idea that Islamic nations
were first and foremost political, economic, and military entities, similar in kind to European nations and subject to the same kind of political
analysis. A change in the genre of news at home affected the perception of
foreign lands abroad: as the "truth" told by newsprint shifted, so too did
the "truth" related about Islamic lands.

In the case of newsprint, that truth was produced dialogically between news readers and news writers and printers. Due to the recurring nature of such publications, such a conversation could evolve along with the genre over an extended period of time. Most of the prose narratives printed about events and peoples in Islamic lands were written with a particular audience in mind and then printed, as was Sandys' *Relation of a Journey begun in 1610* and the various publications describing the Sherleys' adventures in Persia. Sometimes these works were popular enough to be reprinted in new editions during the author's lifetime, but often the original composition and printing were the only opportunity the author had of crafting the "truth" he wished to present to his readers.

In the sixteenth and early seventeenth centuries, however, a new kind of travel publication became popular: collections of prose travel tales printed together in a single volume or set of volumes. Richard Hakluyt's *The Principall Navigations* (1589, 1598) and Samuel Purchas' *Purchas his pilgrimage* (1613, 1625) are the most well known of these compendious sets of travel tales, but there were many others published in the period as well.[52] Since these collections often reprinted material that had previously been printed in a different context, or appropriated for publication texts that were not composed with publication in mind, they pose further complications for scholars seeking to analyze the intersection of a book's ideologies of form and of content. When a text moved from its original scene of composition and reception to this new one, it underwent changes in printing format and paratextual material and acquired a new context as part of a collection that performed a different social function for a different set of readers. The text might remain the same, but its social and ideological implications are likely to have changed, sometimes quite dramatically.

The next two chapters of this book will examine two cases of texts moving from their original context of composition and reception to a new one in Richard Hakluyt's *The Principall Navigations*. More particularly, they will consider what happens to the "truths" offered to readers about Islamic peoples when tales shift settings in this way.

II

4

Turks and Their Paratexts:
The Captivity of Thomas Saunders
and the Ideology of Form

WHEN RICHARD HAKLUYT PUBLISHED HIS TWO-VOLUME collection of travel accounts, *The principall nauigations, voiages and discoueries of the English nation* in 1589, there were few books like it on booksellers' shelves. A reader interested in travel tales might have picked up Richard Willes' 1577 *The history of travayle in the West and East Indies, and other countreys lying eyther way, towards the fruitfull and ryche Moluccaes As Moscouia, Persia, Arabia, Syria, AEgypte, Ethiopia, Guinea, China in Cathayo, and Giapan: vvith a discourse of the Northwest passage,* a partial translation of Spaniard Peter Martyr's *Decades* (translated by Richard Eden), augmented with numerous other English and Continental travel accounts. Or if she had linguistic skills enough to dabble in Continental publications, she might have acquired a copy of the Venetian Giovanni Batista Ramusio's collection of voyages, *Navigationi et viaggi* (1550–1559). She might also have been fortunate enough to purchase Hakluyt's first printed collection of voyage narratives, *Divers Voyages Touching the Discoverie of America, and the Ilands Adjacent unto the Same, Made First of all by our Englishmen, and afterward by the Frenchmen and Britons,* which was published in 1582, although likely in very small quantities.[1] In comparison with the dozens upon dozens of news and travel pamphlets, captivity narratives, and accounts of battles at sea published throughout the late sixteenth century in London, however, large high-end collections of travel accounts spanning the known world were extremely rare. Moreover, none focused exclusively on English travel.

One of the primary characteristics of such a novel publication from the standpoint of the Elizabethan reader must therefore have been simply its newness, and the consequent uncertainty of how to engage with such an unusual book in comparison to the more well-established sub-genres of travel and news pamphlet narratives. Beyond this, it is extremely difficult to state with any certainty what early responses to Hakluyt's collection might have been. There is precious little evidence in the form of marginalia, commonplace books, diaries, or other common reader-response sources of the period to indicate how readers read the *Principall Navigations* and what their impressions might have been regarding the utility, credibility, or entertainment value of its contents.[2] Yet despite this dearth of evidence, scholars routinely ascribe to Hakluyt's work a radical epistemological status, insisting on its iconoclastic potential for setting new standards in reliable and accurate narrative accounts of foreign lands. Emily Bartels gives an exuberant version of this common trope in the literature when she notes that for "anyone [in the period who] wanted the latest scoop on Africa, hot off the press, the place to turn was Hakluyt's *Principall navigations*, which brought the English expeditions to Africa—and Africa as a reality—into England's (literate) public domain. That reality is notably disjointed, sometimes contradictory and elusive, but it nonetheless—and *consequently*—challenged the stereotypes as they had not been challenged before."[3] More often, modern reader impressions are silently conflated with early modern ones as critics describe the "faithful redactions" that make up Hakluyt's compilation as "factual," or in one case, "actual history."[4] The idea that Hakluyt is "adher[ing] to principles of objective historiography" is deeply embedded in the literature.[5]

Given the uncertainty surrounding the reception of Hakluyt's work, this is, at best, an unhelpful if generally unremarked tendency in the literature. These claims are further complicated, however, by the very nature of the *Principall Navigations*. As a compilation of over 250 documents, around 80 of which had been previously published in other venues, the *Navigations* could not (and do not) read like a fully unified work. Readers almost certainly had varying responses to the different accounts within the collection as well as to the collection as a whole. Some of these accounts—for example the merchant company letters—had not been written for publication; they were internal company correspondence. Merchant letters had never (to my knowledge) been published as a group and were not a recognized form of travel writing within the public domain. Other voyages had been printed before as popular pamphlets and still bore many of the characteristics of that form of published travel writing; these received an entirely new generic overlay once included within the handsome folio volumes of the *Navigations*. Furthermore, the *Principall Navigations* as a collection was printed twice, once in 1589 and again a decade later (1598–1600) in a significantly expanded second edition. By the time of its second printing, the *Navigations* would no longer have been unknown as a form of travel writing or as a particular text. The length of time between the two printings indicates that the text was not a best-seller when it first came out; yet by 1602 it was recommended reading material on long-distance merchant voyages.[6] These two bits of evidence make the obvious point that the function of this text within Elizabethan culture was not only varied, but shifted across time. The *Principall Navigations* thus offer a unique challenge to the literary critic seeking to analyze its place in the market for printed travel materials.

These layers of complexity in the composition and reception of the texts that make up Hakluyt's *Navigations* as well as its status as a single work make the most common usage of the text in early modern English studies positively irresponsible as a scholarly practice. I refer here to the now entrenched habit of citing small bits of text (often one or two sentences, occasionally a short passage) garnered from one of the accounts in the *Navigations* as unproblematic evidence for claims either about the nature of an early modern locale/people or about the "English" opinion of such places/peoples. Hakluyt's text has become widely used as a mine in which to dig for little ethnographic gems about sixteenth-century Russia, Africa, Turkey, the Near East, or the Americas.[7] Moreover, in addition to the obvious methodological weaknesses of this practice as a whole, it is uniquely problematic in the case of Hakluyt's voyages due to the ideological pitfalls inherent in making sweeping generalizations about early modern "others." Critics unconsciously replicate early modern stereotypes and prejudices by using such brief statements as representative of the period, to the detriment of early modern non-English societies and/or (ironically) the complexities of early modern English culture itself.

By following what Anthony Payne describes as the neglected "other half of any bibliographical transaction: readership and dissemination, who read the text and how it was read and the extent to which the construction of the text either determined its reading or was itself determined by its anticipated readership,"[8] this first in my pair of chapters on Hakluyt's collection will address both of the problems in the literature described above. By analyzing the changes Hakluyt and his printer made to one previously published voyage narrative in order to fit it to the interrelated goals of the compilation as a text, its printed format as a book, and its audience on the book market, I will highlight the levels of mediation that underlay every account of a foreign land included in the *Navigations*. Such a retracing of the material and textual progress of one tale as it moves from a popular print pamphlet to a principal navigation will impede the easy use of such narratives as a mine for quotable quotes by countering the tendency such practices have of flattening out the historical complexities of production in order to posit the selected bit of text as a transparent representation of early modern society or early modern English thought. It will, in essence, thicken Hakluyt's volumes even further, making it more difficult to extract only the tasty little bits while leaving the shape of the whole of each selection behind. It will also call attention to the careful crafting of each travel narrative for a particular print audience, and the role that audience expectation plays in the production of travel texts.

The second chapter in this pair will further engage the question of audience expectation by considering what Mary Fuller has called the "dull" parts of several of Hakluyt's voyages, namely the navigational, geographical, and economic sections of the Persian materials, which Hakluyt obtained from the Muscovy Company records.[9] Such sections are in large part responsible for modern critical assessment of Hakluyt's collection as an overall reliable and factual set of early modern English observations of foreign lands. By contextualizing these accounts and comparing them to the Persian materials discussed in chapter 2, I will point out the role that intended audience played in the shape of such textual accounts of foreigners, thus linking their content and their form to generic expectations and refuting their claim to a naturally higher truth value. I will then be in a position effectively to question the attribution of factuality to such accounts, utilizing the history of factuality as it has been drawn within the history of science literature. In fine, I hope to restore to the *Principall Navigations* and its collected voyages a materially grounded history within early modern English society and therefore a more complex and interesting place in early modern English studies as well.

In so doing, I will not be refuting the frequent uses of Hakluyt in the postcolonial literature, but rather fully enabling an ideological account of the nature of his texts. As Stephen Cohen recently contended, it is "the materialist insistence on the status of literary forms as social products shaped by specific historical circumstances to perform specific ideological tasks—on forms not simply as containers for extrinsic ideological content, but as practices with an ideological significance of their own" that will enable us most fully to critique the colonialist assumptions and histories that were embedded in English culture during the early modern period.[10] In this instance, I will demonstrate how the form of Hakluyt's material in its original setting of composition and reception, as well as the alterations in form wrought upon such texts for the sake of their inclusion in the collection, shape the presentation of the Islamic nations of Persia and Egypt/the Ottoman Empire. I argue that Hakluyt, by altering the context and paratext of such works through their inclusion in the *Principall Navigations*, shifts their ideological import in a decidedly economic direction, aimed at promoting open and mutually profitable trading relations with England's traditional religious enemies. The claim that Hakluyt's works targeted England's economic advancement through the promotion of trade and colonization has been made numerous times before;[11] what have yet to be fully explored are the social and textual mechanisms by which this goal is accomplished in an Old World context. This chapter, in its account of form and audience in one story's journey from popular pamphlet to "principall navigation," will aim to do precisely that.

A CAPTIVE'S AUDIENCE:
THOMAS SAUNDERS' PAMPHLET NARRATIVE AND ITS READERS

Very few of the texts included in the first edition of the *Navigations* were written for publication in this context.[12] As noted above, such compilations were rare at the end of the sixteenth century, and furthermore, most of the documents selected by Hakluyt for inclusion in his collection had been composed for a quite different audience and social purpose. Some were not even meant for publication. For example, a large part of Hakluyt's primary material came from merchant companies, either through the travelers themselves, as in the case of Anthony Jenkinson and his Persian materials, or through the officials of the company, as in Richard Staper's contributions from Levant Company records. They are texts that were primarily written as reports by factors to their masters back in London, to account for the movement of the company's goods, the eventual profits made from them, and the likelihood of continued trade to the area being possible or desirable. They were not written to be published in an expensively printed, publicly sold, folio volume of "principal navigations, voyages and discoveries of the English nation." I will be addressing the impact this origin had on the form of such documents in greater detail below.

For the moment, I would like to examine another type of transformation undergone by some texts in Hakluyt's collection, namely the move from popular pamphlet to principal navigation.[13] A prime example of this is Thomas Saunders' pamphlet account of an English ship and crew taken into captivity during a routine trading voyage to Tripoli in North Africa. In its pamphlet form, the narrative is entitled *A true Discription and breefe Discourse, Of a most lamentable Voiage, made latelie to Tripolie in Barbarie, in a Ship named the JESUS wherin is not onely shewed the great miserie, that then happened to the Aucthor hereof and his whole companie, aswell the Marchants as the Mariners in that Voiage, according to the cursed custome of those barbarous and cruell Tyrants, in their terrible usage of Christian captives: but also, the great unfaithfulnesse of those heathnish Infidels, in not regarding their promise. Together, with the most woonderfull judgement of God, upon the king of Tripolie and his sonne, and a great number of his people, being all the Tormentors of those English Captives.* As Nabil Matar has pointed out in his introduction to Daniel Vitkus's recently published collection of early English captivity narratives, such stories were often printed by the author in an effort to reestablish his reputation and identity as a loyal Englishman and Christian after a long stay in Islamic lands, under conditions known to inspire conversion to Islam and/or betrayal of national interests.

Having experienced the humiliation of being Christian slaves under Muslim masters, the captives-turned-writers used their accounts to establish a Christian teleology and authorize their reintegration into their national community. The former captive—sometimes aided by a narrator or editor—encouraged the reader to recognize that in the encounter between the powerful Muslims and the enslaved English, what was at stake was the certainty that the Christian God was the true God and that a faithful Englishman would always emerge victorious . . . Captivity accounts were written to assert English identity and authorize national commitment.[14]

They also function to ensure the author's place within these national and religious collectives. Such narratives sought, in effect, to help reintegrate the author within the close-knit English communities within which he moved, and are composed and published with that audience in mind. Thomas Saunders' pamphlet clearly seeks to reaffirm his identity as a Christian and an Englishman, in part through its plot and characterization, and in part through its form.

Saunders' *Lamentable Voiage, made latelie to Tripolie* was published as a twenty-four page quarto pamphlet, and sold at a bookseller's located along the north side of St. Paul's Cathedral. Although its price is not recorded, these physical characteristics, printing, and sales details would put it in the category of what are today usually called "ephemera"—short, cheap publications that were meant to be widely available, and shared not only with the literate purchaser but with an even broader community through the reading aloud of sections of the story to interested parties around St. Paul's. It features an epistle dedicatory addressed to the imperially named Master Julius Caesar, judge of the admiralty and commissioner for piracy charges, who almost surely had a hand in the bureaucracy and logistics surrounding the negotiated release of the English captives and goods from their slavery in Tripoli. The author claims he has dedicated his story to Master Caesar in recognition of the fact that he was "wholie bounden" to the judge for his assistance.[15] To neglect to thank the powerful man in some public way would constitute a depth of ingratitude that even wild beasts would not practice. (Saunders goes on to prove this through a lengthy recounting of a tale about a lion relieved of some pain by a terrified man; the lion returns the favor when the two find themselves in the main arena at a typically bloody Roman entertainment.) Although Saunders' "binding" to the judge is meant to emphasize his obligation to the more powerful man, it also points indirectly to the relationship that exists between the admiralty judge and the English sailor, whose status as an Englishman made him worthy of the judge's efforts.

The pamphlet also features a short address to "the gentle Reader" wherein the author claims that he has been forced to publish the story by "the earnestnesse of such (my friendes) as I might not withstand," even though the author "had thought at the first setting downe in paper, should never have ben put in print" (A3v). This stance of humility and forced publication by importunate friends is a common one, and is frequently used to excuse infelicitous prose and to undergird the truth claims in which "trueth needeth no filed termes" (A3v). This author, like many low-status pamphlet authors, forefronts his lack of rhetorical flourish as a guarantor of credibility: according to the author, neither himself, his "rude speech" (A3r), or the pamphlet are fancy, but this lack of artifice or gentility ought to garner them a higher truth value. He insists that although "the true reports of my troubles . . . be not set out with brave termes, yet is in them set downe nothing but plaine troth" (A3r). Although there is no explicit reference to religion in the opening letters, such claims are rooted in an increasingly self-aware Protestant aesthetic of "plainness," and plain speech in particular. By deploying such a disclaimer in his opening letter, Saunders links himself to a particular religious identity and social strata. Similarly, Saunders uses the mediation of his English "friends" to reattach himself to the wider community; by noting that his was a truth already thought worthy to be told to a wider community by this select group, Saunders links himself to his readers through a shared understanding of what will amuse and instruct English society.

This truth that Saunders is claiming is both an honesty of account—these things really did happen, and as I am telling them here—and also a greater truth shared by the particular community he is addressing and to which he would like to stress his membership. That truth is the religious one advertised on the front page of the pamphlet within its title: that the "wonderful judgement of God" is always forthcoming regardless of the trials to which Christians are put, and the "great unfaithfulnesse of those heathnish Infidels, in not regarding their promise." This moral is the primary theme of the text and, given its explicit advertisement within the very title of the work, it is meant to guide the reader's understanding of the story. The sectarian differences within Christianity are not explicitly noted on this title page, but they mark the text in more subtle ways. In addition to the reference to plain speaking in the epistle dedicatory, the title page features one German black type line: "Together, with the most wonderfull judgement [of God]." While I will discuss the structure and appearance of the title page at greater length below, it is worth noting here that the type chosen for this line is a visual reference to the Protestant Bible and the words selected for black type hint at the favorable judgment Protestants expected to receive from the Deity, in contrast to their Catholic counterparts.

Saunders' narrative is not unusual in its Protestant bent. In addition to the prevalence of Englishmen who identified as Protestant by the later years of the sixteenth century, far fewer Catholic narratives survived because such captives were ransomed relatively quickly by their religious compatriots in

Spain and France. Due to their long engagement in the Mediterranean slave trade (both as masters and slaves), the people of these countries had already established monastic institutions dedicated to the relief and ransoming of Catholics held as slaves in North Africa and the Levant. Protestants had no such institutional organizations, and thus languished in African slavery for far greater periods of time; many were never ransomed at all. As Nabil Matar notes, "the corpus of writings about captivity that survives in English is exclusively about British Protestants . . . Catholics are not present because they were ransomed by continental corelgionists in the same way that French Huguenots were ransomed by the English Protestants."[16]

Saunders makes his allegiances clear in an anecdote he recounts at some length during the looting of the Englishmen's ship in the harbor at Tripoli. All of the Englishmen's belongings, including their clothes, are summarily stripped from them as Saunders notes in one terse series of actions: "there came presentlie above an hundred Turkes aboord of us, and they searched us, & stript our verie clothes from our backs, and brake open our chests and made a spoile of all that we had" (B2v-B3r). Saunders then spends almost the entire page following describing how one "Turk," the "kings cheefe gunner," attempts to take as spoil from the master's mate his Geneva Bible. The author intervenes to save the bible by reporting the theft to the high-ranking King of Tripoli's treasurer, effecting his desires by reminding the Islamic official of their national practice of allowing each man to pursue his own conscience in matters of religion:

> I having the language, went presentlie to the kings treasurer, and told him of it [the theft of the Bible]: saeing, that sith it was the will of God that we should fall into their hands, yet that they should graunt us to use our consciences to our owne discretion, as they suffered the Spaniards and other nations to use theirs, and he granted us [that request]. (B3r)

The bible is returned, but once the treasurer leaves the scene, the theft is repeated and the author once again fetches him back to intervene. Upon the third repetition of this scenario, the author is threatened by the chief gunner, who swears he will revenge further interference. Nothing daunted, "I went the third time unto the kings Treasurer, and told him of it, and he came with me," and promised the gunner "an hundred Bastinadoes" if the Geneva Bible were taken again.[17] In this episode, the author makes clear his religious allegiances, as well as his staunch dedication to defending his faith. The episode concludes with the gunner complaining that he had gotten no booty at all from the ship, which the author notes was ultimately to his benefit, as "there was none, neither Christian nor Turke that tooke the valew of a penniworth of our goods from us, but perished both bodie and goods within seaventeen months following, as heerafer shall plainelie appeare." The margin note gives us the moral of this story in case we missed it: "All that had share of the spoile (shortlie after) by Gods judgement perished" (B3r).

This episode thus repeats in miniature the religious lesson announced on the title page, that we would witness "the most wonderfull judgement of God" upon all the various "tormentors" of the English captives. Thus both the Geneva Bible vignette and the story as a whole function in a manner similar to an exemplar in a sermon: Saunders' story will serve as a real-world proof of the ultimate justice of the Christian God (at least toward Geneva Bible readers). Readers should be instructed and reassured by this confirmation of God's fidelity to his true and loyal worshippers, as well as entertained by the dramatic vagaries of the narrative itself. As Saunders states in his address to the readers: "I commit [this true report of my troubles] to thy favourable consideration, and (I hope) to thy benefit and good likeing." Like so many popular pamphlets, this story was printed for the moral instruction, as well as the delight, of the reader.

In addition to invoking this common trope, Saunders is also engaging another very common reading practice in the pamphlet literature: the entertainment of readers not through a suspenseful tale with a surprise ending, but through the signaling, or in this case, outright announcement of a common generic pattern that readers will enjoy having related to them in spite of, or rather, because of the fulfillment reached at the predicable conclusion of the story. The Christians may be enslaved or tormented by evil sinners or infidels, but God will always redeem them in the end. The reading enjoyment comes from the horror of the torment and the glory of the inevitable redemption. In Saunders' pamphlet this tack is pursued not only through the basic plot summary given on the title page, but also through the quite copious marginal notes, which if read alone would give a full summary account of the plot of the text as well as its moral. This detailed plot summary given in the margins would facilitate a quick description of the pamphlet's contents if the reader did not wish to take the time to read, or read aloud, the entire twenty-four-page text. In other words, it gave exactly the kind of short abstract that could circulate rapidly through Paul's walk and the pubs beyond. The only thing lost in such a telling is the "rude" prose the narrator has already disowned; the true details of the account and its religious moral remain intact.

SAUNDERS' *TRUE DISCRIPTION* IN THE ROLE OF "PRINCIPAL NAVIGATION OF THE ENGLISH NATION"

When Hakluyt reprinted Saunders' 1587 pamphlet in the first edition of his *Principall Navigations* two years later, the title, the epistle dedicatory, the note to the readers, and the marginalia were changed, as well as the format of the physical book itself. But, Hakluyt confined himself to these paratextual changes: the content of the story remained untouched. The effect is one in which the popular captivity account is reframed as something slightly different, or slightly more. No longer a popular pamphlet delivered straight from the author and his publisher to the reader, the story was transformed into a principal navigation of the English nation.[18] Yet, Hakluyt's editorial interventions, conservative by the standards of the time, did not so much change the story as add one further level of mediation between the reader and the author's recorded experience. One might say that the piece undergoes rather a warping of its identity than a wholesale generic change. Changes to the paratextual materials would ensure that the text was read and understood somewhat differently, but given that the text remains the same, many things in the reading experience must have remained constant. In this section, I will seek to explore some of these changes, while remaining cautious in my claims regarding alterations made by Hakluyt to Saunders' story.

Let me begin by summarizing the changes that Hakluyt made to the paratext of Saunders' pamphlet. The most significant changes were to eliminate Saunders' dedication and reader note altogether, and to add to the account three royal letters, one from Elizabeth to the Ottoman Sultan Murad, and two from Murad to his viceroys in North Africa, the second addressed specifically to the viceroy in Tripoli. He also changed the title significantly and greatly abbreviated the marginal notes in the original. The title page of Saunders' original also disappears, as the tale is now included in the middle of Hakluyt's collection. It is prefaced by Hakluyt's own title page and introductory material, and embedded in the middle of multiple other tales of English involvement in the Levant and North Africa. So while the text itself remains unchanged, the paratextual material meant to guide the readers as they engage the narrative has been drastically altered, resulting in a subtle, but I would contend significant, ideological shift in the form of the account.

The primary casualty of Hakluyt's paratextual alterations is the focus on the author and his links to the community. These were originally drawn most clearly in Saunders's dedicatory epistle and note to the reader, both of which Hakluyt eliminated. As discussed above, Thomas Saunders is the main subject of the first five pages of the pamphlet narrative through the personal focus of the title page and opening addresses to Master Julius Casear and the reader. Hakluyt suppresses the role of the author and his unique voice both through the elimination of these pages and also by quite literally shrinking the name of the author in the title. While the pamphlet prints "THOMAS SAUNDERS" in all caps and in the second or third largest font on the page, so that it stands out quite noticeably on the busy title page, Hakluyt puts the author's name last, without caps, and in the smallest available type. He also severs Saunders' claim to eyewitness credibility by removing the parenthetical description of the author included on the pamphlet, "one of those Captives there at the same time." Hakluyt's title simply notes that the account was "written by Thomas Saunders." This is consistent with Hakluyt's stated goal for the collection, which was to highlight exploratory and trading voyages performed by those of the English nation. Saunders' personal identity is less important than his nationality. Indeed, the very inclusion of the tale in the *Principall Navigations* means that its author is English, rendering the inclusion of the particular name of the author even less essential.[19]

The name of the author is not the only thing that has shrunk in this reprinting. From the voluminously descriptive title cited above, Saunders' relation has become merely "The voiage made to Tripolis in Barbarie, in the yeere 1584. with a ship called the Jesus, wherein the adventures and distresses of some Englishmen are truly reported, and other necessarie circumstances observed. Written by Thomas Saunders."

What is lost in Hakluyt's abbreviated version of the title, aside from sheer volume, is the religious lesson in the original, which was emphasized through the adjectives used, the employment of such terms as "infidel" and "tormentors," and the type font on the line "together with the most wonderful judgement" [of God], which clearly evoked the German black type of early print bibles. Furthermore, with the virtual elimination of the plot summary in the title, Hakluyt also prevents the reader from knowing the basic generic pattern of the text. The extensive plot description and the dramatic word choice of the original are generic signalers that this was to be a story of a certain kind, and therefore asked to be read in a certain way. Adjectives like miserie, curssed, barbarous, cruell, terrible, unfaithfulnesse, heathnish, and woonderful indicate that the enjoyment of this text will lie in its dramatic calamities and its reassuringly happy ending. Once the voyage ceased to be "lamentable" and became simply a set of far tamer "adventures and distresses," readers were no longer being encouraged to read the text in the mode evoked by the pamphlet [see figs. 4 and 5].

The changes made to the pamphlet's marginalia function in a similar manner to disturb the traditional moralistic reading of the story. Only two notes are altered, but a full forty-one notes are eliminated, 60 percent of the total notes in the original.[20] There is no discernable pattern to the notes which are retained and kept; the primary effect of eliminating so many notes is to render them incapable of transmitting the plot in a coherent manner. Several big logical gaps in the story appear in the marginal notes

Of a moſt lamentable

Voiage, made latelie to

Tripolie in Barbarie, in a Ship named
the I E S V S:

vvherin is not onely ſhevved

the great miſerie, that then happened the Auĉthor hereof
and his whole companie, afwell the Marchants as the Marriners in that Voiage, according to the curſſed cuſtome of thoſe
barbarous and cruell Tyrants, in their terrible vſage of
Chriſtian captiues: but alfo, the great vnfaithful-
neſſe of thoſe heathniſh Infidels, in not regarding their promiſe.

Together, with the moſt woonderfull iudgement
of God, vpon the king of Tripolie and his ſonne,
and a great number of his people, being all the
Tormentors of thoſe Engliſh Captiues.

Set foorth by THOMAS SAVNDERS,
one of thoſe Captiues there at
the ſame time.

¶ Imprinted at London, by Richard Iones, for Edward
White, dwelling at the Signe of the Gun, by the little
North doore of Paules, the 15. of Aprill. 1587.

4. The cover page of Thomas Saunders' *A true description and breefe discourse of a most lamentable voiage, made latelie to Tripolie in Barbarie* (1587). The Bodleian Library, University of Oxford, Shelfmark 4° C 16(23) Art.BS.

Commonly the Carauans come thither in October from Mecca to Cairo, and from thence to Alexandria, where the merchants be that buy the fpices, and therefore the fpices are brought moft to Alexandria, where each Chriftian nation remaineth at the Confuls houfes. Yet oftentimes the Chriftians go vp to Cairo to buy drugs and other commodities there as they fee caufe. And the commodities there vendible, are all fortes of kerfies, but the moft part blewes, and of clothes all colours except mingled colours and blacks. Pepper is vfually fold for 24. ducats the quintal. Ginger for 14. ducats. You muft take canuas to make bags to put your commoditie in from Alexandria, for there is none. There is alfo fine flaxe, and good ftore of Buffe hides.

The voiage made to Tripolis in Barbarie, in the yeere 1584. With *a ſhip called the Iefus, wherein the aduentures and diſtreſſes of ſome En-glithmen are truly reported, and other neceſſarie circumſtances obſerued. Written by* Thomas Sanders.

This voiage was fet foorth by the right woorſhipfull, fir Edward Oſburne knight, chiefe merchant of all the Turkiſh company, and one maſter Richard Stapers, the ſhip being of the burthen of one hundred tunne, called the Iefus, ſhe was budded at Farunne a riuer by Portſmouth. The owners were maſter Thomas Thomſon, Nicholas Carnabie, and Iohn Gilman. The maſter (vnder God) was one Zacheus Hellier of Black-wall, and his Mate was one Richard Morris of that place: their Pilot was one Anthony Ierado a French man, of the prouince of Maſſils: the purſer was one William Thomſon our owners fome: the merchants factors were Romane Sonnings, a Frenchman, and Richard Skegs feruant vnto the faid maſter Stapers. The owners were bound vnto the merchants by charter partie thereupon, in one thouſand markes, that the fayd ſhip by Gods permiſſion ſhould goe for Tripolis in Barbarie, that is to fay, firſt from Portſmouth to Newhauen in Normandie, from thence to S. Lukar, otherwiſe called S. Lucas in Andeluzia, and from thence to Tripolie, which is in the Eaſt part of Affrica, & fo to returne vnto London.

Man doeth pur poſe, and God both diſpoſe.

But here ought euery man to note and confider the woorkes of our God that (many times) what man doth determine, God doth difappoint. The faid maſter hauing fome occaſion to go to Farunne, tooke with him the Pilot and the Purſer, and returning againe by meanes of a petrie of wind, the boate wherein they were, was drowned, the faid maſter, the purfer, and all the company: onely the faid Pilot by experience in fwimming faued himſelfe: thefe were the beginnings of our forowes.

A new maſter chofen.

After which the faid maſters Mate would not proceed in that voiage, and the owner hearing of this misfortune, and the vnwillingneſſe of the maſters Mate, did fend downe one Richard Deimond, and ſhipped him for maſter, who did chufe for his Mate one Andrew Dier, and fo the faid ſhip departed on her voiage accordingly: that is to fay, about the 16. of October, in An, 1584. ſhe made faile from Portſmouth, and the 18, day then next following ſhe arriued into Newhauen, where

The new maſter died.

our faid laft maſter Deimond by a furfeit died. The factors then appointed the faid Andrew Dier being then maſters Mate, to be their maſter for that voiage, who did chufe to be his Mates, the two quarter maſters of the fame ſhip, to wit, Peter Auftine, and Shillabey, and for purſer was ſhipped one Richard Burges. Afterward about the 8.day of Nouember, we made faile foorthward, and by force of weather we were driuen backe againe into Portſmouth, where we refreſhed our bictuals and other neceſſaries, and then the wind came faire. About the 29.day then next following, wee departed thence, and the firſt day of December by meanes of a contrary winde, we were driuen to Plimmouth. The 18,day then next following, we made foorthward againe, and by force of weather we were driuen to Falmouth, where we remained vntil the firſt day of Ianuarie: at which time the wind comming faire, we departed thence, & about the 20,day of the faid moneth we arriued fafely at S, Lucas. And about the 9.day of March next following, we made faile from thence, and about the

The Iefus arriued in Tripolis.

18,day of the fame moneth we came to Tripolis in Barbarie, where wee were very well interteined by the king of that country, and alfo of the commons. The commodities of that place are fweet oiles: the king there is a merchant, and the rather (willing to preferre himfelf before his commons) requeſted our faid factors to traffique with him, and promiſed them that if they would take his oiles at his owne price, they ſhould pay no maner of cuftome, and they tooke of him certaine tunnes of oile: and afterward perceiuing that they might haue farre better cheape notwithſtanding the cuftome free, they defired the king to licence them to take the oiles at the pleaſure of his commons, for that his price did exceed theirs: whereunto the king would not agree, but was rather contented to abate his price, infomuch that the factors bought all their oiles of the kings cuftome free, and fo laded the fame aboord.

In

as printed in the *Navigations*; these notes cannot be used as shorthand for the text, which now must be read in full for the story to make sense. The opening few notes serve as a prime example of this. When strung together, Saunders' marginal notes for the first two pages of the original printed pamphlet read as follows:

> Man dooth purpose, and god dooth dispose. The Maister and the Purser with all the rest except the Pilot drowned. A new Maister chosen. The new maister died. The Jesus arrived into Newhaven. Another Maister chosen. The Jesus driven backe againe into Portsmouth. After set forward and driven backe againe into Plimmouth. After that driven back to Falmouth. The Jesus arrived into Tripolie. (A4r–v)

The moral of the story is stated at the beginning, and immediately the reader is given multiple examples of God frustrating the plans of the men involved, primarily through poor weather and unexpected deaths. The list of calamities in conjunction with warnings about the contrariness of God's will also instills in the reader a sense of foreboding for the upcoming voyage. Surely this trip is not meant to be. When the text is reprinted in the *Principall Navigations*, the notes run as follows: "Man dooth purpose, and god dooth dispose. A new Maister chosen. The new maister died. The Jesus arrived into Tripolie."[21] The storyline here is somewhat more disturbed. Presumably God did something to the original ship's master since a new one needed to be chosen for the voyage, although what happened is not specified. Once the new master was similarly dispatched, the ship arrives in North Africa. The most logical (if incorrect) conclusion here is that God did not wish the ship to arrive in Tripoli with a master onboard and therefore did everything he could to keep this from happening. It seems clear that one cannot use these notes as a coherent summary of the plot (although it's fun to try); they must instead be used as indicators of major points of interest in the text. Similarly, the moral message regarding the inscrutability of God's will is by no means eliminated in Hakluyt's version of the printed text, but its effect is significantly weakened. In short, the marginalia in Saunders' tale as printed in the *Navigations* always refer the reader back to the full text for both plot and thematic development; unlike in the original pamphlet publication, they cannot stand alone.

With both the title and the margin notes disabled as devices for plot summary, there is no way to know the end of the tale ahead of time. Unlike Saunders-as-pamphlet-narrative, Saunders-as-principal-navigation can be read as a tale of suspense, with the reader uncertain as to the ultimate end to the story or therefore its ultimate moral. Moreover, the two notes that were actually changed in the *Navigations* reprinting both serve to blunt or downplay that original religious moral. In one original pamphlet note, the French factor who is blamed for the ship's confiscation and the crew's enslavement, Romaine Sonnings, is condemned for his behavior in the face of execution in Tripoli: the note reads "Romaine Sonnings the Frenchman turned Turke in hope of his life, and died in the profession of a Turke" (B4r). The religious lesson here is clear: those who think they can save their lives by conversion to Islam (as was generally believed) are not only wrong, but will burn in hell for abjuring Christ right before death. Hakluyt modifies this note to soften the religious warning somewhat: his note reads "A Frenchman turned Turke, in hope of his life, and afterward was hanged" (*PN*, 195). It's not entirely clear here whether the Frenchman had time to recant his conversion to Islam and return to the Christian fold before he was hanged. The word "afterward" is ambiguous in regard to how much time passed between the Frenchman's conversion and death. It is possible to read this merely as a warning that conversion to Islam does not actually guarantee better treatment at the hands of Islamic captors. This is in contrast to the original note, in which the phrase "died in the profession of a Turke" makes the Frenchman's doom, and the moral of this tale, perfectly clear. Thus, in the *Navigations* marginal note, the religious lesson is softened slightly, while the secular one regarding how Christian captives should behave when taken hostage is brought to the fore. This pattern is one that holds in other areas of paratextual change as well, where the changes work simultaneously to blunt the mode of reading enabled by the narrative's original pamphlet format and to insinuate alternative engagements with the text, ones that downplay religion and the personal and promote a sense of national identity and possibility.

The final change made to the pamphlet's account of Saunders' travails is the addition of the queen's letters. You might expect that such missives would function similarly to Saunders's dedication of the tract to the judge of the admiralty, strengthening Saunders' claim as a worthy Englishman by highlighting that his redemption was accomplished through the queen's personal intervention. Indeed, this is one possible interpretation of the new link made in the *Navigations* between Saunders and his queen. Both the positioning and the content of the queen's letters, however, mitigate against this conclusion. Saunders' story ends with a move reminiscent of his insistence in the pamphlet epistle dedicatory that he is "whollie bounden" to the judge of the admiralty; the author claims that his redemption has entailed upon him a whole series of such binding obligations:

> we are bound to praise almighty God during our life, and as dutie bindeth us, to praie for the preservation of our most gratious Queene, for the great care hir Majestie had over us hir poore subjects, in seeking and procuring

of our deliverance aforesaid, and also for hir honorable privie councell, & I espeically for the prosperitie and good estate of the house of the late deceased the Right honorable the earle of Bedford, whose honor I must confesse, most diligentlie at the sute of my father now departed, travelled herein; for the which I rest continuallie bounden to his, whose soule I doubt not but is alreadie in the heavens in joy with the Almightie, unto which place he vouchsafe to bring us all, that for our sins suffered most vile and shamefull death upon the crosse, there to live perpetuallie world without end, Amen. (C4v)

Saunders begins with his obligation to God, works his way down the chain of rank—the queen, her privy council, the Earl of Bedford, his own father—and ends the pamphlet a few sentences later with an "Amen," reminding us that such a social order and its obligations are divinely sanctioned. This set of obligations reinforces the traditional ordering of society and Saunders' place within it. In the *Principall Navigations*, however, although this text is retained untouched, it is now followed by the queen's letter to the Sultan Murad, which is cast entirely in terms of the reciprocal set of obligations the queen shares, not with her loving people, but with the Ottoman sultan. It seems initially that the queen's letter is echoing Saunders' hierarchy and its link to the Christian God, but it suddenly takes a left turn as it veers into praise of the Islamic emperor:

> Elizabeth, by the grace of the most high God, and onely maker of heaven and earth, of England, France, and Ireland Queene, and of the Christian faith, against all the Idolaters and false professors of the name of Christ dwelling among the Christians, most invincible and puissant defender: to the most valiant and invincible Prince, Zultan Murad Can, the most mightie Ruler of the kingdome of Musulman, and of the East Empire the onely and highest Monarch above all, health, and many happie and fortunate yeeres, with great aboundance of the best things. (*PN*, 200)

Following these conventional diplomatic greetings and wishes of health and happiness to the sultan, the queen reminds the Ottoman ruler of their recent agreement, in which the sultan granted to England an ambassador and special trading privileges throughout his territories. She thanks the sultan for this boon, which he "most liberally and favourably granted to our subjects of England," hoping that "by mutuall traffike, the East may be joyned and knit to the West;" this laudable outcome will further result in "most great profits and commodities to both sides, as well to the parties subject to your Empire, as to the Provinces of our kingdome" (*PN*, 200). Following this opening salutation and tracing of the recent diplomatic and trading history between the two nations, the queen finally mentions the incident that we as readers of Saunders' tale have been anticipating. In the third paragraph of her letter, the queen refers to some of "our subjects" who have been "evil intreated and grievously vexed," by some of the sultan's subjects, who were "perhaps ignorant of your pleasure." Given this news, the queen very politely

> desires your Imperiall Majestie, that you will understand their causes by our Ambassadour, and afterward give commandement to the Lieutenants and Presidents of those provinces, that our people may hencefoorth freely, without any violence, or injurie, travel, and doe their busines in those places. (*PN*, 200)

She closes the letter with a promise to perform all those things that she understands will be acceptable to the sultan, may whom "God, the onely maker of the world, most best and most great, long keepe in health, and flourishing."

The letter included as part of Saunders's tale thus never references Saunders at all, or his companions, or even the ship. Indeed, the events of his capture and captivity are framed squarely as an example of a minor violation in an overall solid agreement made previously between the two rulers. In thirty lines of text, only about two and one-half acknowledge the plight of the Jesus and her crew, while the other twenty-eight or so express love and good will toward the Ottoman emperor, good wishes for their mutual advantage in this new diplomatic relationship, and a general review of their joint history. This is unsurprising, since from the queen's perspective the importance of her budding diplomatic and trading relationship with the Porte far outweighs one merchant ship and a group of commoners taken into captivity. The ecumenical language that the queen crafts here was designed to mute religious differences in the effort to establish what would be a very profitable alliance, and one that might be a powerful political counterbalance to growing Spanish power and hostility.[22] This warm, friendly (albeit formal) language toward the "Great Turk" clashes badly with the antagonism Saunders continually displays toward Muslims in his narrative, and therefore presents a strange counterpoint to the voyage that this letter was supposed to supplement or corroborate. The traditional social and religious values in Saunders' pamphlet have been disrupted by the strange complexities of international diplomacy; Saunders himself has become a mere ripple in the delicate and stormy motions of state relations.

This impression is only strengthened by the Turkish letters that follow, which detail the workings and customs of the Ottoman bureaucracy needed to effect the release of the English captives and the restitution of their ship and property. If anything, the sultan emerges as a strong protector of English subjects and their interests within his domain, and yet does so in a way that respects the judgment and integrity of his own subjects. His letter orders his viceroys in Argiers, Tunis, and Tripoli to refrain from taking Christian ships, even when those ships fire upon North African vessels, since the Christians must remain upon their guard against pirate galleys and might therefore be forgiven for mistaking state vessels for rebel pirate ships:[23]

> We therefore command thee, that upon sight hereof, thou doe not permit any such matter in no sort whatsoever, but suffer the said English men to passe in peace, according to the tenor of our commandment given, without any disturbance, or let, by any meanes upon the way, although that meeting with thy gallies, and not knowing them a farre off, they taking them for enemies, should shoote at them, yet shall you not suffer them to hurt them therefore, but quietly to passe. (*PN*, 201)

The scenario detailed here, which was mentioned twice in the sultan's letter to his viceroys, is striking in part because it was not at all the case with the taking of the Jesus. Both sides were perfectly well aware who the enemy was; the English ship was attempting to flee the harbor and the viceroy of Tripoli was trying to keep them there. Eventually a captured Christian gunner, a Spaniard, was promised freedom if he could hit the English ship; the gunner was skilled enough to bring the Jesus to a standstill, at which point she was boarded, her goods confiscated, and her crew taken prisoner. Thus, as in the case of the queen's letter requesting the release of the crew and the restitution of the ship's goods, the sultan's letter is extremely general, and refers to conditions in the Mediterranean at large, rather than the circumstances attending the taking of this one ship. Saunders' tale is once again placed inside a much broader frame (international naval relations in the eastern Mediterranean), a frame in which the Islamic emperor is shown to act fairly—even charitably—toward English sailors within his domains.

The effect of these two letters, when combined with the alterations in the marginalia and the title, is to blunt or run against the grain of the pamphlet's original moral that Turks lie and torment Christians, but that God will vindicate his people in the end. Indeed, the letters directly contradict the assertion that Turks do not keep their word, as the queen's letter is a reminder of an agreement between the two states that the sultan then proceeds to honor. Saunders' narrative has an advantage in this conflict in that it is far longer than the letters that follow (seven and one-half folio pages to the letters' two and one-half), and coming first, it conditions the reader to regard the Barbary inhabitants, their sovereign, and his emperor as faithless, greedy, and violent. Yet, original letters written by two great sovereigns—one of whom was the readers' queen—would far outweigh in status and thus in credit the tale of a commoner. The letters therefore hold their own against the length and priority of Saunders' account, especially given the subtle changes in the paratext made during the pamphlet's migration into a principal navigation. One might also view the letters as having the last word on the matter, since following the letters the collection moves on to a new Levantine voyage. Indeed, the fact that Saunders' tale is embedded in a series of narratives describing the eastern Mediterranean, most of which discuss diplomatic and trading conditions with the Ottoman Empire, further emphasizes the broader national and mercantile contexts in which this story took place.

What ultimately makes possible this shift away from the traditional religious moral of Saunders' title, however, are the details of Saunders' own story. This tale is, in effect, a highly unstable story in that its rhetoric is contradicted by the narrated facts of Saunders' experience. Saunders carefully traces the chain of English letters and communications that effected his release, beginning with his own to his father, then his father's plea to the Earl of Bedford, the earl's visit to London to inform the queen of the matter, and finally the queen's letter requesting their deliverance, which was sent via the merchant Edward Osborne to William Harborne, the queen's ambassador in Istanbul. He must then, however, follow this sequence of events through to the sultan's commission for their release, which was carried by Edward Barton (assistant to the ambassador), a "Justice of the great Turkes," a Turkish soldier, "another Turk," and a Greek interpreter to the viceroy in Tripoli. Upon their interview with the viceroy, the Turkish justice is quoted at length by Saunders; the Englishmen are delivered from slavery and their goods returned to them at the explicit order of the Turkish emperor. The viceroy (here called the King of Tripoli) first asks the group to state their business:

> The Justice answered that the great Turke his Sovereigne had sent them unto him, signifying that hee was informed that a certain English shippe called the Jesus, was by him the said king confiscated, about twelve moneths since, and nowe my saide Sovereigne hath here sent his especiall commission by us unto you, for the deliverance of the said ship and goods, and also the free libertie & deliverance of the Englishmen of the same shippe, whome you have taken and kept in captivitie. And further the same Justice saide, I am authorized by my saide Sovereigne the great Turke to see it done: And therefore I commande you by vertue of this commission, presently to make restitution of the premisses or the value thereof . . . which commission the King with all obedience received. (C3r)

The fact of the Englishmen's release is ultimately unambiguously attributed to the Turkish emperor and the obedience he claims from his subjects, not the English queen or her servants. Even more interestingly, the climax of the story marks a narrative shift from Saunders' focalization, in

which he paraphrases the justice's words in indirect discourse, to a form
of direct quotation in which Saunders-the-author speaks as the justice,
using first person pronouns and possessives. Thus "the great Turke *his*
Sovereigne" becomes "*my* saide Sovereigne the great Turke" (my emphasis). This is an act of imaginative reconstruction; in Saunders' account,
all the English captives are explicitly ordered into the room immediately
after this exchange takes place. As this presumably includes Saunders
himself, he could not have been a first hand witness to the conversation.
It is tempting to speculate on the psychological rationales for this adop-
tion of the persona of the Turkish Justice, especially as this type of shift
in narrative voice is unique in Saunders' narrative. My purpose here is
not to fathom the mind of the author, however, but to note that this structural shift heightens the dramatic effect of the intervention of the Turkish
justice, and renders it a particularly vivid moment in the text. Despite the
role that the English sovereign and her subjects play in the emancipation
of the English captives, it is clearly the good will and power of the Turkish emperor that makes it so. Furthermore, the chain of causality tells the
reader that the sultan does so at the behest of the English ambassador. It
is the friendship that the "Great Turk" bears toward the English queen
and her subjects that effects this release. In contrast to Saunders' repeated
invective against the Muslims he encountered, the story makes clear that
he owes some of these Muslims his gratitude.

As the title indicates, Saunders' narrative quickly retreats from this
rapprochement with the Turkish authorities. Immediately following the
dramatic recounting of the prisoners' release by order of the sultan, Saunders "returne[s] to the kings plagues and punishments which Almightie
God at his will and pleasure sendeth upon men in the sight of the world,
and likewise of the plagues that befell his children and others aforesaid"
(C3v). The long list of misfortunes that follows stretches for two pamphlet
pages, describing how the Viceroy of Tripoli lost half of his three hundred slaves to plague within a month of the Englishmen's capture (what
were those Englishmen carrying?), proceeded to lose to thieves the same
number of camels on the one-month anniversary of their captivity, and
then allowed a Maltese captive to escape with his new brigandine, along
with twelve other Christian captives. Most impressively to the author, the
viceroy "road forth upon the greatest & fairest mare that might be seen,
as white as any swan: he had not ridden 40. paces fro[m] his house, but on
a sudden the same mare fell downe under him starke dead" (C3v). After
smiting so many animals around the viceroy's person, God eventually
arranges the assassination of the viceroy himself, according to Saunders'
account; within three months of the Englishmen's delivery, the "Soldiers
of Tripolie killed the said king." The viceroy's son, "according to the cus-
tom there," sails to Istanbul with the remaining wealth and goods of the

deceased official in order to surrender them to the sultan. The ship is captured on route by a Venetian galley, however, ending in the slaughter of all the Muslims on board and the freeing of all the Christian slaves. And thus, with the plaguing and punishment of the ruler of Tripoli and its inhabitants, and the safe arrival home of Saunders and the remaining few English survivors of this ordeal, "we are bound to praise almightie God during our life" (C4v). The queen and numerous others are then thanked, as discussed above, and the narrative closes in an echo of the Lord's Prayer, "world without end, Amen." Saunders' brief excursion into the mind of the Turkish judge is solidly recouped in these final paragraphs, as the Deuteronomic code, or at least God's solid preference for Christianity, is reinstated. The Tripolitans involved in the enslavement of the Englishmen are punished, while the innocent English are returned safely home. There is no thankfulness to the sultan, nor thanks to God for moving his heart to act on the Englishmen's behalf; the Great Turk and his officials are cut out of the final moments of gratitude as recorded in the narrative. Instead, through the punishment of the "turks" at the hand of the Christian Venetians, a clear division between the two religious populations is reimposed and presented as divinely ordained.

The facts of the story remain, however, as does the vivid climax of the Englishmen's release in Tripoli at the hands of the Turkish judge. By placing the queen's correspondence with the sultan immediately following Saunders' tale, Hakluyt and/or his printer highlight this contradiction within the story and draw back into focus the cooperation between the two rulers and nations rather than the religious divisions between them. As the letters emphasize the broader diplomatic agreements and contexts within which the release was engineered, Saunders' experiences are made to seem as one particular incident situated within a broader scenario of international politics, rather than a paradigmatic instance of the eternal enmity of Christians and Muslims. The paratextual changes made to Saunders' pamphlet in the course of its transformation to a *Principall navigation . . . of the English nation* use the story's internal contradictions to shift the reader's attention from one possible resolution of that tension to another. The pamphlet ignores the sultan's role in effecting the release of the Englishmen in its attempt to place itself within the medieval crusade paradigm; the *Navigations* downplays the particularities of the author's treatment at the hands of certain Muslims in order to emphasize the general geopolitical context in which that situation occurred, and the good that could be brought about through cordial relations with Islamic nations.

This strategy is particular to Saunders' inclusion in the *Navigations.* Other selections do not include the kind of internal contradiction described here. Sometimes the paratextual changes Hakluyt and/or his printer made reinforce the themes and conclusions of the included narrative; sometimes

they contradict them outright. I would argue, however, that most of the
changes made to the accounts in order to include them in Hakluyt's collection have as their aim the generalizing and nationalizing effect that I have
traced in the case of Saunders' tale. Hakluyt does not in fact wish to provide his readers traditional stories with predictable endings about the per-
fidy of foreigners and the justice of God; instead he would like his readers
to be inspired to emulate their queen in establishing profitable relationships overseas and to think about the good of the nation as a whole. Or
simply to think about the nation as a whole—to conceptualize themselves
as Englishmen participating in some larger project than that described in
any one tale. Furthermore, while God is certainly not absent in Hakluyt's
thinking or his collection, there is a general shift in the deity's relationship
to his English subjects. For example, in Hakluyt's version of Saunders'
story, it is not so much God as the queen and the sultan working together
toward their common commercial profit that accomplishes the release of
the English captives and their goods. God is certainly to be praised and
thanked, but Hakluyt's readers are given the lesson that good foreign relations and power projected beyond England's shores are the best guarantee
of bodily salvation and commercial gain. The two are linked together by
the active voyaging of the English and their willingness to think collectively and profitably as a people about their position on the world stage.
Hakluyt accomplishes this through the shift in form represented by his
relatively novel collection of English overseas voyages. The form of the
collection, accompanied by a series of changes to the originals' paratext
that suppress or alter the texts' original generic form and reader expectations, works for Hakluyt as a way to use materials written for other
printing contexts as part of a nationalistic narrative encouraging English
overseas trade and diplomatic relations.

The following chapter addresses this latter point by comparing the inter-
linked form and content of the Persian materials printed in the *Navigations*

with the variety of popular materials discussed in chapter 2, which were printed to describe the Sherley brothers' exploits in that same country. In it I will continue to pay attention to the original context of composition for the set of tales in Hakluyt's collection and the changes that would have occurred upon their inclusion in the compilation. I will also expand my analytic lens somewhat, however, to consider the claims so frequently made for Hakluyt's voyages, namely that they are inherently more historically "accurate," "factual," or "trustworthy" than other prose relations printed at the time. In short, the following chapter will consider the question of whether Hakluyt's voyage narratives were regarded as "more true" than other reports of foreign lands printed at the time.

5

Determining the Facts of the Matter:
Merchant Letters and *The Principall Navigations*

THE PREVIOUS CHAPTER DISPLAYED THE analytic benefits to be derived from attending to the ideological implications of form when studying early modern travel accounts. Through an exploration of the Muscovy Company letters included in Hakluyt's *Principall Navigations*, this chapter will also consider some of the hazards that accompany the exclusion of form—its histories and ideologies—from our analytic armory.

The *Navigations* has undoubtedly received more critical attention in the past two centuries than any other early modern travel text, while its editor holds the honor of being the only early modern figure associated with foreign travel to inspire the creation of a society devoted to the publication and dissemination of travel accounts written by English authors.[1] As described above, most of this critical attention has been uniformly positive, citing Hakluyt's "seriousness" as an editor, crediting him with "compiling archives of history" or collecting the "actual history" of the period.[2] This praise contains an implicit negative comparison to other travel documents from the period, whose histories presumably do not qualify as "actual."

These readers are responding to a significant difference in form between many of the travel accounts published in Hakluyt's collection and those previously published in the period, whether in collections like Willes' *The history of travayle* or singularly as popular pamphlets, elegant folio books, or anything in between. Although the *Principall Navigations* included many medieval accounts, some previously printed popular pamphlets, and a selection of first person narratives similar to many published at the time, it also published, for the first time, a large selection of merchant company documents, which differed in form and content from most previous travel publications. It is primarily these materials, I would argue, that have inspired so many critics to accord Hakluyt's collection a higher truth value than other travel materials printed at the time. Indeed, a recent description of these merchant accounts makes explicit the connection between trade company letters and the *Principall Navigations*' status in the current scholarly literature: "those who traveled for the sake of trade helped to produce *a body of knowledge* that would serve the purpose of profit. The texts compiled by Richard Hakluyt and Samuel Purchas are the best-known examples of this *data-gathering*." Borrowing from the lexicon of science and information technology, the author reinforces the idea that merchant letters contain material that is neutral and factual by anachronistically using the term "data-gathering." This elides the many layers of mediation that sit between the original observation of such "data" and its communication to us in the form of a collection of materials printed in 1589. It also overlooks the complex and often vexed social negotiations involved in the construction of any "body of knowledge," especially that treating foreign lands and peoples.[3]

It is easy to fall into the mistake of using such language to describe merchant company letters since their most notable feature is the prevalence of seemingly short, value-neutral statements treating the material conditions of travel, such as weather, topography, speed of travel, and physical objects desirable as trading commodities, e.g., wool, silk, currants, pepper, etc. They bear a strong formal verisimilitude to the types of locutions that today we call "facts," i.e., "truth, reality . . . a thing known for certain to be true; a datum of experience . . . a thing assumed or alleged as the basis for inference."[4] In other words, statements modern readers classify as "facts" are read as somehow elemental, beyond interpretation, the building block of raw data upon which interpretation is built.[5] They communicate "reality" or, in a historical context, something that "actually" happened or existed. As the merchant accounts in the *Navigations* are filled with statements bearing a formal resemblance to the modern fact (and indeed, contain little else), I would argue that a kind of formal misrecognition has occurred in the critical literature, wherein the many merchant accounts are read as "factual," in a way that would have made little sense to early modern readers or authors.

The word *fact* does routinely appear in sixteenth- and seventeenth-century texts, but its definition at the time was quite different from the current primary meaning for the term. Derived from *faiçt*, the medieval past participle of the French verb *faire* ("to make, to do"), in Hakluyt's time a fact was something done, an action completed, a deed accomplished. The word originally entered English through the juridical system, which since the Norman Conquest had employed French as its transactional language. The common phrase *matters of fact* referred at the turn of the seventeenth century to the domain of witnesses in the courtroom, who were called upon to clarify the specifics of past deeds, or facts (in this case, criminal actions) so that the jury might come to a conclusion regarding what really happened: the facts of the matter. The early modern fact, therefore, was a highly contested deed, in which firsthand witnessing was the most credible evidence for its occurrence, followed by secondhand or thirdhand accounts, and finally documentary evidence.[6] It is, for example, in this sense that the term is used in the treaty between Queen Elizabeth I and the Ottoman Sultan Murad III, as printed in Hakluyt's *Navigations*: "If any [Englishman] shall commit any great crime, and flying thereupon can not bee found, let no man be arrested, or detained for another mans fact, except he be his suretie."[7]

Although the primary meaning of the word *fact* shifted across the early modern period, studies tracing the history of factuality usually date the origins of its modern understanding to the middle or end of the seventeenth century. Thus, readers of Hakluyt's late-sixteenth-century collection were unlikely to have used the presence or absence of facts as we know them to evaluate the truth status of the narratives in his volumes. Given this chronology, several questions present themselves, namely: if these fact-like statements in the merchant account are not modern facts, what are they? How would they have been read?

Many scholars writing on Hakluyt's collection have made claims regarding its early modern reception, although these claims are not often stated explicitly. This reluctance to engage the issue directly is understandable, given the notorious difficulties attending determining how books were read in previous centuries. Tracking down evidence for reader response to a particular work is an even more daunting task. So few critics try, preferring instead to limit their treatment of the reception of the *Navigations* to a few enthusiastic adjectives; those who have made a more extended effort, such as James P. Helfers—upon whom Hakluyt's collection "impresses a sense of specificity, factuality, and comprehensiveness"—often end up with a combined discussion of (what is clearly a modern) reader response, and implied motivations on Hakluyt's part. Indeed, the latter are much discussed in the literature; proving that Hakluyt "intended . . . to provide as much information as possible (whether foreign or domestic) for English explorers and colonists to use," however, does not prove that the *Principall Navigations* was read that way by most of its audience.[8] Moreover, Hakluyt frequently acted as a consultant for trading companies and the crown and as an earnest petitioner for Crown support of navigational instruction and colonial funding. The oral advice he gave, the letters he exchanged and passed around, and the colonial tracts he circulated through manuscript publication to the relevant parties, all accomplished this purported goal of facilitating informational exchange between merchant and colonial travellers—without printing or selling anything. The elaborate presentation of both historical and contemporary travel texts to the public via the printing press seems more likely to have been done for propagandistic purposes: to stir up interest, enthusiasm, and national pride. (Indeed, the phenomenal rise of small investors in merchant companies during the decade immediately following the second edition of the *Navigations* might well be a reflection of the book's success in this vein.[9]) But, it is not important here either to prove or disprove critical guesses on Hakluyt's intent in publishing the *Navigations*—indeed, they are in the end forever unknowable.[10] The point is that few to no critics make any effort to place Hakluyt's collections within their generic context, or to discuss them as a set of printed books in a marketplace of (dis)similar commodities. Instead, most tend implicitly to project modern evaluations and approval upon a set of texts that, according to early modern travel-history-writing standards, were neither fish nor fowl.[11]

To the extent that comparisons with other early modern travel histories are made, they are usually made (briefly) with the other vast collection of tales published shortly after Hakluyt's death, Samuel Purchas' *Hakluytus Posthumous, or Purchas, his Pilgrimes*. In what are usually rather judgmental essays, critics deplore Purchas and praise Hakluyt for two main reasons: first, the editorial prose of the former is condemned for its fussiness, and that of the latter feted for its transparency (allowing the "business-like air" of his sources to come through); second, Purchas is reviled for his indiscriminate hacking and rewriting of (so-called) genuine historical documents while Hakluyt is lauded for his commitment to empiricism—a point then related to his noninterventionist editorial style. Purchas has recently been well defended by Helfers, who points out that the two editors wrote for disparate audiences and for quite different reasons.[12] Helfers, however, does not treat the anachronistic application of the criteria of empiricism to these two early modern travel collections, which is often the strongest claim that Hakluyt's proponents make on his behalf.

Hakluyt's insistence that those who had travelled were responsible for bringing "certayne and full discoverie of the world" to "us"—presumably the armchair travellers of the day—and his decision to "refer every voyage to his Author, which both in person hath performed, and in writing hath left the same," has been regarded by critics as indicative of his integrity as an editor and his devotion to high documentary standards.[13] Indeed, this quotation is usually seen as sufficient evidence for the attribution of empiric superiority (and is often the only evidence marshalled on its behalf).[14] Yet, it seems worthwhile to be cautious when awarding accolades for precocious empiricism. After all, at least 10 percent of the material in the second edition of the *Navigations* is antiquarian, and the majority of the "Ambassages, Letters, Privileges, and other necessarie matter of circumstance appertaining to the voyages" cannot precisely be classed as empirical observation of foreign lands.[15] Hakluyt's guardian and inspiration, his cousin Richard Hakluyt the lawyer, had along with John Dee debated the possibility of navigating a northeast passage to Cathay—that is, to China, by sailing along the northern coast of the Asian continent, basing their arguments entirely upon such authors as Pliny and Ishmael Abulfeda.[16] Empirically gathered knowledge was desirable, but it was not always privileged over other, more traditional forms of knowledge. If anything, classical and contemporary works provided competing models of authority and knowledge acquisition throughout the period of Hakluyt's life.[17]

Moreover, there is another explanation for Hakluyt's attribution of each tale he printed in the *Navigations*, one that this book has sought repeatedly to highlight: credibility. Hakluyt published his collection within a subgenre of history that was growing more and more unstable as readerly interest shifted from having social truths related in an entertaining fashion—philosophy by example—to the credibility that could be extended to particular facts—that is, highly contested deeds—included within the histories.[18] By the time Hakluyt was collecting his tales, travellers were notorious for stretching the truth; as William Parry writes at the opening of his history of Anthony Sherley's travels, "It hath beene, and yet is, a proverbiall speech amongst us, that Travellers may lie by authority."[19] Despite this rooted scepticism toward travel histories, the intensity surrounding the debates over the usefulness of travel and the reliability of travel reports—quarrels that were revisited in nearly every narrative of any length and rhetorical seriousness—speaks to the urgency perceived as inhering in such questions. Reputations, both personal and national, were at stake, as well as a great deal of money in the form of trade. Hakluyt's statement of support for empirically-inspired narrative—that those who had travelled were responsible for bringing the world back to English readers—should thus be seen as being mediated by an important consideration: the bearers of such discoveries were never merely neutral carriers of information. On the contrary, each must "answere for himselfe, justifie his reports, and stand accountable for his owne doings."[20] The identities and reputations of the travellers themselves must always stand as the guarantor of the truth of the "facts" they reported. Empirical evidence was useful in large part because contemporary voyages provided a stock of firsthand witnesses, whose testimony could be judged as more or less credible based on the standing of the witness himself.

Thus, critics who tout the great leap toward empiricism and factuality made with the publication of the *Navigations*, citing its instant and sustained popularity as evidence for their claim are—insofar as they are considering seventeenth-century standards at all—confusing epistemology with credibility. Many of the voyages' similarities to modern conventions of nonfiction prose writing were not indicative of a superior truth value accorded to the tales at the time. Empiricism was only beginning to join authority as an arbiter of truth, and the probability of particular short statements (facts) were not yet the main standard of truthfulness in a tale. But if the *Principall Navigations*' epistemological status was uncertain (or at least beyond current scholarly evaluation), its credibility was not. What counted for a narrative's credibility was the social standing of its author(s), and Hakluyt's compilation—filled as it was with writings from the queen, her ministers, major noblemen, and wealthy merchants—had status in excess.

Therefore, putting aside anachronistic attributions of factuality or empiricism, let us return once again to the many merchant reports published by Hakluyt in his *Navigations*, and pursue the question of their perceived truth value through a comparison to other true travel tales from the period and with an eye toward the social credibility of their authors. If these fact-like statements in the merchant account are not modern facts, what are they? How would they have been read? Why are the merchant accounts in particular so relentlessly filled with them? And what have been the effects of our critical misrecognition of such statements? What have been the ramifications, in this case, of not paying attention to questions of form? The remainder of this chapter will address these questions first by exploring the formal features and content patterns of the Muscovy Company materials treating voyages to Persia that are printed in the *Navigations*, and then comparing them to patterns in form and content in the group of separately published accounts of the Sherley brothers' voyages to Persia. The statements in the Muscovy materials that resemble modern facts will be discussed in detail, and linked to the social function these written documents were meant to perform. These statements, which I will be calling "particulars," will then be placed in the context of early modern history writing; they will be differentiated from early modern "facts," which performed an important role in determinations of credibility (both of individuals and texts), but one distinctly different from that played by "facts" in modern knowledge regimes. As in the case of Thomas Saunders' pamphlet, I will consider the changes made to the merchant company letters as they were crafted into principal navigations and, given the high credibility such authors collectively possessed in English society, the impact that their inclusion had on the genre of travel writing as a whole and its claims to tell a true tale about a foreign land and people.

Persian Tales

Several of the published accounts of the Sherley brothers' travels in Persia have been discussed in detail above. It is worth returning to that collection of materials, however, in order to paint in broader brush strokes their form and content differences with the Persian tales printed in *The Principall Navigations*. The Sherley materials are fairly heterogeneous in genre, featuring one stage play, a short anonymous news pamphlet reporting the "success" of the voyage, a personal account of the journey published by one of Sir Anthony Sherley's men, two pamphlets commissioned by

the family to tell their story and whip up support for the Sherleys' political position on Persia, and an autobiographical narrative written by Sir
Anthony himself.[21] Despite this variety of genres, authors, and circumstances of publication, there are at least three features shared by all of
these accounts: the inclusion of dialogue or reported speech, a reliance on
moralistic or prescriptive statements to guide the reader's opinion on the
facts described, and the organization of the narrative around the actions
of the protagonists.

First, all of these accounts at some point slow down their summary
narrative in order to include extended scenes of conversation between
the voyagers and their foreign hosts. These scenes are presented in several different narrative formats. Least popular but still frequent are the
set speeches that are reprinted verbatim for the reader as direct speech.
Two good examples of this ancient historical practice are the opening
speech given by Anthony Sherley upon his presentation to the Persian
shah as printed in the anonymous 1600 pamphlet—"I humblie beseech
your Majestie, when you have read the Historie of the inward thoughtes of
my mind"—and the brief pep talk recorded in Nixon's 1607 pamphlet as
given by Robert Sherley to a group of Persian soldiers preparing to charge
a Turkish enemy under his command—"I need not (worthy Gentlemen,
and souldiers of Persia) seeke to encourage you."[22] Nixon's lengthy piece
also contains an unusual instance of direct dialogue when we are introduced to "a certain Jew" who has "found the meanes to come and speake"
with the third Sherley brother, Sir Thomas, while the latter lay in prison in
Constantinople after an unsuccessful privateering venture in the Mediterranean: "after a few salutations, the Jew reasoned with him in this manner.
As you are a stranger both by your birth, and language, to this Nation; so
you also seeme to bee strange and ignorant of their Natures & Conditions.
I have heard of your long imprisonment, and though I know not the cause,
yet I grieve much at the manner of your handling."[23] Direct speech, either
in set pieces or in dialogue, is rather rare in these early modern histories
of travel, and tends to be reserved for moments of greater significance,
traditionally at battles, royal courts, or when treating matters of religion.

The most common form of representing cross-cultural conversation
was indirect narration by either a topical observer or omniscient narrator.
These indirect reports seem to vary in distance from the conversation itself
depending upon how much space is dedicated to the interaction. Sometimes the exchange is reported quite closely, as in this hostile conversation
between Thomas Sherley and the Turkish "Bashaw" holding him captive:
"[The Bashaw] demanded . . . why in that hostile maner against the law
of Armes, and condition of the League betwixt both kingdomes, without any leave or admittance, hee [Sherley] had landed a forcible power,
with purpose to spoyle and prey in that part of the Turkes Dominion. Sir

Thomas answered, that being violently driven into wants by the fortunes of the sea and his long travels, hee was compelled to land, onely to refresh his men, and the rather in that country which hee knew to bee friend unto his King. The Bashaw replyed againe, that his entrance was against the law."[24] Often, however, only the occurrence of the conversation and its broad topic and outcomes are described, as when the eyewitness William Parry writes that "Sir Anthony made his Oration: which being ended, the king [Shah Abbas I] discoursed with him of his travelles, of his native countrey, the manner of governement there, and of diverse other things that accidentally became the subject of their discourse."[25]

The majority of both the directly and indirectly reported conversations between the English voyagers and their foreign interlocutors focuses more heavily on the English side of the dialogue, often just summarizing foreign responses. This tendency is perhaps unsurprising, given that foreign replies would very often have to be either translated or just surmised by the writer. There are some considerable exceptions to this rule, however, as in Sir Anthony Sherley's autobiographical account of his dealings at the Persian court. Many pages are given to reporting conversations between Sherley and the shah, who is given long passages of direct speech in reply to Sherley's comments. Most notable is the twenty-page dispute between Sherley and the various members of the shah's council, several of whom speak quite suspiciously and disparagingly of Sherley in front of the shah, whose reply ends the long conversational episode.

In terms of tone and content, these scenes of cross-cultural communication are sometimes exaggerated and antagonistic, sometimes quite intricate and ambiguous, sometimes formal and florid. Regardless of the tone, however, all the accounts of the Sherley voyages include several detailed and lengthy presentations of Anglo-Persian interaction, specifically in the form of verbal exchange. This is, in fact, the principal concern of several of the Sherley accounts: the anonymous pamphlet of 1600, Nixon's 1607 piece, and Anthony Sherley's long autobiographical narrative center on the words and deeds of the English travelers and their foreign counterparts. Due to the nature of the genre, it is also of course the prime—although not the only—mode of presentation in Day, Wilkins, and Rowley's collaboratively written play. Thus, well over half of the Sherley texts devote the majority of their narrative space to cross-cultural conversation.

The second feature common to all of the Sherley texts is the presence of overt moralistic statements, either on foreign lands and peoples, the Sherleys' conduct and particular circumstances, or the nature of travel itself. Although the treatment of the Sherleys and their story differs from pamphlet to pamphlet (as does the story itself), all of the works wax moralistic or prescriptive in their discussion of the various subject matter. Readers are instructed, sometimes quite heavy-handedly, about the appropriate

response to the foreign cultures, events, and characters to which they are
introduced in the course of the narrative. This can take the form of sar-
casm, complaint, open preaching, or a prayer in which the reader is invited
to join with the author in beseeching God to enact some particular event.
Unsurprisingly, the preacher John Cartwright provides an excellent example of the latter two approaches, often employed in combination: "As for
the miserable thraldome that the poore Christians doe endure under the
Turkish tyranny, we (thanks be given unto God) in these Northerne parts
of the world may behold with safety, but not without pitie, when we rightly
consider, how that the people among whom our Saviour himselfe con-
versed . . . are now become a cage of uncleane birds: filthy spirits doe possesse them."[26] Unclean birds are one of the milder metaphors deployed by
the preacher, who tends to be rather colorful in his judgments. Yet despite
his purple prose, the preacher remains serious in intent, which is more than
can be said for the panegyric framed and translated by Thomas Middleton in preparation for Robert Sherley's return from Persia. Both Sherley
and Persia are praised unreservedly in a kind of written formal posturing
that often crosses the border into the slightly ridiculous, as in "Englands
Complaint to Persia for her Sherley": "[England:] O Persia! thou glorious
kingdome, thou chiefe of Empires; the Palace sometimes where Wisdome
onely kept her Court, the land that was governed by none but wisemen:
Yet must I tell thee . . . that against all Law of Nations, thou robbest me of
my subject."[27] Readers are also lectured on the good results, both for traveler and nation, of voyaging, as in William Parry's long opening apologia
for traveling and travel writing; self-justifications on the part of the voyagers are also ubiquitous, especially in the case of Anthony Sherley's journey, which was taken under somewhat obscure and controversial auspices.
The examples of this tendency are almost innumerable, for at bottom they
indicate an expectation about the relation of foreign events and places that
includes the instruction of the reader, or at least the presentation of judgments on the part of the author. Clearly these authors expected that they
should evaluate the foreign lands and adventures they described, as well
as provide a narration of images, conversations, and events.

The final characteristic that all of the Sherley texts share is perhaps the
most obvious: all center on the figures of the Sherleys themselves. The
unifying device of the narrative is the thoughts, words, and deeds of the
main characters; the vast majority of each tale is taken up with an account
of these figures. The foreign swirls about them, intimately interacting
with them, acting upon and being impacted by the English voyagers.
These exchanges, and specifically the manner in which the more familiar
English character handles them, form the main interest of all of the Sherley texts. Structurally, this organizational strategy often gives a narrative
arc to the journey, with various departures and destinations functioning

as beginning and ending points for each tale. Thus, the Sherley texts all share several characteristics: they center on the figures of the Sherleys themselves, and specifically on their interactions with foreigners; these interactions are portrayed—often quite extensively—as verbal exchanges between the English and their Levantine and Persian hosts; and, finally, the accounts are interlarded with evaluative language, comments, and lengthy instructional passages that attempt to guide the readers' reactions to the material presented.

In contrast, the material in Hakluyt's volumes depicting English travel to Persia cannot as a group be said to share these characteristics. To begin, the Persian texts in the *Navigations* feature no fewer than seventeen separate protagonists, often appearing in groups of four or five, any one of which might pick up the narration or step into the role of dominant character. There are roughly sixteen separate entries in the *Principall Navigations* depicting the six voyages taken by Muscovy Company factors into Persia between the years 1558 and 1579.[28] Each piece tends to recount some small aspect of the Englishmen's journey into, through, or out of Persia, and might pick up or break off at any given point within the voyage. This tendency is largely due to the format of the tales, which are most often letters sent back to London from various cities along the way. Written by company agents to their masters back in London, these letters are meant to update the latter as to the good behavior and success (or failure) of the former in the task for which the voyage was made: to trade.

The bulk of these letters tend to utilize two main organizational strategies that for the moment I will dub the travel log and the trade report. The travel log is a chronological account of a journey that follows the speaker and the company's goods as they move across the foreign domain in various forms of transportation. It is occasionally peppered with one- or two-sentence references to geographical features along the way, but otherwise continues unbroken for pages at a time. This strategy transmits valuable information to the company in the form of distance, means, and duration of travel, as well as possible transport difficulties, whether geographical, seasonal, or sociopolitical. These details were obviously crucial considerations when planning trading voyages that might take years and absorb an enormous amount of the company's capital and goods; timing and risk were central business concerns, then as now. Crucial as this information might have been to the Muscovy Company merchants, travel log passages make remarkably poor reading for all those not planning a voyage through early modern Asia:

> The 18 day in the morning about seven of the clocke, the pavoses [small ships] being discharged, departed away toward Astracan, the winde then at Southeast, they road still with the shippe, and observing the elevation of the

pole at that place, found it to be 45 degrees 20 minuts. The 19 day, the winde Southeast, they road still. The 20 day the winde at Northwest they set saile about one of the clocke in the morning, and stered thence South by West, and Southsouthwest, about three leagues, and then ankered in sixe and a halfe water, about nine of the clock beforenoone, at which time it fell calme: the elevation of the pole at that place 45 degrees 13 minuts. The 21 having the winde at Northwest, they set saile and stered thence South by West, and South untill eleven of the clocke, and had then nine foote water: and at noone they observed the latitude, and found it to be 44 degrees 47 minuts: they had they three fathoms and a halfe water, being cleare off the flats.[29]

While it is not the case that entire voyages are described in this manner, there are long sections of this type of narration in nearly every Persian voyage. It is easily identifiable by both its predictable content—latitude, leagues, depths, directions, landmarks, and problems with the route or vehicle—and its regularity of form. Although they are written out in prose paragraphs and describe travel across land as well as sea, travel logs clearly derive from daily ship's log entries, which were being rapidly and explicitly regularized by trading companies.[30] They follow a strict chronological order, are usually composed in an anonymous plural (either first or third person), and are never longer than a few sentences, regardless of the events described. Deaths of company members from illness are given little elaboration; violent attacks are handled in only slightly greater detail:

> The 19 November the winde being Northerly, there was a great frost, and much ice in the river: the next day being the 20 of November the ice stood in the river, and so continued until Easter day. The 22 of December departed this life John Moore the gunner of the shippe. Thursday the seventh. . . . Robert Golding desirous to understand what might be done at Shamakie, which is a daies journey from Backow, went thither, from whence returning, he was set on by theeves, and was shot into the knee with an arrow, who had verie hardly escaped with his life and goodes, but that by good hap he killed one of the theeves horses with his caliver, and shot a Turke thorow both cheeks with a dag. On the sixt day of August. . . .[31]

The tendency to give daily weather conditions and death equal narrative attention is a strong testament to the perceived purpose of writing for the authors of Hakluyt's Persian material. Deaths are registered, but not commented upon or discussed in detail because the point of the documents is to encourage replication of the voyage and to assist in preparation for such later attempts. Unlike navigational directions or weather conditions, the details of a particular man's death are fairly irrelevant to this purpose; sicknesses affecting a significant percentage of the party, especially if interpreted as due to weather, location, or traveling conditions, might be considered a significant factor to consider in further voyages to the area,

but singular deaths inevitably less so. Hakluyt's Persian tales do not edi-
torially comment on daily events; the authors make no attempt to teach a
moral lesson or to lend broader significance to anything that occurred during the course of the journey. The point of the letters written from Asia to
the Muscovy Company governors was simply to account for the transport
and sale of Company goods, and any events that did not directly impact
upon that purpose are noted in the briefest manner possible.

Indeed, the majority of narrative space is given to the loading, unloading, shifting, showing, and selling of English goods (mainly wool cloth),
with the concomitant assessment, purchase, shifting, unloading, and loading of Persian goods (mainly silk cloth), a narrative strategy I will call the
trade report. The point of the trade report is identical to that of the travel
log: to account for the transport and sale of company goods. In the trade
report, however, any attempt at narrative chronology is abandoned, as are
a great majority of the details of transporting people and goods from one
location to another. The setting of the letter shifts from one city to another
with little acknowledgement of time taken or distance traveled. Long
deliberations unconnected to any narrative of events save trading are routinely included—for example, on the possibility of importing yew trees
for bows or the seasonal harvesting of raw silk. Description of geography
is generally limited in the trade report, and any more general cultural
description appears largely in the service of trade, as per the instructions
given to voyagers bound for Asia by Richard Hakluyt the lawyer: "Take a
speciall note of theyr apparell and furniture, and of the substance that the
same is made of, of which a merchant may make a gesse, as well of their
commoditie, as also of theyr wants."[32] Unlike the Sherley accounts, which
began with the brothers' departures and ended with their arrival at some
European destination, there is usually no narrative arc whatsoever in the
trade report; Hakluyt's printing of Laurence Chapman's account of the
fourth company voyage to Persia is an excellent example, when, after cat-
aloging the cost of various forms of cloth and spices, the account abruptly
ends, "for want of further matter to inlarge." This organizational strategy
is truly object-oriented, and often breaks out into actual enumeration of
products or currency exchange rates, such as the lists of "Commodities to
be caried out of England into Persia" and "Commodities to be brought out
of Persia for England" appended to the final letter of the third voyage.[33]

In both the travel log and the trade report, foreign peoples are described
only tangentially, and purely in reference to trade. In these accounts, native
inhabitants tend to fall into four categories: thieves of various kinds, merchants, sailors or caravan leaders, and nobility or rulers. Nearly all of
these groups are described solely in terms of whether they are hindrances
or helps to travel and trade, and are then described only with taciturn suc-
cinctness. The exception to this rule is the more extensive treatment given

to certain nobles and monarchs through whose territory the voyagers needed to pass or wished to trade within. For example, fuller details are given of the English interactions with local governors, who often provide the travelers with good entertainment, armed escorts, and permission to pass through their territory. These rulers were crucial not only to the success of the trip at hand, but also to the permanent trade route the Company hoped to set up. Without the active friendship of such individuals, such a trade line would become impossible, and therefore much ink is spilled on the precise dealings the English have with each ruler. Moreover, many of the local governors and kings routed all desirable commodities through themselves, keeping a corner on the market of such products as raw silks. Thus, such rulers were not only enforcers of order but lucrative trading partners as well.

The most extended discussions are reserved for the Persian shah, from whom the Muscovy Company sought broad privileges in the hope of setting up an alternate trade route for Eastern silks and spices. The traditional route through Ottoman territory was controlled by the Turks and the Venetian factors working within their domains; the English sought to divert goods across the Caspian Sea and north through Russia, whose ruler had by that time entered into a close relationship with the company.[34] These reported conversations are unique in the Persian letters, as they are practically the only occasions when authors admit to speaking in depth with any of the hundreds of foreigners with whom they must have come in contact during their years-long journeys. Even when others are mentioned, the interactions are only implicit in the text or, at most, are described in the third person by a speaker who relates few to no details, preferring instead to retain the neutral stance of uninvolved witness or passive mouthpiece of important trade information. It is therefore quite striking when discussions with the shah are reported in considerable depth, and occasionally even lapse into direct speech. In many respects, these royal interviews are the climax of both the travel log and trade report, as the outcome of such interactions will determine the state of trade in the area for years to come and, thus, are ostensibly the *raison d'être* for the journey. The first such conversation with the shah did not go well, culminating in a religious debate that marks one of the only extensive sections of directly reported speech in all of Hakluyt's Persian material:

> hee reasoned with me much of religion, demaunding whether I were a Gower, that is to say, an unbeleever or a Muselman, that is, of Mahomets lawe. Unto whom I answered, that I was neither unbeleever nor Mahometan, but a Christian. What is that sayd hee unto the king of Georgians sonne, who being a Christian was fled unto the sayd Sophie, and hee answered that a Christian was he that beleeveth in Iesus Christus, affirming him to bee the sonne of God, and the greatest prophet: Doest thou beleeve so sayd

the Sophie unto me: Yea that I doe, sayd I: Oh thou unbeleever sayd he, we have no neede to have friendship with the unbeleevers, and so willed me to depart.[35]

Later interviews were more successful, but regardless of the outcome of the conversation, all of the accounts agree in reserving the most extensive narrative coverage for this particular cross-cultural exchange. Even then, however, the report is limited to matters of trade, politics, and religion; as one narrator put it, all other matters are "here omitted."[36] Indeed, trade was too centrally embedded in these voyages and in the minds of those involved for any cultural observations entirely to escape its pull. As Mary Fuller writes, "there was alongside the process of material exploitation and profit, the loop of voyage, report, repeated voyages, repeated invest-ment, a process of textual generation and accumulation with which Hak-luyt is identified": in the company documents included in the *Principall Navigations*, trading and writing were intertwined and mutually genera-tive activities.[37]

MERCHANT COMPANY LETTERS AS NAVIGATIONS, VOYAGES AND DISCOVERIES OF THE ENGLISH NATION

To the average modern reader, the tales in the *Principall Navigations*, graced by "so business-like an air," seem considerably more trustwor-thy than the Sherley texts, which smack of exaggeration, if not outright falsehood.[38] Dialogue seems suspicious (especially so given the elision of translators), so-called verbatim speeches appear entirely fabricated, and evaluative comments render the whole narrative overly biased in tone. As I have argued throughout this book, however, early modern standards of credible writing were not based primarily upon such criteria, and were instead grounded in the author/audience relationship that established (or failed to establish) trust and credit for a particular tale. Similarly, the short, seemingly value-neutral bits of information that appear to modern readers to guarantee the gravity and reliability of the Muscovy company materi-als had another name and another generic function in the early modern period. The small, well-bounded epistemological units that today we call "facts" were in the Renaissance more often referred to as "particulars," and their presence characterized the genre of history writing, both natural and civil (which included prose relations of both past and current events).[39] But, these details—which in a modern fact-based regime of knowledge production are considered the collective repository of a text's claims to be true—were in the Renaissance much less important to the social pro-cess of evaluating a story's truthfulness. Both classical and medieval precedents for history writing presented such particulars as subordinate to overarching moral lessons, rendering them far less crucial to the truth-value of a given text. Historical particulars were therefore altered, eliminated, or added by authors when such changes were seen as reinforcing the rhetorical effect on the reader of a particular moral or religious truth. As Jonathan Sell notes, "rhetorical textbooks even advised embellishment of the truth, or plain lying, by means of the insertion of fictitious elements in a description in order to lend it vividness."[40] A fact-based regime guards these particulars, noting changes, labeling certain details historically false and others true; earlier regimes of knowledge production viewed particulars largely as the vehicle by which a greater moral or religious truth was communicated. Thus even a clear lack of fidelity to narrative particulars did not necessarily impugn an early modern history's claim to truthfulness.

Most of the travel narratives analyzed in this book so far, including the Sherley materials, place themselves fairly clearly in this tradition of history writing (coranto-style newsbooks form the main exception). Many of the voyages in the *Navigations* similarly situate themselves within this prose tradition. The merchant accounts do not, however, and are in that respect quite unusual printed travel publications. Letters from abroad were occasionally published, often as news pamphlets, but merchant reports to company masters were, to my knowledge, not among those. This type of letter differed from those more commonly published in that they had a much narrower topical focus than other news/travel letters sent by family, friends, intelligencers, or noblemen travelling in service to more powerful masters. As described above, their focus upon navigation and commodities was quite relentless. At the point of composition, these authors could have had little suspicion that their letters would be published in a collection of "voyages"—taking a place alongside printed material similar to that describing the Sherley brothers—and were not written with that context, or that readership, in mind.[41]

Linked to that change in readership was a change in the paratext that guided readers' engagement with the material in the Muscovy Company factor letters. The letters would originally have arrived in the hands of their specific addressees with the seal unbroken, awaiting their first London readers. The heading would indicate the respect and greetings of the writer and inform the reader of the exact date and location where the letter was written. The hand would likely be familiar to many of the readers, as the company members chosen for the voyage would be well known to those who received their reports, and multiple letters were sent over the course of a single voyage. The letter itself would bear the marks of its travel, arriving folded, possibly stained, wrinkled, or damaged; in some cases, the lines would show signs of their scene of composition—for example, irregularities in letters or lines unavoidable when writing on a violently rocking boat. The closing would again note the respect of the writer for his readers and the signature would stand as the unique guarantor of the author's identity and his status within the company. Both the signature and the letter as a whole served as a symbol or proxy for the author, a substitute for his presence in London, which marked both an absence undertaken at the company's behest and his efforts to be of present service even while gone. The readership of such letters would be somewhat limited, being primarily the secretaries and masters of the Muscovy Company.

The publication of such letters in the *Principall Navigations* therefore represents a major shift in paratext and readership. Whether Hakluyt altered the text of any of the letters before printing them is, unfortunately, impossible to ascertain. Nearly all of the early Muscovy Company records were destroyed in a fire, and thus Hakluyt's printed versions are the only versions extant. Matthew Day has highlighted the changes Hakluyt made to Giles Fletcher's account of Russia; changes may have been made to the Persian materials for similar reasons.[42] But while the kind of side-by-side comparison one can do with Saunders' account cannot be done here, there are clear additions made to the letters as part of their inclusion in a printed collection of travel tales. These changes in paratext, meant to guide a new set of readers in their engagement of the reprinted letters, can still tell us much about the ideological work accomplished through these texts by means of Hakluyt's decision to include them in his collection.

The most obvious changes rendered to the letters are those made in the medium, from handwritten loose-leaf pages to printed pages in a folio-sized book. This translation into print marks a shift in economic function, from their original purpose as carriers of actionable information regarding trading conditions in foreign markets and the best means of transporting goods to those markets, to their new status as saleable commodities. By the time the letters were printed in 1589, the trading information included within them was too old to be of any practical use in trading; Hakluyt rescues these letters from obsolescence by recycling them into a kind of entertainment that can be sold in the stalls of London booksellers. The arrival of these letters in the field of printed travel relations has significant ramifications for the genre, most of which I will discuss in detail later in this chapter. For the moment, it is enough to note that this economic shift coincides with a shift in readership and reader expectations.

The authors of letters—even business letters—have the advantage of writing to a well-known audience, with whom the author usually shares both a bank of specialized knowledge (whether through shared history, acquaintances, or professional training) and a general understanding of the function of the letter, i.e., the reason for writing. These links, which existed in the original letters, are lost when the Muscovy Company letters are printed for general consumption in Hakluyt's volumes. Muscovy agents' letters were suddenly being read by many individuals who knew nothing about foreign trade or the way in which the company was pursuing its trade in Persia. Nor did they necessarily know any of the individuals involved, whether authors, addressees, or persons mentioned in the text of the communiqués. A shared context for understanding was lost, and the letters were not revised with this new audience in mind. Instead, they were headed and annotated.

This is the second set of the major changes Hakluyt made to these letters in printing them, and they were clearly made with an eye toward assisting readers uninitiated in the details of foreign trade and unfamiliar with the members of the Muscovy Company in particular. The table of contents lists the letters by the name(s) of some of the voyagers, the year they travelled, and their association with the company: "The voyage of Thomas Alcocke, George Wrenne, and Richard Cheiny servants to the Company of Moscovie Marchants in London, into Persia. An. 1563." Occasionally the names listed are differentiated by rank within the company, with "agents" being of higher status than mere "servants," as in "The voyage of Arthur Edwards Agent for the Moscovie Company, Iohn Sparke, Laurence Chapman, Christopher Fawcet, and Richard Pingle servants into Persia. 1568."[43] In the body of the *Navigations* each voyage is introduced by number, so—unlike the original recipients of the letters—readers of the collection would be able to place each set of texts in a broader narrative of engagement with Persia. They would, for example, know when reading the "Advertisements and reports of the 6. voyage into the partes of Persia and Media," that its author was narrating the final voyage the Muscovy Company would authorize to the region. Each letter or document is also introduced in detail through its heading, with the recipient identified and described, and the overall subject of the letter summarized: "A letter of Arthur Edwards to M. Thomas Nicols, secretarie to the worshipfull companie trading into Russia and other the North parts, concerning their preparation of their voyage into Persia."[44] Readers were therefore briefed on the relative status of both the author and the recipient of the letter, which would help to orient them as to the likely function and tone of the letter, attempting to compensate for the shared knowledge lost through the reprinting of these letters for a general audience.

Hakluyt also sought to assist readers in understanding the trade details, vocabulary, and geographical information taken for granted by the original author by providing extensive glosses on the text in the margins. When Arthur Edwards references "Jeraslave," the gloss informs us that "Jeraslave [is] a towne upon the River of Volga." Casual or incomplete mentions of individuals involved in the voyage or the company are given a line of identification: "Richard Johnson chiefe of the third voyage into Persia." Company servants sometimes refer to one another in their letters in order to praise or blame various individuals for their performance and general behaviour, and Hakluyt subtly takes sides in these debates through his marginal glosses. For example, the rather bland gloss on Richard Johnson is given in response to Arthur Edwards' clear critique of the man in his first letter to Nicol: "your Agent . . . appointed (as chiefe for your voyage to Persia) Richard Johnson. For my part I am willing, as also have been and shall be content, to submit myself under him, whome the Agent shall appoint, although hee were such a one as you shoulde thinke in some respects unmeete."[45] By Edwards's third letter, however, Hakluyt concurs with the author's criticism of Johnson. Edwards complains

> The bils of debts that richard Iohnson left with me, had neither the parties name, nor summe of money in two of them, and in other bils, but his owne name. If I had not used discretion, in causing to be written in our priviledge, that such debts as are owing, should be paide any of us in the absence of the other, some men would not have paid one penny, but onely to Richard Iohnson, who hath written but his owne name onely in the bils.

Hakluyt opts to provide readers with a gloss on this report: "Richard Johnsons great negligence."

Most of the glosses, however, do one of two things: they orient the reader in the story by summarizing major events and noting dates and geographical landmarks, or they provide readers with obscure bits of information about trading in Asia. Readers are pointed to "the value of a tumen" ("200. shaughes is a tumen, reckoning every shaugh for 6. pence Russe") and told "what a batman is" ("the batman being 7.li. which may be 6.li. and a half of English waighte"). We are advised that "Daras [is] a great mart for silk" and, in case we are planning our own trip to the area, that "Gilan [is] 7 dayes sayling from Astracan."[46] Although such details were originally included in the letters because they would be of practical use to the company in its trading decisions, they would be of no use or value to the readers of the *Navigations*. Yet Hakluyt not only includes them by printing them in the text of the letters, he highlights them through his marginal glosses, which indicates that he expected readers to be interested in such information, or wished to generate that interest. Part of the fascination such details might hold for the readership of a compilation of English voyages to foreign lands would simply be the strangeness of the details. Currency and weight units were used on a daily basis in London, and to imagine the use of different units could be enjoyable in its oddness. I would argue, however, that another reason for reader interest in such obscure details lay in the Muscovy Company itself. As one of Hakluyt's marginal glosses notes, these letters contain "The secret doings of the Moscovie company."

The gloss is referring to a passage that discusses how to keep such secrets safe from other national merchants in the area, not revealing those secrets to the reader. Arthur Edwards recommends that the company send along one "(if they can get some such) as can speake the Portingall tongue" as then they could "bye a slave that can speake this language and the Portingal tongue also." This would allow business transactions with the Persian merchants to take place independently of the Russian merchants or their servants, who facilitated such exchanges at the point of Edwards's writing and were rival traders in the area. The company servant and slave could

> then interprete unto us in all your secret doings, not making the Russes privie: for they are sorie that we doe trade into these parts. For wee are better beloved then they are: because they are given to be drunkards they are much hated of these people. It is to be wished that none should serve your worships in these parts that be given to that kinde of vice.[47]

This is probably not the secret doings that the reader might have hoped for upon reading Hakluyt's gloss of the passage. Although technically the note is in line with others in describing the topic of the passage, readers might be forgiven for being misled by Hakluyt's marginalia here.

Hakluyt's marginal notes are not provided with anything approaching regularity, and indeed are often quite poorly spaced along the side of the page, with several notes crammed together and then long blank spaces with nothing written next to the primary narrative. This indicates that no regularized method compelled Hakluyt to summarize the passage quoted above as "the secret doings of the Moscovie company"; he could have left it unnotated like so many others, or he could have glossed it with something referring to the languages involved, or the drunkenness of the Russian merchants. Instead, Hakluyt chooses to play off the curiosity of his readers: who wouldn't wish to know the secret practices of one of the wealthiest trading companies in London?

It was this curiosity, I believe, driven by the high credit of the merchants involved in the Muscovy Company and additional interest in the distant locale in which they operated, that provided much of the draw of these merchant accounts. Without the sense that one was gaining insider information about how a lucrative trade was conducted, details like "2000. peeces of kersies to be sent to Persia" in 1567 (twenty-two years prior to the publication of the *Navigations*) would simply not have been very interesting.[48] Nor would much of the text of the letters themselves. Although there is enough commentary on the nature of Persian geography and culture to satisfy someone seeking a description of that land, the primary focus of the letters, as I argue above, was trade. Most of the letters embed any cultural commentary within their trade assessments, so some knowledge of trading terminology and currency exchange is necessary to understand the full meaning of many passages in the narrative:

> Your London reds are not to be sent hither: for they will not give above 18. shaughes their arshine. Here be reds of more orient colour being Venice die. The people are given much to weare cloth: the common people specially were carseis: and the Marchants of more wealth weare broad cloth. You shall doe well to sende five or sixe broad clothes, some blackes, pukes, or other sadde colours, that may be affoarded at 20. shaughes the ashine and not above.[49]

Such narratives may, as Sir Walter A. Raleigh noted so many years ago, "hold the promise of Empire"[50]; for early modern readers they probably just held the promise of money. Although none of the trading information printed in the *Navigations* was current, and the trade route had been closed in the 1580s by wars between Persia and its powerful Ottoman neighbors, when open, this route had been fairly lucrative, and the Russian trade to its north even more so. This trade was how some of London's wealthiest had achieved or greatly augmented their wealth, and their business practices, trade routes, political negotiations, and pricing decisions were open to public scrutiny for the first time in Hakluyt's collection. So while narratives by more well-known adventurers such as Drake or Gilbert usually offered the reader a more exciting adventure story that glorified the larger-than-life leader of such expeditions, the merchant company materials glowed with the allure of the company's wealth. The individual figure of the traveller and/or author in these accounts is superseded by the collective; their importance is their role in generating the riches of the company. This partial dissolution of individual identity is achieved through their collective printing, their designation in the headings as leaders of the nth Muscovy Company voyage to Persia, and their status as "servants" or "agents" for the company.

Just as individual travellers were collapsed into the company, the activities of the company were claimed by Hakluyt for the nation as a whole. Although the wealth of the Muscovy Company remained the clear possession of company members, their trading success is claimed as success for England as well. They take their part alongside the heroic histories of its noblemen and soldiers and become part of the navigations, voyages, and discoveries of the English nation. Indeed, by the second edition of Hakluyt's collection, their activities had been elevated to the very title of the collection, as the "navigations, voyages, and discoveries of the English nation" became the "navigations, voyages, *traffiques* and discoveries of the English nation," making international trade as important a part of England's national identity as the discovery of new lands or such feats of navigational prowess as Drake's circumnavigation. Hakluyt's marginal notes repeatedly use their pronouns to nationalize the company's actions, so that "the Shaugh [is] desirous to bargaine for *our* commodities," "a house given *our men* in Shamakie by the King," and "Cozamomet [is] a noble man that favoured *our nation*" (my emphasis).[51]

The claim Hakluyt made for merchant company trading activities being part of England's national identity by including company letters in a compendium of more traditional narratives brought together to represent the geographical intrepidity of the English shifted not only the formal ideology of the letters cum navigations, they also broadened the formal parameters of the genre of travel writing. If the letters were read differently in their new context and with their new paratext, the idea of what constituted a travel narrative was also altered by this new type of prose placed in the midst of older, more familiar modes of printed narration. "Business" letters may have been a very old prose genre but they were new to the medium of print, and they were not normally considered as similar in kind to travel tales written as "histories," with their central heroic figure, copious moral instruction, and carefully crafted narrative arc. In allocating a significant amount of space to such pieces and placing them alongside older forms of travel writing, Hakluyt shifts the parameters of printed prose travel writing to include a genre not previously regarded as such in the print market. Given the high credibility accorded to the wealthy London merchant companies, his inclusion of these letters arguably also affected certain readers' expectations for what a "true" tale of foreign lands might look like, and the formal conventions it might follow.

Postscript

HISTORIANS WHO TREAT THE HISTORY OF FACTUALITY LOCATE a shift in the understanding of this concept in the seventeenth century in which "a fact" moves from its traditional meaning of an (often highly contested) deed, to the modern notion of a fact as "a datum of pure experience, purified of opinion and generalization."[1] This generic change is traced through numerous "fact-based" discourses, such as witnessing/law, natural philosophy, and history.[2] According to this narrative, all areas where prose accounts were pressed into service as a means for discovering the "truth" about the world experienced a similar change, further dividing them from lyric poetry, drama and other overtly poetic forms: "the truth of poetry was thought to lie in its ability to capture universal moral truth and did not turn on epistemological questions of evidence, error, or partiality as the truth of history did. As more attention was placed on 'matter of fact' and the evidence for matters of fact, imaginative forms were more clearly contrasted to history." According to intellectual historian Barbara Shapiro's work, travel narratives and news reports, as subgenres of history, also developed an emphasis on these matters of fact, devoting more narrative space to these particulars (things done or observed), and less to moral or religious instruction.[3]

The institutionalization of a select number of forms in fact-based genres also helped to settle which modes of narration would become most closely associated with a credible story. The establishment of gentlemanly norms of speech in the natural philosophic community, and ultimately in the nascent Royal Society emphasized that truth must be sought through a particular set of linguistic conventions, even as it relied upon relations of trust between its noble practitioners.[4] Lorraine Daston explores the role of the fact in this community, considering the function of its brevity in the establishment of natural philosophic theories adjudicated credible. She concludes that

> several factors conjoined to make written accounts of observations, especially the subset of observations called "matters of fact," short and disjoint. As Bacon had remarked of aphorisms, short forms set forth in no particular order lent themselves to combination and recombination, in contrast to systematic expositions that served one theory only. Moreover, in cases of controversy, the simpler the matter of fact, the greater the hope that agreement might be reached at least on that point.[5]

The form of these observations, and in particular their brevity, became a crucial factor in the generation of assent among natural philosophers in seventeenth-century England. Stabilizing the formal features of scientific knowledge helped to stabilize the formation of the knowledge itself.

These narratives about the division in history, natural philosophy and related areas of knowledge dovetail with many accounts of the origins of the English novel. Robert Mayer in particular has drawn upon accounts of the changes in history writing in the period, including the gradual cessation of what we would call imaginative discourse inserted within a history for reasons of emphasis or moral clarity. As such imaginative discourse falls out of use in history writing, it becomes associated primarily with the novel. Mayer insists that "writers persistently asked readers of fiction to situate their imaginative works in relation to the discourse of history, and the history-fiction problematic was, therefore, an ever-present preoccupation of writers and readers of the texts that we now associate with the early English novel."[6] Travel writing and news reports in particular are seen to play an important role, as many early novels, like Behn's *Oroonoko* and DeFoe's *Robinson Crusoe*, borrow heavily from such subgenres of travel writing as captivity narratives and merchant accounts.[7]

This schema, in which the increasing factuality of certain modes of writing, such as history or news, force a distinction between "factual" and "fictional" genres, in part through greater formal regularization of the former, fits well with many aspects of the history of travel writing. There were, for example, numerous schemes to regularize the form and content of travel narrations to help stabilize the production of knowledge from abroad and separate it off from "fictional" accounts. Thomas Palmer's massive Ramian chart stands as one of the more extreme examples of this effort to regulate travel writing, although there are numerous *ars apodemica* publications that prescribe the manner of writing down one's travels.[8] Trading company masters, who funded repeated voyages and the necessary agents and factors to man them, sought and succeeded in disciplining the form used by their servants in reporting events abroad. From the earliest voyages to Russia and beyond, company travellers received instructions on what to observe in their notes, as when William Boroughs, a company master, and two consultants, John Dee and Richard Hakluyt the laywer (elder cousin to Richard Hakluyt the editor of the *Principal Navigations*), provided Arthur Pet and Charles Jackman with advice on how to organize their reports of their attempted journey to Cathay by means of the Northern Passage:

> When you come to Orfordnesse . . . do you set off from thence, and note the time diligently of your being against the said Nesse . . . do you at the ende

of every 4. glasses at the least (except calme) sound with your dipsin lead, and note diligently what depth you finde, and also the ground . . . note what depth you did prove, [if you] could finde no ground (this note is to observed all your voyage, as well outwards as homewards . . . And so likewise doe you note the depthes into harboroughs, rivers, etc.

Such details were required to be set down and delivered to the masters upon return to England, and constituted the primary proof of good conduct and a successful accomplishment of the task at hand: "These orders if you diligently observe, you may thereby perfectly set downe in the plats, that I have given you your whole travell and description of your discovery, which is a thing that will be chiefly expected at your hands."[9] As the word "plat" indicates, Burroughs provided Pet and Jackman with a chart or predetermined arrangement of their observations which they were expected to use in the recording of their observations while travelling. The word "plat" was also used to indicate the plot of a piece of literature, highlighting the links between voyaging and writing, mapping the space of a stage or the narrated time of a prose relation and mapping the lived experience of moving across the globe.[10]

The disciplining of the company travel account resulted in the kinds of travel tales discussed in chapter 5. Backed by the credibility of the wealthy trading companies, such standardized accounts, with their attention to small facts and other particulars and their disinterest in expansive accounts of conversations with local inhabitants, harrowing escapes and other admirable actions of the narrator, gradually acquired a very high epistemological standing among written accounts of foreign travels used by those in positions of power in English society, and seemed to confirm the gradual movement toward modern notions of factuality and truth production. Given their high social status, other travel tales would come to be judged by their resemblance to these company records and the high standard of factuality they set.

Or would they? The types of captivity narrative pamphlet publications described in chapter 4 not only continued to be published throughout the seventeenth century, they actually increased in number and in popularity. The number of Englishmen and women taken captive and sold as slaves in North African markets grew dramatically across this century, rendering the type of social work performed by captivity narratives written upon the author's return even more urgent.[11] A hiatus in their publication from 1625–1640 occurred due to their interpretation by Charles I as a critique of his domestic taxation and efficacy in foreign warfare and diplomacy; after this gap, they came back at full intensity, and without a noticeable move toward a greater "factuality."[12] In the realm of news print, the story is even more complicated, as foreign news print was banned along with domestic by Charles I in the early 1630s; this ban was eventually broken with great fury and enthusiasm by a highly partisan series of writers, who do not by any means always prefer the coranto newsbook form discussed in chapter 3. Gentlemen travellers like Sandys more and more frequently voyaged across Europe and the Near East in an itinerary that came to be known as the Grand Tour, and each of them wrote about their journeys in their own idiosyncratic style. These varied histories do not fit comfortably into a simple narrative arc about the consolidation of the modern fact in travel discourse.

What does seem clear is the point I have sought to make across this book: different communities established practices for determining authorial (and textual) credibility that matched the specific social and cultural situations of those involved. Different kinds of truths remained paramount for each of these communities, and the varying subgenres of foreign reporting developed to privilege and promote those values. Rather than the hegemonic rise of *the* modern fact, this book has maintained that the answer to whether travel narratives would be judged on the formal features of the high-status trading company report is simply that it depended upon who was doing the judging. The London newsreading population assessed the truth of their true stories from abroad in a different manner than did George Sandys' gentle audience, which differed again from the practices employed by the merchant companies. The varying socio-textual practices employed in each community do not necessarily coincide with one another, and they do not always run in a straight line toward our modern conceptions of factual discourse.

Much current work within English literary studies smoothes over of the complexity of English society and its many modes of evaluating the truth value of written material. The focus on the study of "English" representations of Muslims in this period ("how *the* English portrayed that [Mediterranean] world") precludes from view how the variations in the ways that Muslims are depicted in English writings of the period might be associated with different strata of English society.[13] Much of the specific local work done by these texts is elided, as an analysis of content is more or less separated off from the particular communities that produced and consumed the physical books, pamphlets and manuscripts that were the means by which this content was communicated.[14] Ironically, although there has been considerable attention to the complexifying of "Muslims" in English writings of the period—the term "Turk," for example, has been thoroughly dissected and the variations in nationality, language, and "race" among so-called Turks vigorously explored—there has been little effort to unpack what is meant by "English" writings in the period.[15] Discussions of the constructions of English "nationhood" have been useful in this regard, but they are too infrequently linked to work on the representation of foreigners in "English" writings and neglect to consider how different versions of "Englishness" might consistently align with certain versions of "Turkishness." In contrast, this study has delineated specific reading and writing communities and the practices within those communities by which writers represented Muslims and laid claim to "true knowledge" of these foreign lands and peoples.

With the hegemonic "culture of fact" disaggregated into a multiplicity of communities and practices within English society, it becomes necessary to revisit such claims as Meyer's regarding the origins of the novel. Meyer states that "writers persistently asked readers of fiction to situate their imaginative works in relation to the discourse of history, and the history-fiction problematic was, therefore, an ever-present preoccupation of writers and readers of the texts that we now associate with the early English novel."[16] But who were these writers and readers, and what practices of truth telling and assessment did they employ? To which one of the many subgenres of history writing does the "history-fiction problematic" refer for these writers and readers? Did early novels address specific communities, employing their individualized forms of narrative truth telling? Or were novels instrumental in joining together several subgenres and communities of practice into a broader understanding of what constituted "factual" versus "fictional" writing?

Different kinds of questions also need to be asked of early modern dramas and their contributions to English depictions of Islamic peoples. How did the plays' obvious "poetic" status affect the work they did domestically as audiences composed of Englishmen and women with varying access to political and economic power watched these representations? Characters in stage plays are frequently used as *representations of* an undifferentiated "English" conception of (carefully delineated kinds of) Muslims; but to what extent do these plays also *create* such conceptions and linked practices as manifested in the different areas of English life? In particular, what do they contribute to the knowledge that grounded the actions of early English traders, sailors, investors, settlers, and colonial governors? Were any of the many "true" genres more or less influential in this development, and with which populations (the noblemen who ventured money; the merchants who provided ships, expertise and resources; the commoners who populated the vessels and settlements)? Like *the* fact or *the* true tale, early English imperialism (and proto-imperialism, para-colonialism, etc.) requires unpacking into early English imperialisms: the multiplicity of "racist" or imperialist practices and ideas that existed among the many strata of English society. Those ideologies were formed not only by the popular stage plays of the era, but also the many true tales printed during this period. It is therefore time that we look more closely at the work both of these genres are being asked to do in the particular communities that created and consumed them.

Notes

1. Stephen Cohen, "Between Form and Culture: New Historicism and the Promise of a Historical Formalism," in *Renaissance Literature and its Formal Engagements*, ed. Mark David Rasmussen (New York: Palgrave, 2002), 32.

2. Recent studies on drama include Daniel Vitkus, *Turning Turk: English Theater and the Multicultural Mediterranean* (New York: Palgrave Macmillan, 2003); Richmond Barbour, *Before Orientalism: London's Theatre of the East, 1576–1626* (New York: Cambridge University Press, 2003); Matthew Dimmock, *New Turkes: Dramatizing Islam and the Ottoman in Early Modern England* (Grand Rapids, MI: Ashgate, 2005); Jonathan Burton, *Traffic and Turning: Islam and English Drama, 1579–1624* (Newark: University of Delaware Press, 2005); and Matthew Birchwood, *Staging Islam in England: Drama and Culture, 1640–1685* (Cambridge: D. S. Brewer, 2007).

3. Birchwood, *Staging Islam in England*, 7.

4. Brinda Charry and Gitanjali Shahani, eds., *Emissaries in Early Modern Literature and Culture: Mediation, Transmission, Traffic, 1550–1700* (Burlington, VT: Ashgate, 2009), 11; Nabil Matar, *Turks, Moors and Englishmen in the Age of Discovery* (New York: Columbia University Press, 1999), 5–7; and Imtiaz Habib, *Black Lives in the English Archives, 1500–1677: Imprints of the Invisible* (Burlington, VT: Ashgate, 2008).

5. There are a few notable exceptions to this, including Gerald MacLean's impeccable *The Rise of Oriental Travel: English Visitors to the Ottoman Empire, 1580–1720* (New York: Palgrave Macmillan, 2004) and Linda McJannet's *The Sultan Speaks: Dialogue in English Plays and Histories about the Ottoman Turks* (New York: Palgrave Macmillan, 2006), which treats several prose histories, particularly Richard Knolles' *Generall Historie of the Turkes*, in great detail and with real acumen.

6. The phrase "relentless mentioning" is from Paul Gagnon, "Why Study History?" *The Atlantic Monthly* (Nov. 1988), 60.

7. Goran V. Stanivukovic, ed., *Remapping the Mediterranean World in Early Modern English Writings* (New York: Palgrave Macmillan, 2007), 4.

8. Ibid, 11–12.

9. For a contemporary English translation of *De orbe novo*, see Francis Augustus MacNutt, *De Orbe Novo: The Eight Decades of Peter Martyr D'Anghera* (New York: B. Franklin, 1970). The excerpt discussed here has also been reprinted in Andrew Hadfield, ed., *Amazons, Savages and Machiavels: Travel and Colonial Writing in English, 1550–1630: An Anthology* (Oxford: Oxford University Press, 2001), 241.

10. Richard Eden, *The decades of the newe worlde or west India conteynyng the navigations and conquestes of the Spanyardes, with the particular description of the moste ryche and large landes and ilandes lately founde in the west ocean perteynyng to the inheritaunce of the kinges of Spayne. . . . Wrytten in the Latine tounge by Peter Martyr of Angleria, and translated into Englysshe by Rycharde Eden* (London: Guilhelmi Powell [for William Seres], 1555), A2r–v. To be clear, my use of this particular introduction is simply meant to serve as one example of the type of error often made by scholars of this

173

period. While it illustrates my point quite sharply, it should be seen as just one instance of a larger trend in the field.

11. In addition to the formidable body of work by Nabil Matar, culminating in his trilogy—*Islam in Britain* (Cambridge: Cambridge University Press, 1998), *Turks, Moors and Englishmen in the Age of Discovery* (New York: Columbia University Press, 1999), and *Britain and Barbary, 1589–1689* (Gainesville: University Press of Florida, 2005)—see, for example, Daniel Vitkus's treatment of religious conversion and race in "Turning Turk in *Othello*: The Conversion and Damnation of the Moor," *Shakespeare Quarterly* 48 (1997): 145–76; or Patricia Parker's exploration of gender and travel through the discovery tropes of "dilation" or "bringing to light" in "Fantasies of 'Race' and 'Gender': Africa, *Othello* and Bringing to Light," *Women, 'Race' and Writing in the Early Modern Period*, ed. Margo Hendricks and Patricia Parker, eds. (London : Routledge, 1994), 84–100. More recent examples include Bernadette Andrea's "From Invasion to Inquisition: Mapping Malta in Early Modern England" and Jonathan Burton's provocative "Emplotting the Early Modern Mediterranean," both found in *Remapping the Mediterranean*, Stanivukovic, 245–271 and 21–40, respectively. The latter makes a strong methodological case for the use of non-English sources, and insists that the historical formalist approach runs the risk of reproducing the limited viewpoint of its subject and eliding the influence of foreign sources on the text in question (see page 26 in particular). Given that the type of horizontal approach Burton employs here tends to miss the impact of domestic local and material processes on the text in question, it would seem useful to find a way in which the two approaches could complement each other.

12. Vitkus, *Turning Turk: English Theater and the Multicultural Mediterranean*, 10.

13. In addition to McJannet's and MacLean's studies mentioned above, Mary Fuller's chapter on John Smith in her new book is an excellent example of the possibilities inherent in this approach: Mary C. Fuller, *Remembering the Early Modern Voyage: English Narratives in the Age of European Expansion* (New York: Palgrave Macmillan, 2008). Andrea Frisch also performs several fascinating extended studies of French travel accounts in service of her argument regarding witnessing in the period: Andrea Frisch, *The Invention of the Eyewitness: Witnessing and Testimony in Early Modern France* (Chapel Hill: University of North Carolina Department of Romance Languages, 2004).

14. Jonathan P. A. Sell broaches some important questions regarding the nature of truth in travel writing, but as his project focuses on wonder and is designed primarily to defend the capacity of rhetoric to communicate a nonliteral truth that he terms "consensual truth," it differs substantially in approach from this study. See Jonathan P. A. Sell, *Rhetoric and Wonder in English Travel Writing, 1560–1613* (Aldershot, England: Ashgate, 2006).

15. See Chapter 5 for an extensive discussion of anachronistic attributions of "factuality" to Richard Hakluyt's *Principall Navigations* and the implications of treating this collection as a source for historical facts.

16. Matar's differentiation of dramatic representations from "evidence that has survived about the *actual* interaction between Britons and Muslims," and his description of the former as entirely homogenized and stereotyped have provoked several critical responses by those studying primarily dramatic texts. Unfortunately, although Matar makes this critique in an effort to encourage further work on nondramatic texts, he maintains the hierarchy between "literary" and "non-literary" texts by insisting that play texts be "*supplemented* by and *contextualized* within" nondramatic accounts (my emphases). Making a distinction between different types of texts treating Anglo-Muslim interactions is indeed important, but it needs to be historicized rather than anachronistically applied using contemporary generic categories. See Matar, *Turks, Moors and Englishmen*, 6–7; Dimmock, *New Turkes*, 10 and Burton, *Traffic and Turning*, 18–22.

17. Burton, *Traffic and Turning*, 18–19. Gerald MacLean has similarly insisted that early modern English literary scholars interested in Anglo-Islamic relations must begin to read more widely and deliberately in Ottoman history. See Gerald MacLean, *Looking East: English Writing and the Ottoman Empire Before 1800* (New York: Palgrave, 2007), 1–23.

18. Ben Jonson, *Volpone*, 5.4.4–6. John Cartwright, *The preachers trauels Wherein is set downe a true iournall to the confines of the East Indies, through the great countreyes of Syria, Mesopotamia, Armenia, Media, Hircania and Parthia. . .* (London: printed by William Stansby for Thomas Thorppe, and are to bee sold by Walter Burre, 1611), 70–71. "Gulled story" in Jonson's play could be scanned as either "the story of Sir Politic Would-be's gulling" or "the story that gulls others because it is untrue." In the context of the line, the former makes more sense to me.

19. See, for example, Andrew Hadfield's use of fictional and factual in *Literature, Travel and Colonial Writing in the English Renaissance, 1545–1625* (Oxford: Clarendon Press, 1998): "The interrelationship between fictional and non-fictional writing is especially significant when one is dealing with colonial texts, because it cannot be assumed that the fiction is a reflection of a reality, textual or otherwise, and that it comes after the fact. The most important English book of travel writing of the late Middle Ages was *The Travels of Sir John Mandeville*, a work which clearly owed as much to medieval romances as it did to factual observation, and which inspired Columbus's decision to try to circumnavigate the globe by sailing west to find Cathay," and "[n]umerous subsequent works, whether fictional or factual, can be related to More's text . . ." (7, 11).

20. Barbour, *Before Orientalism*, 7.

21. Daniel Goffman, Afterword, in *Remapping the Mediterranean World*, Stanivukovic, 274.

22. Classic works in this field include J. G. A. Pocock, *The Ancient Constitution and the Federal Law: A Study of English Historical Thought in the Seventeenth Century. A Reissue with a Retrospect* (Cambridge: Cambridge University Press, 1987); F. Smith Fussner, *The Historical Revolution: English Historical Writing and Thought, 1580–1640* (New York: Routledge and Paul, 1962); Arthur Ferguson, *Clio Unbound: Perception of the Social and Cultural Past in Renaissance England* (Durham, NC: Duke University Press, 1979); and Joseph Levine, *Humanism and History: Origins of Modern English Historiography* (Ithaca: Cornell University Press, 1987).

23. Fuller, *Remembering the Early Modern Voyage*, 19.

24. Charry and Shahani, *Emissaries in Early Modern Literature and Culture*, 5.

25. Ibid, 10.

26. Mikhail M. Bakhtin/ Pavel N. Medvedev, *The Formal Method in Literary Scholarship: A Critical Introduction to Sociological Poetics*, trans. Albert J. Wehrle (Baltimore: The Johns Hopkins University Press, 1978), 8.

27. Cohen, "Between Form and Culture," 32–33.

28. A possible exception to this is provided by merchant companies, whose vetting processes nevertheless do not depart significantly from the general rule in which accounts are evaluated in reference to their author's reputations and not their formal features. They will be discussed in further detail below.

29. See Barbara Shapiro, *Beyond "Reasonable Doubt" and "Probable Cause": Historical Perspectives on the Anglo-American Law of Evidence* (Berkeley: University of California Press, 1991), 188.

30. Steven Shapin, *A Social History of Truth: Civility and Science in Seventeenth-Century England* (Chicago: University of Chicago Press, 1994), 69.

31. Thomas Palmer, *An Essay of the Meanes how to make our Travailes, into forraine Countries, the more profitable and honorable* (London, 1606), chart.

32. Notwithstanding formal prohibitions, there were clearly women who traveled in this period. There are records of women in some of the early seventeenth-century colonies in America, and women were among those taken from English shores during raids by Mediterranean pirate crews and sold into slavery in North Africa. To my knowledge, however, there are no written accounts of female voyagers until at least the mid-seventeenth century, and none written by the women themselves until the latter half of that century.

33. William Parry, *A new and large discourse of the Travels of Sir Anthony Sherley Knight, by Sea and over Land, to the Persian Empire. Wherein are related many strange and wonderful accidents: and also the Description and conditions of those Countries and People he passed by: with his returne into Christendome. Written by William Parry, Gentleman, who accompanied Sir Anthony in his Travells.* (London: Printed by Valentine Simmes for Felix Norton, 1601), A3r.

34. Craig Muldrew, "Interpreting the Market: The Ethics of Credit and Community Relations in Early Modern England," *Social History* 18.2 (May, 1993): 169.

35. For a more detailed discussion of such instruments of credit, see chapter 2.

36. Cohen, "Between Form and Culture," 32.

37. Barbara Shapiro, *A Culture of Fact: England 1550–1720* (Ithaca, NY: Cornell University Press, 2000) and *Probability and Certainty in Seventeenth-Century England: A Study of the Relationships Between Natural Science, Religion, History, Law, and Literature* (Princeton: Princeton University Press, 1983); Shapin, *A Social History of Truth*; Lorraine Daston, "Why are Facts Short?" *Max-Planck-Institut für Wissenschaftsgeschichte Preprint 174: A History of Facts*, (Berlin, Germany: 2002) 5–21. This article was later published in Italian as "Perché i fatti sono brevi?" *Quaderni Storici* 108.3 (2001): 745–70.

38. Frisch, *Invention of the Eyewitness*, 12.

CHAPTER 1. WASTE AND EMPIRE

1. Stephen Cohen, "Between Form and Culture: New Historicism and the Promise of a Historical Formalism," in *Renaissance Literature and its Formal Engagements*, Mark David Rasmussen (New York: Palgrave Macmillan, 2002), 23.

2. James Ellison performs an extensive and thoughtful reading of the religious and political implications of Sandys' work, including its relations to the ideas of his brother, the parliamentarian Sir Edwin Sandys. Ellison asserts that Sandys' "open-mindedness and willingness to learn from their experiences abroad was not the norm, and that their attitudes were quite remarkable for the time" (52). James Ellison, *George Sandys: Travel, Colonialism and Tolerance in the Seventeenth Century* (Cambridge: D. S. Brewer, 2002). I will argue here that their attitudes toward the morality of land use were decidedly in line with other progressive gentry of the time, which in this case aligned them with values and beliefs less admired today. I am not seeking to besmirch Sandys' character with this reading, but neither am I interested, as Ellison seems to be, in defending it.

3. Jonathan Haynes notes this deliberate orientation of Sandys' text towards his peers: "He is very conscious of playing the role of field representative for the learned classes in England . . . he always has their interests in mind" (62). Jonathan Haynes, *The Humanist as Traveler: George Sandys' Relation of a Journey begun an. Dom. 1610* (London: Associated University Press, 1986).

4. Quoted in James Ellison, *George Sandys: Travel, Colonialism and Tolerance in the Seventeenth Century* (Cambridge: D. S. Brewer, 2002), 109. Ellison also notes the link between the publication of the *Relation* and Sandys' appointments within the Virginia Company, although he argues that this connection was likely due in some large

part to Sandys' experience at various Levantine industrial sites: "It was common for Renaissance gentlemen to compose detailed accounts of their travels as a proof of their qualifications for high office, and it is probable that Sandys' fascinating accounts on the industries of the Mediterranean were an important factor in his achievement of high office within the Virginia company . . . Many . . . passages might be quoted from *A Relation* in which Sandys points out new markets, studies local patterns of trade, and reports intelligently on local business conditions. These passages may well have a bearing on Sandys's appointment to the post of Treasurer" (109). This claim seems valid to me only insofar as the "industries" explicitly cited by Ellison were those acceptable to pursue as a gentleman, specifically silkworm cultivation, which was likely considered agricultural in nature (similar to beekeeping), and glassblowing, which was an exception to the rule forbidding noble participation in industrial crafts due to its extreme rarity as a skill. I did not note extensive commentary in *A Relation* on any industry that would not be considered noble, and indeed the majority of Sandys' discourse on the economics of the Levant is dedication to agricultural production. In the one place he registers trading patterns, he explicitly breaks off early, claiming that this was "no part of my skill or profession." See George Sandys, *A relation of a journey begun an. Dom. 1610. Foure bookes. Containing a description of the Turkish Empire, of Ægypt, of the Holy Land, of the remote parts of Italy, and ilands adioyning* (London: Printed [by Richard Field] for W. Barrett, 1615), 86. Future references to this text will be made parenthetically.

5. Sandys, *A Relation*, Epistle dedicatory.

6. Efterpi Mitsi also notes how Sandys' account is "structured through contradictions, especially when traveling in Greece, whose ambiguity is both geographical (situated at the threshold between East and West) and cultural (its noble past set against its ignoble present)." Mitsi seeks to explore Sandys' humanist account of the landscape as a series of translations and/or appropriations that create an "alternate space" that is neither fully classical nor fully contemporary. See Efterpi Mitsi, "A Translator's Voyage: The Greek Landscape in George Sandys's *Relation of a Journey* (1615)," *Studies in Travel Writing* 12 (2008): 49.

7. Bosworth has similarly noted the way in which Sandys portrays travel as the perfect preparation for a position of high responsibility in government, citing his focus on "the broadening effects of travel as a propaedeutic to public service." See Clifford Edmund Bosworth, *An Intrepid Scot: William Lithgow of Lanark's Travels in Ottoman Lands, North Africa and Central Europe, 1609–1621* (Aldershot, England: Ashgate, 2006), 3.

8. This situation echoes criticism of landowners back in England who were rapidly converting cropland into pasturage for sheep. Landlords were accused of causing the "decay of tillage" in the land, which would eventually result in the starvation of England's people. For a detailed discussion of these complaints against such "improvement" of land by landowners, see Andrew McRae, *God Speed the Plough: The Representation of Agrarian England, 1500–1660* (Cambridge: Cambridge University Press, 1996), 23–56. This chapter is much indebted to McRae's intelligent and important discussion of the changes in English land-use ideology in the period. I will be returning to the connections between England's agricultural debates and Sandys' descriptions of Mediterranean husbandry below. This also parallels exactly the situation that Sandys would find (and join) in Jamestown, where English settlers were so insistent upon planting the cash crop of tobacco that they not infrequently starved, or were forced to pay extortionate prices for grain when they could not barter or steal from the surrounding native communities. See Edmund S. Morgan, *American Slavery, American Freedom: The Ordeal of Colonial Virginia* (New York: W. W. Norton, 1975), 108–30.

9. The grammar of this sentence, noting that something could be "waste" *and* "unhusbanded," implies that they are not mere synonyms as I am using them here. This points

to the more technical and complex legal definition of the word "waste" in early modern England, of which I will speak more extensively below. For the moment, the modern sense of "underutilized" will suffice.

10. Jess Edwards, "'Nature in Defect': Yielding Landscapes in Early Modern Discourses of Enclosure and Colonisation," *Studies in Travel Writing* 4 (2000): 5–6.

11. Ibid., 7.

12. McRae, *God Speed the Plough*, 42–43.

13. Edwards, "Nature in Defect," 8.

14. *A Prymmer or boke of private prayer nedeful to be used of al faythfull Christianes*, P5a-P6a. Quoted in McRae, *God Speed the Plough*, 39–40.

15. Robert Crowley, *An informacion and Peticion agaynst the oppressours of the poore commons of thys realme compiled and imprinted for this onely purpose that amongest them that haue to doe in the Parliamente some godlye mynded men, may hereat take occation to speake more in the matter then the authour was able to wryte* (London, 1548), A4b. Quoted in McRae, *God Speed the Plough*, 40.

16. McRae, *God Speed the Plough*, 79.

17. Sir Samuel Sandys attempted to "improve" his lands at Ombersely in Worcestershire by enforcing "archaic manorial by-laws strictly, and so claim[ing] the forfeiture of the tenant's copyhold for a technical default," a practice described by Heal and Holmes as one of many "ingenious or nefarious schemes" employed by landlords that were "checked by the courts." Both Sir Samuel and Sir Miles Sandys "became locally infamous for their rapacity. Samuel Sandys acknowledged that he intended to exploit the manor of Ombersely 'for his best profit' even though this might lose him the good will of the tenants. He let his demesne lands 'to the very uttermost value,' and sought both to secure the forfeitures of copyholds on technicalities, and to increase the revenue from the fines and dues from customary land. His brother, Miles, had purchased a number of fenland manors previously held by the bishop of Ely. Sandys, like other newcomers to this under-exploited area, had ambitious schemes for the enclosure and drainage of his lands. To silence the opposition of the tenantry, he pursued a campaign of legal intimidation based on the resurrection of antiquated manorial dues that included demands for labour services. His oppression of his Willingham villagers, fourteen of the 'gravest, auncientist and most harmlesse' of whom were imprisoned on trivial suits, was accompanied by a series of disputes with neighbouring landlords over engineering operations that frequently drained his lands at the expense of flooding theirs. One of the local gentry wrote nostalgically of a time of harmonious social relations on the Isle, 'before Sir Miles for our punishment planted himself in this countrie.'" See Felicity Heal and Clive Holmes, *The Gentry in England and Wales, 1500–1700* (Stanford: Stanford University Press, 1994), 107.

18. Edwards notes that "waste" land is not necessarily obvious to the eye, but must be proven to be so in a court of law, which would determine if current usage contravened its ancient and traditional usage. The effect of Sandys' doubled vision of ancient text and contemporary eye-witness when describing Ottoman lands, however, is in part to render waste visible by displaying the gap between ancient and contemporary usage. The fact that such waste is made visible through ekphrastic passages in ancient texts and described with a combination of woodcuts and Sandys' own ekphrases of contemporary landscapes makes the relationship between land, text, and visuality extremely complicated.

19. McRae, *God Speed the Plough*, 194.

20. In contrast to the eight usages of the first person singular to denote actions taken by Sandys the traveler in Book I, Sandys uses it thirty-nine times to reference a writing decision or make a polite remark to the reader requesting permission for an opinion ("if I may"), acknowledging his uncertainty on a subject ("I know not whether"), or issuing a clarification ("I mean").

21. Both Haynes and Mitsi note this distance between the traveler and the landscape, but they read this primarily as evidence for Sandys' "bookish[ness]" or his interest "in being accurate, critical and useful," which Haynes attributes to Sandys' "piety and Christian ideology," as well as his humanism. Mitsi quotes this passage from Haynes without qualification, and describes Sandys' persona in the *Relation* as that of "a scholar, busy searching for the appropriate matching of actual with literary *loci*" (53). See Mitsi, "A Translator's Voyage," and Haynes, *The Humanist as Traveler*, 45.

22. For an extensive discussion of this idea in relation to English colonization of the Americas, see Edwards, "Nature in Defect."

23. For a detailed description of the Virginia colony at this time, including the events leading up to the massacre and George Sandys' activities in Virginia, see Morgan, *American Slavery, American Freedom*, 92–107.

24. George Sandys to Sir Miles Sandys, (30 March 1623) Manchester Papers, No. 321, in *The Records of the Virginia Company of London*, ed. Susan Myra Kingsbury (Washington DC: Government Printing Office, 1935), 4: 70–72.

25. George Sandys to Samuel Wrote, (28 March 1623) Manchester Papers, No. 319, in Kingsbury, *The Records of the Virginia Company of London*, 4: 64–68.

26. Morgan, *American Slavery, American Freedom*, 109. For a complete description of the tobacco boom years and their many contradictions, including George Sandys' role in them, see Morgan, 108–30.

27. James Ellison notes in the *Oxford Dictionary of National Biography* that "Sandys's remarkably frank letters to friends and relatives about the appalling conditions in the colony after the uprising had the misfortune to be impounded in London and used as evidence of Sir Edwin's mismanagement of the company." See James Ellison, "Sandys, George (1578–1644)," *Oxford Dictionary of National Biography* (Oxford University Press, 2004), http://0-www.oxforddnb.com.library.unl.edu:80/view/article/24651.

28. This information is taken from Ellison, "Sandys, George (1578–1644)," *Oxford Dictionary of National Biography*.

29. The most recent biographer of the Sherley family, D. W. Davies, entitled his account *Elizabethans Errant: The Strange Fortunes of Sir Thomas Sherley and His Three Sons, As Well in the Dutch Wars as in Muscovy, Morocco, Persia, Spain, and the Indies* (Ithaca: Cornell University Press, 1967). Jonathan Burton, in his efforts to balance out the relentlessly Anglocentric accounts of the Persian embassy that Anthony and Robert Sherley participated in, notes the many scathing descriptions of Anthony's character in the literature ("an inveterate and unscrupulous intriguer, a sententious hypocrite devoid of all real sentiment, being incapable of single-minded devotion to any person or cause," "His impudence was colossal, his self-conceit fantastic") before describing his efforts at achieving patronage and position as "misadventures." See Jonathan Burton, "The Shah's Two Ambassadors: The Travels of the Three English Brothers and the Global Early Modern," in *Emissaries in Early Modern Literature and Culture: Mediation, Transmission, Traffic, 1550–1700*, ed. Brinda Charry and Gitanjali Shahani (Burlington, VT: Ashgate, 2009), 26. I should note that nothing in my reading about the Sherleys causes me to disagree with these assessments of Anthony's character; my point is that dismissing literatures associated with "failed" historical actors obscures the more interesting question of why such actors and texts did not move their contemporaries and thereby become, and become known as, successful.

CHAPTER 2. "THE ROBE OF TRUTH"

1. I should note that the Sherleys were not the only leaders of these expeditions, and that the use of the term "ambassador" or "embassy" is somewhat misleading since

such emissaries were understood to have different functions in Persia and in European countries. In the embassy of 1600–1601, the Persian Husein Ali Beg was designated a leader along with Anthony Sherley, a situation that caused considerable internal strife as the party passed through Europe. In treating this episode, Jonathan Burton has aptly reminded scholars of English literature and of the Sherleys in particular to push beyond the bounds of merely English sources, especially when telling stories involving historical actors from other nations. See Jonathan Burton, "The Shah's Two Ambassadors: The Travels of the Three English Brothers and the Global Early Modern," in *Emissaries in Early Modern Literature and Culture: Mediation, Transmission, Traffic, 1550–1700.* ed. Brinda Charry and Gitanjali Shahani (Burlington, VT: Ashgate; 2009), 23–40.

2. An exception to this general characterization of the literature is the work that has been done on the composition and reception of Walter Raleigh's *The discouerie of the large, rich, and bevvtiful empire of Guiana* (London: Robert Robinston, 1596). See for example, Mary Fuller, "Ralegh's discoveries: the two voyages to Guiana" in *Voyages in Print: English Travel to America, 1576–1624* (Cambridge: Cambridge University Press, 1995).

3. I will restrain myself from offering any examples from the contemporary publishing market.

4. Ultimately the Sherley brothers' popularity with the minor businessmen of Jacobean society was not enough to save the fortunes of the Sherley family, but it must for a brief period have smoothed the small transactions of daily life and bought the family time to gain back favor in the circles of power after it had been lost. The quote is from Samuel Purchas, *Purchas His Pilgrimes*, (London, 1625; repr. Glasgow: MacLehose and Sons, 1905), I: 374. This passage is noted in Anthony Parr, "Foreign Relations in Jacobean England: The Sherley Brothers and the 'Voyage of Persia,'" Jean-Pierre Maquerlot and Michèle Willems, eds. *Travel and Drama in Shakespeare's Time* (Cambridge: Cambridge University Press, 1996), 14.

5. Parr, "Foreign Relations in Jacobean England," 18.

6. This account of Sir Thomas Sherley's activities in the Netherlands, as well as many other biographical details in this chapter, come from D. W. Davies, *Elizabethans Errant: The Strange Fortunes of Sir Thomas Sherley and His Three Sons, As Well in the Dutch Wars as in Muscovy, Morocco, Persia, Spain, and the Indies* (Ithaca: Cornell University Press, 1967), 21.

7. It should be noted that skimming off the top of funds meant for soldiers' pay and provisioning was an extremely common practice in this period. Sir Thomas distinguishes himself only by the ingenuity of his embezzling and the amount he managed to acquire, far more than the 10 percent considered legitimate. For the various methods employed by commanders to make money while at war, see Davies, *Elizabethans Errant*, 16–20.

8. Rowland Whyte to Sir Robert Sidney, 8 March 1597 in A. Collins, *Letters and Memorials of State in the reigns of Queen Mary, Queen Elizabeth, King James, King Charles the First, part of the reign of King Charles the Second, and Oliver's usurpation* (London: T. Osborne, 1746), II: 27–28; Rowland Whyte to Sir Robert Sidney, 12 March 1597 in *Historical Manuscripts Commission Report on the Manuscripts of Lord De L'Isle and Dudley, Preserved at Penshurst Place, Kent* (London: HMC Historical Manuscripts Commission, 1934), II: 238–39. Quoted in Davies, *Elizabethans Errant*, 44.

9. Mario Biagioli, *Galileo Courtier: The Practice of Science in the Culture of Absolutism* (Chicago: University of Chicago Press, 1993), 328.

10. Lawrence Stone, *The Crisis of the Aristocracy, 1558–1641* (Oxford: Clarendon Press, 1965), 514.

11. In addition to notes signed by untrustworthy debtors, there were other dangers for unwary purchases of such credit instruments: "Fictitious bills were in circulation at that

time with the connivance of businessmen. It even became common for a man to draw upon his own credit—which left the door open to many abuses." See Fernand Braudel, *The Structures of Everyday Life: The Limits of the Possible*, trans. Siân Reynolds, (New York: Harper & Row Publishers, 1981), 472.

12. Carl Winnerlind, "Credit-Money as the Philosopher's Stone: Alchemy and the Coinage Problem in Seventeenth-Century England," in *Oeconomies in the Age of Newton*, ed. Margaret Schabas and Neil De Marchi (Durham, NC: Duke University Press, 2003), 236–37.

13. Francis Drake, commendatory poem to Sir George Peckham's, *A true reporte, of the late discoueries, and possession, taken in the right of the Crowne of Englande, of the new-found landes: by that valiaunt and worthye gentleman, Sir Humfrey Gilbert Knight. Wherein is also breefely sette downe, her highnesse lawfull tytle therevnto, and the great and manifolde commodities, that is likely to grow thereby, to the whole realme in generall, and to the aduenturers in particular. Together with the easines and shortnes of the voyage. Seene and allowed* (London: John Charlewood for John Hinde, 1583). The poem continues: "Hee, that for vertues sake, will venture farre and neere:/ Whose zeale is strong, whose practize trueth, whose faith is void of feere,/ If any such there bee, inflamed with holie care./ Heere may hee finde, a readie meane, his purpose to declare:/ So that, for each degree, this Treatise dooth unfolde:/ The path to Fame, the proofe of zeale, and way to purchase golde."

14. Barbara J. Shapiro, *A Culture of Fact: England 1550–1720* (Ithaca: Cornell University Press, 2000), pp. 36–37.

15. Sir Anthony Sherley, *Sir Antony Sherley his relation of his trauels into Persia. The dangers, and distresses, which befell him in his passage, both by sea and land, and his strange and vnexpected deliuerances. His magnificent entertainement in Persia, his honourable imployment there-hence, as embassadour to the princes of Christendome, the cause of his disapointment therein, with his aduice to his brother, Sir Robert Sherley, also, a true relation of the great magnificence, valour, prudence, iustice, temperance, and other manifold vertues of Abas, now King of Persia, with his great conquests, whereby he hath inlarged his dominions. Penned by Sr. Antony Sherley, and recommended to his brother, Sr. Robert Sherley, being now in prosecution of the like honourable imployment. Printed for Nathaniell Butter, and Ioseph Bagfet* (London, 1613), A2r–v.

16. *A true report of Sir Anthony Shierlies* [sic] *iourney ouerland to Venice from thence by sea to Antioch, Aleppo, and Babilon, and soe to Casbine in Persia: his entertainment there by the great Sophie: his oration: his letters of credence to the Christian princes: and the priuiledg obtained of the great Sophie, for the quiet passage and trafique of all Christian marchants, throughout his whole dominions. Printed by R. B. for I. I.* (London, 1600), Br.

17. William Parry, *A new and large discourse of the trauels of sir Anthony Sherley Knight, by sea, and ouer land, to the Persian Empire Wherein are related many straunge and wonderfull accidents: and also, the description and conditions of those countries and people he passed by: with his returne into Christendome. Written by William Parry gentleman, who accompanied Sir Anthony in his trauells.* Printed by Valentine Simmes for Felix Norton (London, 1601).

18. William Shakespeare, *Twelfth Night, Or What You Will* (Cambridge: Cambridge University Press, 2003), 2.5.148–49 and 3.4.232–36. Elizabeth Story Donno, editor of the latest Cambridge edition of the play, notes that these two references have been "taken to reflect current interest in the accounts (published 1600 and 1601) of Sir Anthony Sherley's adventures when serving as an ambassador for the shah." Leslie Hotson argues for the earlier performance date in *The First Night of Twelfth Night* (New York: Macmillan, 1954); that it was performed on February 2, 1602 is certain.

19. Anthony left his brother Robert, who had remained in Persia as Anthony's surety, to bear the brunt of the shah's displeasure. The embassy continued on without Anthony to Spain, where several of the Persians in the company converted to Catholicism and stayed behind. One, the secretary Uruch Beg, composed his own relation of the journey from Persia in Spanish (or had it transcribed). This unpublished account was edited and translated into English in the 1920s by Guy Le Strange and printed under the title *Don Juan of Persia: A Shi'ah Catholic, 1560–1604* (New York: Harper & Bros., 1926). Anthony never returned to England; he spent the rest of his life working as an intelligencer and government agent for numerous different monarchs, most notably King Phillip III of Spain.

20. This was Thomas' fifth expedition. Previous voyages had resulted in the capture of several neutral vessels, which eventually had to be reinstated and the owners repaid for lost cargo. See Davies, *Elizabethans Errant*, 61–73.

21. Although his letters of mark from England expressly forbid him from entering the Mediterranean, Thomas ignored this and sailed directly for Italy and the court of the Grand Duke of Tuscany, where he stopped and acquired an additional license from that prince which permitted him to attack Turkish vessels and territory. English merchants operating in the Levant were extremely unhappy about this as it damaged their trade in the region.

22. The ship sailed off. Davies notes with irony that Sherley achieved considerable fame as a pirate after his capture, since his three ships continued to operate independently in the Mediterranean, and word of their attacks spread more widely than word of his capture: "Sherley's name became the terror of the seas. The very model of the fearless buccaneer, he would apparently plunder a village one day and strike like lightning at a settlement a hundred miles away the next" (175). For a detailed account of this episode, see Davies, *Eliabethans Errant*, 172–180.

23. Sir Thomas Sherley the younger to the King, Spring or Summer, 1607, in *Historical Manuscripts Commission Calendar of the Manuscripts of the Most Honourable the Marquis of Salisbury* (London: HMC Historical Manuscripts Commission, 1965), XIX: 174. Quoted in Davies, *Elizabethans Errant*, 182.

24. Anthony Nixon, *The three English brothers Sir Thomas Sherley his trauels, vvith his three yeares imprisonment in Turkie: his inlargement by his Maiesties letters to the great Turke: and lastly, his safe returne into England this present yeare, 1607. Sir Anthony Sherley his embassage to the Christian princes. Master Robert Sherley his wars against the Turkes, with his marriage to the Emperour of Persia his neece* (London: Adam Islip, 1607); and John Day, William Rowley, and George Wilkins, *The trauailes of the three English brothers Sir Thomas Shirley Sir Anthony Mr. Robert. As it is now play'd by her Maiesties Seruants. Ptinted [sic] for Iohn Wright, and are to bee sold at his shoppe neere Christ-Church gate* (London: George Eld for John Wright, 1607). The play has been recently edited and reprinted in Anthony Parr, ed., *Three Renaissance Travel Plays* (Manchester: Manchester University Press, 1995). Parr collates four of the extant copies of the quarto publication of the play. I will be citing from his edition. In his introduction to the volume, Parr also concludes that Sir Thomas likely commissioned both the pamphlet and play in order to "keep the absent brothers in the public eye" by "circulating their story as widely as possible" (8–9). I argue that Thomas had a personal stake in commissioning these productions as well.

25. Rowland Whyte to the Earl of Shrewsbury, 17 September 1607 in *The Sussex County Magazine* 9 (1935): 708. Quoted in Davies, *Elizabethans Errant*, 182–83.

26. This explanation was given by Thomas when questioned by royal officials in the Tower. PRO, State Papers, Foreign, Turkey, SP 97/5, fol. 257, 1607 (the questions put to Thomas Sherley in the Tower and his answers). Quoted in Davies, *Elizabethans Errant*, 183–84.

27. Namely, the 1600 anonymous news pamphlet, Parry's 1601 autobiographical account, and Nixon's pamphlet. There was a pamphlet published about one of Thomas' earlier privateering ventures in 1602 entitled *A True Discourse, of the late Voyage made by the Right Worshipfull Sir Thomas Sherley the younger, Knight: on the coast of Spaine, with foure ships and two pinnasses . . . wherein is shewed the taking of three townes, Boarco, Tanaredo and Fyguaro, with a castle and a priorie. Written by a gentleman that was in the voyage. Printed for Thomas Pauyer* (London, 1602). There is also the possibility that the playwrights spoke to Sir Thomas directly, or had access to his unpublished manuscript, *Discours of the Turkes*. The latter was printed in 1936 as *Discours of the Turkes by Sr. Thomas Sherley*, Sir E. Denison Ross, ed. (London: Camden Miscellany, 1936).

28. Sir Philip Sidney, *Defence of Poesy*, eds. Geoffrey Shepherd and R. W. Maslen, 3rd ed. (Manchester: Manchester University Press, 2002), 85.

29. This early-sixteenth century English misnomer for the shah first appears during the time of the powerful Safavid Dynasty, which ruled Persia from 1500–1736. It comes either from a corruption of "Safavid" itself, or from the epithet given to the earliest Safavid ruler, *Ṣafī-al-Dīn*, or "pure of religion."

30. Day et al., *The Three English Brothers*, 1.1.21–23.

31. Ibid., 1.1.117–18, 120–27.

32. Parr also notes the New World echoes of this scene. See *Three Renaissance Travel Plays*, "Introduction," 16–17.

33. Day et al., *The Three English Brothers*, "Prologue," 5–25.

34. For this claim regarding the nature of medieval and Renaissance histories, see Suzanne Fleischman, "On the Representation of History and Fiction in the Middle Ages," *History and Theory* 22 (1983): 278–310.

35. Day et al., *The Three English Brothers*, "Dedication," lines 1–4, 8–11. Parr believes the dedication to be aimed more at the constituency around Prince Henry's court than his father's, as the prince was "promoting an aggressive and interventionist foreign policy," in an effort to find and fund military excursions that would allow the young nobility to show their martial worth and win glory. See Parr, *Three Renaissance Travel Plays*, "Introduction," 9–10.

36. For an interesting discussion of the dramatic structure of the play, see H. Neville Davies, "*Pericles* and the Sherley Brothers," in E. A. J. Honigmann, ed., *Shakespeare and His Contemporaries* (Manchester: Manchester University Press, 1986, 94–113). Parr notes the difficulties both Nixon and the playwrights had in presenting some of the less heroic deeds of the Sherleys. See Parr, "Introduction," *Three Renaissance Travel Plays*, 18–19.

37. "Sampsonia" was the daughter of a Circassian (Georgian) chieftain, who was baptized "Teresa" when she married Robert Sherley in 1608. She accompanied Robert on his European embassy and provoked much curiosity at European courts. Her portrait was painted by Van Dyke; it is reproduced in Davies, *Elizabethans Errant*. A second set of portraits also exists of the Sherleys, by an unknown artist, likely painted during their stay in England in the 1620s. For a contemporary take on Lady Teresa Sherley, see Bernadette Andrea, "Lady Sherley: The First Persian in England?" *Muslim World* 95.2 (2005): 279–95.

38. For a full discussion of this aspect of the play, see Anthony Parr, "Foreign Relations in Jacobean England: The Sherley Brothers and the 'Voyage of Persia,'" in *Travel and Drama in Shakespeare's Time*, ed. Jean-Pierre Maquerlot and Michèle Willems, (Cambridge: Cambridge University Press, 1996), 14–31.

39. Day et al., *The Three English Brothers*, 1.1.74–79.

40. Ibid, 1.2.230–32; 1.2.238–40.

41. Ibid, 1.1.78–79.

42. Ibid, 1.1.142–147.

43. See Nabil Matar, "English Renaissance Soldiers in the Armies of Islam," *Explorations in Renaissance Culture* 21 (1995): 81–94.

44. Fears of secret conversion were rife, and many Englishmen who returned from extended time in the Mediterranean and Middle East were regarded with considerable misgiving. For further discussion, see for example, Nabil Matar, "'Turning Turk': Conversion to Islam in English Renaissance Thought," *Durham University Journal* 86.55, n. 1 (January 1994): 33–41, or for an insightful treatment of conversion to Islam in support of a reading of *Othello,* see Daniel Vitkus, "Turning Turk in *Othello*: The Conversion and Damnation of the Moor," *Shakespeare Quarterly* 48 (1997): 145–176.

45. *Sir Anthony Sherley his relation,* 5.

46. Day et al., *The Three English Brothers,* 1.1.142–44.

47. The poem was published in English as *His Maiesties Lepanto, or heroicall song being part of his poeticall exercises at vacant houres. Printed by Simon Stafford, and Henry Hooke* (London, 1603).

48. *His Maiesties Lepanto,* B4r.

49. Early modern Mediterranean pirate crews conducted raids as far north as Iceland, not excepting the southern coasts of England and Ireland. Contrary to the impression given by their popular description as "Barbary" pirates, most pirate crews were ethnically and nationally mixed, drawing members from across North Africa, the Middle East, and Europe (again, not excepting England). Indeed, without the maritime technologies brought by Northern European pirates, Mediterranean-based pirate ships would not have been able to sail up the Atlantic coast. For more extensive discussions of early modern pirating, see Nabil Matar, "Introduction" to *Piracy, Slavery, and Redemption: Barbary Captivity Narratives from Early Modern England,* ed. Daniel Vitkus (New York: Columbia University Press, 2001), 1–52; Daniel Vitkus, "The Circulation of Bodies: Slavery, Maritime Commerce and English Captivity Narratives in the Early Modern Period," in *Colonial and Postcolonial Incarceration,* ed. Graeme Harper. (New York: Continuum, 2001), 23–37; Christopher Lloyd, *English Corsairs on the Barbary Coast* (London: Collins, 1981); Barry Richard Burg, *Sodomy and the Pirate Tradition: English Sea Rovers in the Seventeenth-Century Caribbean* (New York: New York University Press, 1995).

50. Parry, *A new and large discourse,* D2r.

51. Ibid, D2v.

52. Nixon, *The three English brothers,* H2v.

53. Ibid, H4r–Ir.

54. It is worth noting that the Ottoman Empire allowed considerably greater religious freedom to its Jewish and Christian minorities than European nations ever extended to its Jewish or Islamic populations, which were usually banned from practicing openly, expelled, and/or viciously persecuted. For a discussion of the specific position occupied by religious minorities in the Ottoman Empire during the period under discussion, see Roderic H. Davison, *Turkey: A Short History,* 3rd ed. (Huntingdon, England: Eothen Press, 1998), 51–54.

55. Nixon, *The Three English brothers,* K4v.

56. Day et al., *The Three English Brothers,* 1.1.157–9; 1.2.191–193.

57. Ibid, 5.13.170–202.

58. Thomas Sherley the younger to Giovanni Bassadonna at Venice, 6 July 1607, and Sir Thomas Sherley the younger to the Earl of Salisbury, September 1607, in *Historical Manuscripts Commission Calendar of the Manuscripts of the Most Honourable the Marquis of Salisbury* (London HMC Historical Manuscripts Commission, 1965), XIX: 173, 474. Quoted in Davies, *Elizabethans Errant,* p. 181, 182.

59. This information is included in G. B. Shand, "Source and Intent in Middleton's *Sir Robert Sherley*," *Renaissance and Reformation* 19 (1983): 257–264.

60. Thomas Middleton, *Sir Robert Sherley, Sent Ambassador in the Name of the King of Persia, to Sigismond the third, King of Poland and Swecia, and to other Princes of Europe. His Royall entertainement into Cracovia, the chife Citie of Poland, with his pretended Comming into England. Also, The Honourable praises of the same Sir Robert Sherley, given unto him in that Kingdome, are here likewise inserted. Printed by I. Windet, for John Budge, and are to bee sold at his Shop at the Great South doore of Pauls* (London, 1609), 12.

61. Ibid.

62. See Shand, "Source and Intent."

63. Parr, "Foreign Relations in Jacobean England," 16.

64. Middleton, *Sir Robert Sherley, Sent Ambassador*, 4.

65. Ibid, 9.

66. Ibid, 9–10.

67. Ibid, 8.

68. Ibid, 1.

69. Ibid, 8.

70. Ibid, "To the Reader," unnumbered page 2.

71. For investment in overseas ventures in this period, as well as a breakdown by social group, see Theodore K. Rabb, *Enterprise & Empire: Merchant and Gentry Investment in the Expansion of England, 1575–1630* (Cambridge, MA.: Harvard University Press, 1967); see especially 35–55.

72. For the imperative to conspicuous consumption, see Norbert Elias, *The Court Society*, trans. Edmund Jephcott (New York: Pantheon Books, 1983); for the shift in wealth from the landed to the merchant members of society, see Stone, *The Crisis of the Aristocracy*; for the "diluting" of the nobility in France by their engagement in activities traditionally relegated to commoners (such as trade), see Guy Chaussinand-Nogaret, "Aux origines de la Révolution: noblesse et bourgeoisie," *Annales: Économies, Sociétés, Civilisations* 30.2 (1975): 265–278, the author refers to this process as "le suicide moral et culturel de la noblesse" (265).

73. Purchas, *Purchas His Pilgrimes*, I: 374.

Chapter 3. True News

1. Ian Atherton, "The Itch Grown a Disease: Manuscript Transmission of News in the Seventeenth Century," *Prose Studies* 21.2 (1998): 39–65; Richard Cust, "News and Politics in Early Seventeenth-Century England," *Past & Present* 112 (1986): 60–90; see also Adam Fox, "Rumour, News and Popular Political Opinion in Elizabethan and Early Stuart England," *Historical Journal* 40.3 (1997): 597–620.

2. See for example: "Newes from Vienna" (1566); "News from divers countries" (1597); "Novem. 22. Numb. 42. The Continuation of our weekly Newes" (1624); "A coranto Relating divers particulars" (1622); "Good newes from Florence" (1614); Cortano, "Good newes for Christendome" (1620); "July 16. Numb. 9. The continuation of the most remarkable occurrences of newes" (London, 1630); "Novemb. 28. Numb. 9. Briefe abstracts out of diuerse letters of trust Relating the newes of this present weeke" (1622); Buonaccorsi, "A Jewes prophesy, with newes from Rome" (1607); R. S. "The newe propheticall King of Barbary Or The last newes from thence" (1613).

3. See for example: "Letters sent from Venice. Containing the certaine and true newes" (1571); "A true discourse wherin is set downe the wonderfull mercy of God" (1593); "True

and most certaine newes, sent from Vienna in Austria" (1595); "True newes of a notable victorie obtayned against the Turkes" (1598); "A relation Strange and true, of a ship of Bristol" (1622); "Newes from Turkie and Poland. Or A true and compendious declaration" (1622); "A true and credible report of a great and very dangerous fight at sea" (1600).

4. For example, I will not examine broadsides in this chapter even though they were frequently read aloud and passed along in ways similar to pamphlet news, primarily because they were not particularly insistent about their truth status and were not usually tied to current events.

5. "An Excellent Discourse of an exployt of Jhon Ffox an inglishman who had ben prisoner .14. yeres under the Turkes. and killing the gaoler Delivered .266 Christians that were also prisoner[s] under the said Turkes. Printed by Thomas Dawson and Stephen Peele," (London, 1579) cited in ed. Edward Arber, *A Transcript of the Registers of the Company of Stationers of London,* vol. II, p. 357, (London and Birmingham: privately printed, 1875–1894), under 22 July 1579; "The woorthie enterprise of John Foxe, in delivering 266. Christians out of the captivitie of the Turkes at Alexandria," printed in *The principall navigations, voyages, and discoveries of the English nation,* ed. Richard Hakluyt, (London, 1589); Anthony Munday, "The Admirable Deliverance of 266. Christians by Iohn Reynard Englishman from the captivitie of the Turkes, who had beene Gally slaves many yeares in Alexandria," (London, 1608).

6. It is therefore almost always to the 1620s serial news publications in quarto that the term "newsbook" refers, a convention I will follow here. I refer to other sizes of printed news as "pamphlets."

7. The earliest citations I have found dated from the 1530s; there may be news pamphlets published previous to this era. For an early example of news printing, see, "The tryumphant vyctory of the imperyall mageste agaynst the Turkes: the xxvi day of Septembre in Steurmarke by a capytayne named Michale meschsaer. Cum privilegio. Translated and emprynted out of Frenche into englysshe by Robert Copland dwelling in Flete strete by Flete brydge at the sygne of the Rose garland, for Rychard bankes bookseller" (London, 1532).

8. Göran Leth traces the links between the Netherlands and early coranto printers in England in "A Protestant Public Sphere: The Early European Newspaper Press," in *Studies in Newspaper and Periodical History, 1993 Annual,* ed. Michael Harris, (Westport, CT: Greenwood Press, 1994), 67–92. For an early example of the coranto-style format in England, see the 1597 pamphlet "News from divers countries."

9. John Cleveland, *A Character of a London Diurnall* (London, 1644), A2r. "Sippet" is the diminutive form of "sop," a piece of bread used to mop up gravy and to dip in soup. Sippets were little bits of bread used in the same way, often toasted or fried to help them hold up when dropped in hot liquids. I think of them as a kind of early modern crouton.

10. Some news pamphlets were acknowledged to be simple transcriptions of letters, often written by one gentleman to his patron, while others hid their epistolary origins and were printed as short dramatic recountings of current events. See for example the heading and signature in, Buonaccorsi, "A Jewes prophesy, with news from Rome" (1607). Occasionally news was printed in diary format, as from a soldier on the battlefield. See for example the compendious "Newes from Turkie and Poland" (1622); see also the diary-like tendencies of "A true discourse wherin is set downe the wonderfull mercy of God" (1593). Another variation on the news story's structure included scenes of news reception at foreign courts, thereby giving the reader not only the original news, but the further news of its interpretation by others. See for example Prevost, "Letters sent from Venice" (1571); and "True newes of a notable victorie" (1598).

11. Thomas Blundeville, *The true order and Methode of wryting and reading Hystories* (1574), F2v–F3r.

12. Prevost, "Letters sent from Venice" (1571). For further examples of this practice, see the peace treaty contained in "Newes from Turkie and Poland" (1622), or the two speeches by the French king and his rebelling Protestant subjects in "Novemb. 28. Numb. 9. Briefe abstracts out of diuerse letters of trust" (1622). For examples of prayers printed under a separate heading at the end of a news pamphlet, see "Newes from Vienna" (1566) and "The estate of Christians" (1595). For prayers incorporated into the beginning or end of the text, see "True newes of a notable victorie" (1598), "A True relation of taking of Alba-Reglais" (1601), and Buonaccorsi, "A Jewes prophesy, with news from Rome" (1607).

13. I will be returning to this tendency to end with a prayer, supplication, or exhortation to the "Christian Reader" later in the chapter. For petitions and/or exhortations, see R. S. "Late newes out of Barbary" (1613), "True newes of a notable victorie" (1598), and "Newes from Rome, Venice, and Vienna" (1595).

14. Eugene Kintgen, *Reading in Tudor England* (Pittsburgh: University of Pittsburgh Press, 1996), 35.

15. Rudolf II, "A Great and Glorious victorie" (1595), unnumbered page 3.

16. Ibid, unnumbered page 2.

17. Ibid, unnumbered page 3.

18. Blundeville, *The true order and Methode of wryting and reading Hystories*, H2v–H3r.

19. Fritz Levy also notes that "while newsletters and pamphlets certainly go back at least to the 1590s, the real growth of the news industry paralleled England's involvement in the Thirty Years' War;" Levy's primary interest, however, is in quantity and geographic reach rather than the format of news. See Fritz Levy, "How Information Spread among the Gentry, 1550–1640," *Journal of British Studies* 21.2 (1982): 23.

20. For example, the 1597 publication "Newes from divers countries" is organized in coranto fashion.

21. According to Joseph Frank, these are two of the editors who have been identified as working to translate and arrange the news printed in the main London newsbook of the decade. See Frank, in Chapter 1, *The Beginnings of the English Newspaper 1620–1660*, (Cambridge, MA: Harvard University Press, 1961) p. 1–18. Thomas Gainsford trained at the Inner Temple before serving in the English army in the Low Countries sometime between 1584 and 1588. He was constantly in debt, and sought to relieve his financial situation by frequent military engagements in the Netherlands and Ireland, as a courier to the Continent, and eventually by writing. He composed several histories, a commonplace book, a guide to letter-writing, a prose romance, and an elegy, among other works. After failing to find patronage, Gainsford began to work for Nathaniel Butter, translating and editing news. He died of spotted fever in 1624. For more on Gainsford, see Sir Sidney Lee's entry in the *Dictionary of National Biography*, eds. Sir Leslie Stephen and Sir Sidney Lee (Oxford: Oxford University Press, 1917), 7: 808; see also S. A. Baron's more recent article on Gainsford in the *Oxford Dictionary of National Biography* (Oxford: Oxford University Press, 2004). The Reverend William Watts (1590?–1649) probably worked as a translator and editor late in the newsbook's life, around 1630. Watts was a Cambridge-trained churchman, who served as chaplain at Caius College, for Prince Rupert, and to Sir Albertus Morton, among others. He traveled extensively and was an excellent linguist. He was given two livings, one in Norfolk and one in London. An active royalist during the mid-century Civil War, Watts died of disease while attending Prince Rupert in 1649. For more on Watts, see Charlotte Fell-Smith's entry in the *Dictionary of National Biography*, ed. Sir Leslie Stephen and Sir Sidney Lee (Oxford: Oxford University Press, 1917), 20: 986; also, Jason McElligott's entry on Watts in the *Oxford Dictionary of National Biography* (Oxford: Oxford University Press, 2004).

22. Readers of early modern newsbooks were primarily a motley mix of low-ranking gentlemen who collected and vetted news for patrons (so called "intelligencers") and the shop owners, tradesmen, sailors, and "masterless" men (and women) of London, who gathered at St. Paul's to read the news or hear it read by another. The former group had a personal political interest in the news; the latter were often concerned with its politico-religious implications. Doubtless both groups derived considerable entertainment from the news as well.

23. Quoted in Cyndia Susan Clegg, *Press Censorship in Elizabethan England* (Cambridge: Cambridge University Press, 1997), 58.

24. "A continuation of more newes from the Palatinate" (1622), cited in Folke Dahl, *Bibliography of English Corantos and Periodical Newsbooks 1620–1642* (London: The Bibliographical Society, 1952), citation #62.

25. "March 19. Numero 18. Newes from Europe," cited in Frank, *The Beginnings of the English Newspaper*, 11.

26. "Novemb. 20. Numb. 4. The affaires of Italy" (1623).

27. I read this unusual use of "exoneration" as an attempt to explain in further detail the actions of those featured in the news pamphlet, in order to render the account more comprehensible and possibly also for the sake of guiding (or mitigating the violence of) the readers' reactions to these actions.

28. Quoted in Frank, *Beginnings of the English Newspaper*, 9–10.

29. "Weekely newes, containing the propositions of the ambassador of the Emperor at Wolffenbuttel" (1623), cited in Dahl, *Bibliography of English Corantos*, citation #96.

30. "Newes of Europe, with the severall particulars of each countrey" (1624), cited in Dahl, *Bibliography of English Corantos*, citation #141.

31. "Numb. 28. The continuation of our weekely newes" (1625), 5. Quoted in Levy, "How Information Spread among the Gentry," 22–23.

32. "March 28. Numb. 1. Good and true tydings out of the Indies" (1625), cited in Dahl, *Bibliography of English Corantos*, citation #166.

33. "September 2. Numb. 37. The continuation of our forraine avisoes" (1631), cited in Dahl, *Bibliography of English Corantos*, citation #236.

34. "October. 20. Numb. 44. The continuation of our late avisoes from forreine parts" (1631).

35. Unfortunately for the Reverend, the rumors from Antwerp were soon confirmed by numerous subsequent letters from the Continent. But I think we may rest assured that, although most of London could soon "demonstrate where" Tilly was, the good Reverend was unlikely to have renounced his Protestantism in repentance as he promised.

36. "Weekely newes from Germanie" (1623), cited in Dahl, *Bibliography of English Corantos*, citation #136.

37. "The strangling and death," (1622), cited in Dahl, *Bibliography of English Corantos*, citation #58.

38. For an interesting discussion of the grossly Protestant bias of coranto printers, see Leth, "A Protestant Public Sphere."

39. Quoted in Frank, *The Beginnings of the English Newspaper*, 10. Frank neglects to attribute this quote to a specific edition, and unfortunately I have as yet been unable to trace it.

40. Clegg, *Press Censorship in Elizabethan England*.

41. "Septemb. 14. A relation of many memorable passages from Rome, Italy, Spaine, France, Germany, the Low-Countries, the Palatinate, and other places" (1622), cited in Dahl, *Bibliography of English Corantos*, citation #75.

42. For a sophisticated and detailed discussion of royal censorship from the reign of Elizabeth I through that of Charles I, see Clegg's three-volume study: *Press Censorship in Elizabethan England* (Cambridge: Cambridge University Press, 1997), and *Press*

Censorship in Jacobean England (Cambridge: Cambridge University Press, 2001), *Press Censorship in Caroline England* (Cambridge: Cambridge University Press, 2008).

43. For example, Gainsford's editorial note in "Novemb. 20. Numb. 4. The affaires of Italy" (1623): "Gentle **Readers**, for I am sure that you would faine be known by that Character, how comes it then to passe that nothing can please **you**? . . . If **we** afford **you** plaine stuffe, **you** complaine of the phrase, and peradventure cry out, it is Nonsense; if **we** adde some exoneration, then **you** are curious to examine the method and coherence" [etc., my emphasis]. I disagree with Leth that the "we" that appears in English newsbooks is uniformly indicative of a united Protestant news industry or, as Leth puts it, "a brother speaking to brothers." In the editorial replies to readers discussed here, it seems clear that the editor is using the pronoun to distinguish those who produced the news from those who consumed it. See Leth, "A Protestant Public Sphere," 79.

44. John Cartwright, *The preachers trauels Wherein is set downe a true iournall to the confines of the East Indies, through the great countreyes of Syria, Mesopotamia, Armenia, Media, Hircania and Parthia. With the authors returne by the way of Persia, Susiana, Assiria, Chaldaea, and Arabia. Containing a full suruew of the knigdom* [sic] *of Persia: and in what termes the Persian stands with the Great Turke at this day: also a true relation of Sir Anthonie Sherleys entertainment there: and the estate that his brother, M. Robert Sherley liued in after his departure for Christendome. With the description of a port in the Persian gulf, commodious for our East Indian merchants; and a briefe rehearsall of some grosse absudities* [sic] *in the Turkish Alcoran. Penned by I.C. sometimes student in Magdalen Colledge in Oxford,* (London, 1611), 78.

45. "Novemb. 28. Numb. 9. Briefe abstracts out of diuerse letters of trust" (1622), 3–4.

46. Ibid., (1622), 4.

47. Although the ships that assaulted Christian merchant vessels had their ports in North Africa, their crews often hailed from many different nations, including Christian countries like England. Armed vessels from Christian ports also regularly assaulted peaceful North African ships and towns. For a discussion of Mediterranean piracy, see Nabil Matar, introduction to *Piracy, Slavery, and Redemption,* ed. Daniel Vitkus, (New York: Columbia University Press, 2001), 1–54.

48. "Novemb. 28. Numb. 9. Briefe abstracts out of diuerse letters of trust" (1622), 6. "Ward and Sampson" were notorious English pirates who had reputedly converted to Islam and successfully attacked many Christian ships from their North African base. There are multiple references to their activities in the news, and several single-story pamphlets published about their exploits, as well as a stageplay about Ward and a Dutch confederate: Robert Daborne's *A Christian turn'd Turke: or, The tragicall liues and deaths of the two famous pyrates, Ward and Dansiker* (London, 1612).

49. "The fourth of September. Newes from sundry places, both forraine and domestique" (1622), 6.

50. *New Shorter Oxford English Dictionary* (Oxford: Oxford University Press, 1996) S. V. Fact. For a discussion of "false facts," see Barbara Shapiro, in Chapter 2, *A Culture of Fact: England 1550–1720* (Ithaca: Cornell University Press, 2000), 34–62.

51. For a discussion of early modern calls for crusade persisting well into the seventeenth century, see Franklin Le Van Baumer, "England, the Turk, and the Common Corps of Christendom," *American Historical Review* 50.1 (1944): 26–48.

52. For example, Richard Willes' *The history of travayle in the West and East Indies, and other countreys lying eyther way, towardes the fruitfull and ryche Moluccaes As Moscouia, Persia, Arabia, Syria, AEgypte, Ethiopia, Guinea, China in Cathayo, and Giapan: vvith a discourse of the Northwest passage* (London, 1577), or Richard Hakluyt's first collection, *Divers Voyages Touching the Discoverie of America, and the Ilands Adjacent unto the Same, Made First of all by our Englishmen, and afterward by the*

Frenchmen and Britons (London, 1582). There were also several foreign collections of travel narratives available for those who could read Latin, French, or Italian.

CHAPTER 4. THOMAS SAUNDERS

1. The lack of surviving copies of this work suggests a short print run, although this is by no means conclusive evidence. *Divers Voyages* was also divided into three sections, some of which are missing in surviving copies, which may indicate that each was intended originally as a separate tract. For these points and a more detailed discussion of this work and the physical evidence presented by the surviving copies, see Anthony Payne, "Richard Hakluyt and His Books," in Anthony Payne and Pamela Neville-Sington, *An Interim Census of Surviving Copies of Hakluyt's* Divers Voyages *and* Principal Navigations (London: The Hakluyt Society, 1997).

2. Matthew Day cites two instances of the *Navigations* having been read straight through from cover to cover, as indicated in the marginal notes in Antony Linton's copy, and those in the copy currently at Langleat House. See Day, "Hakluyt, Harvey, Nashe: The Material Text and Early Modern Nationalism," *Studies in Philology* 104, no. 3 (Summer 2007): 289 n. 33.

3. Emily Bartels, *"Othello* and Africa: Postcolonialism Reconsidered," *William and Mary Quarterly*, 3rd series, 54, no. 1 (1997): 54. Bartels's revised version of this essay does not include a description of Hakluyt's work in these terms. See Emily Bartels, Chapter 2 in *Speaking of the Moor: From Alcazar to Othello* (Philadelphia: University of Pennsylvania Press, 2008), 45–64.

4. T. J. Cribb, "Writing Up the Log: The Legacy of Hakluyt," in *Travel Writing and Empire: Postcolonial Theory in Transit*, ed. Steve Clark (London: Zed, 1999), 107.

5. James P. Helfers, "The Explorer or the Pilgrim? Modern Critical Opinion and the Editorial Methods of Richard Hakluyt and Samuel Purchas," *Studies in Philology* 94, no. 2 (1997): 167.

6. For the latter claim, see Mary Fuller, *Voyages in Print: English Travel to America, 1576–1624* (Cambridge: Cambridge University Press, 1995), 147.

7. For a sustained example of this practice, see Jack D'Amico, *The Moor in English Renaissance Drama* (Tampa: University of South Florida Press, 1991).

8. Anthony Payne, "Richard Hakluyt and His Books," *Hakluyt Society Annual Talk 1996* (London: The Hakluyt Society, 1997), 4.

9. Mary Fuller, Lecture at conference "Richard Hakluyt (ca. 1552–1616): Life, times and legacy" held at the National Maritime Museum, Greenwich, UK, May 15–17, 2008.

10. Stephen Cohen, "Between Form and Culture: New Historicism and the Promise of a Historical Formalism," in *Renaissance Literature and its Formal Engagements*, ed. Mark David Rasmussen (New York: Palgrave, 2002), 32. Cohen speaks here of the mediating possibilities of form in literary historical analyses in general; the specific application of these possibilities to postcolonial studies in the early modern period is my own.

11. See for example Pamela Neville-Sington, "'A very good trumpet': Richard Hakluyt and the Politics of Overseas Expansion," in *Texts and Cultural Change in Early Modern England*, ed. Cedric Brown and Arthur Marotti (New York: St. Martin's Press, 1997), 66–79; Richard Helgerson, *Forms of Nationhood: The Elizabethan Writing of England* (Chicago: University of Chicago Press, 1992); T. J. Cribb, "Writing Up the Log."

12. Although the vast majority of Hakluyt's authors were unaware that their works would be included in such a collection, a small number of the voyages may have been written explicitly for that purpose. The account of Drake's circumnavigation included in some of the 1589 editions of the *Principall Navigations* was likely designed for inclusion

in Hakluyt's work; the "Dogge" narrative in *Principall Navigations* (817), also presents some internal evidence of having been composed for the occasion. I am grateful to Colm MacCrossen for pointing out these exceptions to the rule.

13. Very few of Hakluyt's 1589 *Principall Navigations* selections come from previously printed popular pamphlets. Even fewer of these are still extant. Aside from Saunders' narrative, the best surviving candidates for what might be considered a popular printing are "The woorthie enterprise of Iohn Foxe, in deliuering 266. Christians out of the captiuitie of the Turkes at Alexandria" (available only as a 1608 reprinting of a lost 1579 pamphlet), "The third voyage of Sir Iohn Hawkins made with the Iesus of Lubecke, one of her Maiesties Ships to the West India," "The second voyage of Sir Martin Grobisher to the same coastes," "The third and last voyage of Sir Martin Frobisher, to Meta Incognita," "The discourse of syr Humfrie Gilbert knight, to prooue a passage by the Northwest to Cathaya, and the East Indies," "The discourse of Master Christopher Carlile to satisfie and incourage our Marchants, and people in general about the action of planting in America," and "The discourse of Thomas Harriots, touching Virginia." For details of the original publications, and a comprehensive survey of the origins of all of Hakluyt's selections in both editions of the *Navigations*, see the classic D. B. Quinn, ed., *The Hakluyt Handbook*, (London: The Hakluyt Society, 1974), II: 341–460.

14. Nabil Matar, "Introduction: England and Mediterranean Captivity, 1577–1704," in *Piracy, Slavery, and Redemption: Barbary Captivity Narratives from Early Modern England*, ed. Daniel Vitkus (New York: Columbia University Press, 2001), 36–37. See also Daniel Vitkus, "The Circulation of Bodies: Slavery, Maritime Commerce and English Captivity Narratives in the Early Modern Period," in *Colonial and Postcolonial Incarceration*, ed., Graeme Harper, ed. (New York: Continuum, 2001), 33–34.

15. Thomas Saunders, *A true Discription and breefe Discourse, Of a most lamentable Voiage, made latelie to Tripolie in Barbarie, in a Ship named the JESUS wherin is not onely shewed the great miserie, that then happened to the Aucthor hereof and his whole companie, aswell the Marchants as the Mariners in that Voiage, according to the cursed custome of those barbarous and cruell Tyrants, in their terrible usage of Christian captives: but also, the great unfaithfulnesse of those heathnish Infidels, in not regarding their promise. Together, with the most woonderfull judgement of God, upon the king of Tripolie and his sonne, and a great number of his people, being all the Tormentors of those English Captives*, (London, 1587), A3r. All further references will be made parenthetically.

16. Matar, "England and Mediterranean Captivity," 33.

17. Interestingly, in the course of these exchanges, the chief gunner is revealed to be a *renegado*, or a Christian who had converted to Islam. The treasurer attacks the gunner by questioning his dedication to his adopted religion: "thou villaine, wilt thou turne to christianitie againe"? (B3r) As gunners were particularly scarce in North Africa, they were highly valued converts; captured gunners who converted to Islam could expect quite good treatment and remuneration as well as their freedom. Indeed, so tempting was the pay, many Christian soldiers with expertise in artillery voluntarily traveled to the Barbary States to offer their services. For more on this, see Matar, "England and Mediterranean Captivity," 17–18; also, Nabil Matar, "English Renaissance Soldiers in the Armies of Islam," *Explorations in Renaissance Culture* 21 (1995): 81–95.

18. This is not to imply that Saunders' experiences in North Africa, the composition of his account of them, or the publication of that text was in any way unmediated or transparent. Indeed, although there is no indication that Saunders did not write his own tale, ghostwriting or oral dictation were frequent enough practices in the preparation of such popular pamphlets for the press that they cannot be entirely ruled out. Publishers also made cuts or added material without the author's supervision when

they felt it was necessary to facilitate the process of printing or the marketing of the pamphlet.

19. Hakluyt includes these names, as he states in his preface, so that every author can "answere for himselfe, justifie his reports, and stand accountable for his owne doings" (3v). I will discuss the implications of this decision more fully below.

20. These changes might have been made by Hakluyt as he prepared the materials for the printer. They also might have been done by the printer himself, as the type was being set. Although the latter practice was common, in this case I lean toward the former scenario, largely because there is plenty of room for the full set of marginal notes to have been included, and those retained are spaced so irregularly as not to contribute to the aesthetic balance of the page in any way. It is in any case immaterial to my argument whether they were made by Hakluyt or the printer, as I am here attempting to trace the effect these changes had on the experience of reading, not to consider their origins.

21. Richard Hakluyt, ed. *The principall nauigations, voiages and discoueries of the English nation made by sea or ouer land, to the most remote and farthest distant quarters of the earth at any time within the compasse of these 1500. yeeres: deuided into three seuerall parts, according to the positions of the regions wherunto they were directed. . . . Whereunto is added the last most renowmed English nauigation, round about the whole globe of the earth.* 2 vols. (London: George Bishop and Ralph Newberie, 1589), 192. Future references will be made parenthetically as follows: (*PN*, #).

22. As preparations for a Spanish attack on England became obvious in the late 1580s, Elizabeth pressed Murad to attack the Spanish Empire from the east or to send direct military aid to England. Despite the sultan's keen interest in retaining England as an ally against their joint enemy, Murad held off sending any support to the beleaguered queen. Following the Armada's defeat, Elizabeth publicly distanced herself from this alliance in an effort to rebuild a reputation that had become somewhat tarnished within Christendom for her willingness to engage "the infidel" to help fight against other Christians. For more details on Elizabeth's delicate balancing act in this matter, see Franklin Le Van Baumer, "England, the Turk, and the Common Corps of Christendom," *American Historical Review* 50, no. 1 (1944): 26–48.

23. This was a forgivable mistake on the part of English trading vessels given that much piracy was a state-sponsored enterprise in North Africa, bringing in significant revenue for several of the so-called Barbary States. At the point that this letter was written, most pirate crews still sailed in traditional Mediterranean galleys; by the turn of the century, English and Dutch naval technologies and sailors would have revolutionized the pirate fleets and turned them into more maneuverable ocean going vessels able to operate in the Atlantic as well as the Mediterranean. For a discussion of the role of piracy in the North African states, see Matar, "Introduction: England and Mediterranean Captivity." For a discussion of the shifting naval technologies in the Mediterranean and the role of northern Europeans in these developments, see Vitkus, "The Circulation of Bodies;" see also Ralph Davis, "England and the Mediterranean, 1570–1670," in *Essays in Economic and Social History of Tudor and Stuart England in Honour of R.H. Tawney*, ed. F. J. Fisher (Cambridge: Cambridge University Press, 1961), 117–37.

CHAPTER 5.   *THE PRINCIPALL NAVIGATIONS*

1. Mary C. Fuller traces Hakluyt's posthumous legacy in *Voyages in Print: English Travel to America, 1576–1624* (Cambridge: Cambridge University Press, 1995), 141–174.

2. George Bruner Parks, *Richard Hakluyt and the English Voyages*, ed. James A. Williamson (New York: American Geographical Society, 1928), 182; T. J. Cribb, "Writing Up

the Log: The Legacy of Hakluyt," in *Travel Writing and Empire: Postcolonial Theory in Transit*, ed. Steve Clark (London: Zed Books, 1999), 107.

3. Daniel Vitkus, *Turning Turk: English Theater and the Multicultural Mediterranean, 1570–1630* (New York: Palgrave Macmillan, 2003), 21, my emphases.

4. *New Shorter Oxford English Dictionary* (Oxford: Oxford University Press, 1996), S. V. "Fact."

5. For an extended discussion of the character of the ontological entity we call a "fact" and an argument regarding its history in this period, see Lorraine Daston, "Why are Facts Short?" *Max-Planck-Institut für Wissenschaftsgeschichte Preprint 174: A History of Facts*, 5–21. This article was later published in Italian as "Perché i fatti sono brevi?" *Quaderni Storici* 108, no. 3 (2001): 745–70.

6. The progress of the *OED*'s definitions for *fact* broadly trace the shift in meaning of the term from its early modern sense of "something done" to the more familiar usages common to the eighteenth, nineteenth, and twentieth centuries: "1. A thing done or performed. a. in neutral sense: An action, deed, course of conduct. Occas. = effect. Also, action in general; deeds, as opposed to words. *Obscure*. b. A noble or brave deed, an exploit; a feat (of valour or skill). *Obs*. c. An evil deed, a crime. In the 16th and 17th c. the commonest sense. *Obs*. [According to the *OED* this sense of *fact* as "deed" is most prevalent in the sixteenth and seventeenth centuries.] . . . 4. a. Something that has really occurred or is actually the case; something certainly known to be of this character; hence, a particular truth known by actual observation or authentic testimony, as opposed to what is merely inferred, or to a conjecture or fiction; a datum of experience, as distinguished from the conclusions that may be based upon it. [The *OED* attributes this sense of *fact* primarily to the late seventeenth, eighteenth, and nineteenth centuries.] . . . 6. a. That which is of the nature of a fact; what has actually happened or is the case; truth attested by direct observation or authentic testimony; reality. [The *OED* examples list this sense as occurring most heavily in the eighteenth and nineteenth centuries.]"Oxford English Dictionary, 2nd ed., S. V. "Fact."

7. Quoted from "The interpretation of the letters, or priuilege of the most mightie and Musulmanlike Emperour Zuldan Murad Chan, granted at the request of Elizabeth, by the grace of the most mightie God, and only Creator of heaven & earth, of England, France and Ireland Queene, confirming a peace and league betwixt both the said princes and their subjects," in Hakluyt, *PN* (1589), 170.

8. James P. Helfers, "The Explorer or the Pilgrim? Modern Critical Opinion and the Editorial Methods of Richard Hakluyt and Samuel Purchas," *Studies in Philology* 94. 2 (Spring 1997): 165. On the whole, Helfers provides an excellent discussion of critical mistreatments of both Purchas and Hakluyt. The tendencies I criticize here are shared by almost all those who treat Hakluyt extensively in their work.

9. See Theodore Rabb, "Investment in English Overseas Enterprise, 1575-1630," *The Economic History Review*, n.s., 19.1 (1966), 74. Rabb quotes the impressive statistic that "one out of every 30 gentlemen, knights and peers in the country contributed to some kind of overseas venture in this period" and that out of 3,800 investors able to be classified according to social position, "little more than 23 percent turned out to be gentry or nobility," which strongly supports his argument that these voyages "drew on the resources of the entire nation, both landed and mercantile wealth." Many critics have noted the propagandistic function of Hakluyt's publications, linking it to colonial and nationalistic discourses at the time. David Boruchoff has recently pushed back against this trend, however, arguing for a more ecumenical religious interpretation of *The Principall Navigations*. See Boruchoff, "Piety, Patriotism, and Empire: Lessons for England, Spain, and the New World in the Works of Richard Hakluyt," *Renaissance Quarterly* 62.3 (Fall 2009): 809–858.

10. I think there is considerable evidence for modern critical claims that Hakluyt's collection was well received and used by company travelers to further their own voyages. See, for example, Fuller's claims that "by 1602, the *Principall Navigations* was already becoming recommended equipment on long-distance trading voyages" (*Voyages in Print*, 147); Anthony Payne's survey of Hakluyt's "impact and readership" in "'Strange, Remote, and Farre Distant Countreys': The Travel Books of Richard Hakluyt," in *Journeys through the Market: Travel, Travellers and the Book Trade*, eds. Robin Myers and Michael Harris (New Castle, D. E.: Oak Knoll Press, 1999), 20–21; and Pamela Neville-Sington's assertion that "eye-witness descriptions of long sea voyages were of considerable strategic value" in "'A Very Good Trumpet': Richard Hakluyt and the Politics of Overseas Expansion," in *Texts and Cultural Change in Early Modern England*, eds. Cedric C. Brown and Arthur F. Marotti (New York: St. Martin's, 1997), 69. Nevertheless, anachronistic suppositions about epistemological standards in early modern history writing and unsupported assertions of contemporary approval do not assist in proving these claims, and often hinder them.

11. Anthony Payne notes the uncertain genre of Hakluyt's collections in "Richard Hakluyt and His Books," *Hakluyt Society Annual Talk, 1996* (London: The Hakluyt Society, 1997), 10–12.

12. For a survey of contemporary criticism on Purchas in relation to Hakluyt, see Helfers, "The Explorer or the Pilgrim?" 167–68; see also Fuller, *Voyages in Print*, 150.

13. Hakluyt, *PN* (1589), 3v.

14. Note specifically the language used to discuss the generation of the *Navigations* in, for example, Neville-Sington, "A Very Good Trumpet," 68; Cribb, "Writing Up the Log," 104–05; Fuller, *Voyages in Print*, 2; see also Bartels, "Othello and Africa," in n. 3 chapter 4 above. This sentiment was recently rearticulated by Richmond Barbour, who described Hakluyt's collections (along with those of Eden and Purchas) as examples of "visionary empiricism;" see Richmond Barbour, *Before Orientalism: London's Theatre of the East, 1576–1626* (Cambridge: Cambridge University Press, 2003), 6. Payne, in "Strange, Remote, and Farre Distant Countreys," makes the connection between empiricism and reliability explicit when he prefaces the usual quotation used to discuss Hakluyt's intentions with "Hakluyt is quite clear about the organization of his work and its grounding in reliable first-hand reports" (18).

15. The *Navigations* are divided into "Voyages" and "Ambassages, Letters, Privileges, and other necessarie matter of circumstance appertaining to the voyages." See Hakluyt's division of material at the head of the *Navigations*. Although the main body of the 1589 edition of the *Principall Navigations* employs an Arabic page numbering system (one number per page), the introductory matter is done according to its print fold, indicated with an asterisk and number in the epistle dedicatory. The table of contents is left entirely unnumbered. I have chosen to continue the *# designation when citing all introductory matter; all references to introductory matter will hereafter be indicated as in the manner used here, unnumbered pages *5r–*8v.

16. For an account of this debate, see E. G. R. Taylor, ed., *The Original Writings & Correspondence of the Two Richard Hakluyts* (London: The Hakluyt Society, 1935), 1–66. Hakluyt prints three of the letters exchanged between Mercator, Dee, Richard Hakluyt the lawyer, and the men undertaking the expedition, Arthur Pet and Charles Jackman, in the *Navigations*: see pages 459–66, 483–85.

17. Anthony Grafton, April Shelford, and Nancy Siraisi provide an example of this phenomenon in the realm of travel writing in *New Worlds, Ancient Texts: The Power of Tradition and the Shock of Discovery* (Cambridge, MA: Harvard University Press, 1992).

18. Evidence of this shift can also be seen in the early modern genre of news pamphlets and newsbooks. This trend will be further discussed in the postscript below.

19. William Parry, *A new and large discourse on the Trauels of sir Anthonie Sherley* (London, 1601), 3.

20. Hakluyt, *3v. For a similar reading of this quotation, see Fuller, *Voyages in Print*, 151.

21. The main narratives that deal with the Sherley brothers' exploits in Persia are detailed in chapter 2. The Sherleys also appear in Purchas' *Pilgrims*, but the majority of the material on their initial voyage in and out of Persia is simply an edited reprint of William Parry's pamphlet, Anthony Sherley's history, and the preacher John Cartwright's secondhand account of the Sherleys. There are some newly printed stories, but these deal exclusively with Robert's later activities as Persian ambassador, both within the borders of Persia and on his journey back through Europe.

22. *A true report of Sir Anthony Shierlies iourney ouerland to Venice* (London, 1600), A3v–A4r; Anthony Nixon, *The three English brothers. Sir Thomas Sherley his travels, vvith his three yeares imprisonment in Turkie: his inlargement by his Majesties letters to the great Turke: and lastly, his safe returne into England this present yeare* (London, 1607), K3v.

23. Nixon, *The three English brothers*, D4v.

24. Ibid., D2r.

25. Parry, *A new and large discourse*, 30.

26. John Cartwright, *The Preachers Travels. Wherein is set downe a true iournall, to the confines of the East Indies, through the great countreyes of Syria, Mesopotamia, Armenia, Media, Hircania and Parthia. With the authors returne by the way of Persia, Susiana, Assiria, Chaldœa, and Arabia. Containing a full suruew of the Knigdom [sic] of Persia . . . Also a true relation of Sir Anthonie Sherleys, entertainment there: and the estate that his brother, M. Robert Sherley liued in after his departure* (London, 1611), 73.

27. Thomas Middleton, *Sir R. Sherley, sent ambassadour in the name of the King of Persia, to Sigismond the third, King of Poland and Swecia . . . His Royall entertainement into Cracovia . . . with his pretended Comming into England*, (London, 1609), 9.

28. All of the Persian material printed in Hakluyt, *PN* (1589) can be found in 1:361–85, 413–25, and 440–55.

29. Hakluyt, *PN* (1589), 443.

30. For further details on the log as a rising narrative form, see Fuller, *Voyages in Print*, 1–15.

31. Hakluyt, *PN* (1589), 442–46.

32. Hakluyt, *PN* (1589), 460. The instructions are described as "Notes in writing, besides more privie by mouth, that were given by M. Richard Hakluyt, of Eiton in the countie of Hereford, Esquire, Anno 1580: To M. Arthur Pet, and to M. Charles Jackman, sent by the merchants of the Moscovie companie for the discoverie of the Northeast straight, not altogether unfit for some other enterprises of discoverie, hereafter to be taken in hand." The Richard Hakluyt usually referred to as "the lawyer" or "of the Middle Temple" was Richard Hakluyt the editor's elder cousin and legal guardian from a very young age. He was also the younger Hakluyt's inspiration to pursue geography as a practical course of study: see Hakluyt, *PN* (1589), *2r. The one exception to this rule regarding cultural description is the selection entitled "Further observations concerning the state of Persia, taken in the foresayd fift voyage into those partes, written by M. Jeffrey Ducket, one of those agents employed in the same." It is not in letter format, and instead is arranged by topic; it does not place the English travelers within any of the descriptions, nor does it have a narrative arc. It is perhaps best described as a brief ethnography, and is quite dissimilar from the other Persian materials associated with the Muscovy Company.

33. Hakluyt, *PN* (1589), 416, 379–80.

34. The English trading voyages to Persia took place between the early 1560s and 1581; this period coincided with the reigns of Tahmasp I (1524–76), Isma'il II (1576–77), and Mohammed Shah (1578–87) in Persia. In Russia, the Muscovy Company had formed a strong alliance with Ivan IV, "The Terrible" (1533–84), who facilitated their voyages down the Volga to the Caspian Sea.

35. Hakluyt, *PN* (1589), 370–71.

36. Hakluyt, *PN* (1589), 370.

37. Fuller, *Voyages in Print*, 149.

38. Sir Walter Raleigh, "The English Voyages of the Sixteenth Century," in *The Principal Navigations, Voyages, Traffiques & Discoveries of the English Nation*, ed. Richard Hakluyt, 12 vols., (Glasgow: MacLehose, 1905), 12:120.

39. I understand *facts* to be verbal and epistemological constructs that purport to describe things or events. One characteristic of these constructs is that facts are understood to be in some way short, small, or bounded enough so that they can function like bricks in a wall, as singular building blocks of knowledge. In "Why are Facts Short?," Daston argues that this brevity is due to the historical function facts came to serve within scientific communities looking to build consent and avoid violent quarrel over various interpretations of aspects of the natural world.

40. Jonathan P. A. Sell, *Rhetoric and Wonder in English Travel Writing, 1560–1613* (Aldershot, England, 2006), 32.

41. The East India Company would later maintain a tightly closed archive, and very carefully regulate who had access to shipboard journals and company reports; an even tighter watch was kept over what was published. For an extensive discussion of the "writing culture" of the East India Company, see Richmond Barbour's *The Third Voyage Journals: Writing and Perfomance in the London East India Company, 1607–1610* (New York: Palgrave Macmillan, 2009). I am particularly excited by this publication, as it makes more widely available travel materials that are generally kept in archives (presumably in part due to their "dullness") and yet are crucial to understand the English generation and regulation of "true" information from foreign lands.

42. Matthew Day, "Hakluyt, Harvey, Nashe: The Material Text and Early Modern Nationalism," *Studies in Philology* 104, no. 3 (Summer 2007): 281–305.

43. Hakluyt, *6v, *7r.

44. Hakluyt, *PN* (1589), 376.

45. Ibid., 376.

46. Ibid., 378.

47. Ibid., 379.

48. Ibid., 382.

49. Ibid., 379.

50. Sir Walter Alexander Raleigh, "The English Voyages of the Sixteenth Century," 12:120.

51. Hakluyt, *PN* (1589), 382, 377, 378.

POSTSCRIPT

1. Lorraine Daston, "Why Are Facts Short?" *Max-Planck-Institut für Wissenschaftsgeschichte Preprint 174: A History of Facts*: (Berlin, Germany: 2002) 18.

2. Barbara Shapiro has studied all of these realms that treat "matters of fact," and has written on their interconnections in *A Culture of Fact, England 1550–1720* (Ithaca, NY: Cornell University Press, 2000). As an intellectual historian, Shapiro is most concerned

with the changing standards of truthfulness in the abstract: absolute and moral certainty, probability, "reasonable" judgment, and the development of the idea of the fact.

3. Shapiro, *A Culture of Fact*, 41.

4. Steven Shapin argues that practices of gentlemanly civility are crucial to the formation of accepted practices for knowledge production within the Royal Society and highlights the role that trust plays within all such communities. See Steven Shapin, *A Social History of Truth: Civility and Science in Seventeenth-Century England* (Chicago: University of Chicago Press, 1994).

5. Daston, "Why Are Facts Short?" 16.

6. Robert Mayer, *History and the Early English Novel: Matters of Fact from Bacon to Defoe* (Cambridge: Cambridge University Press, 1997), 2–3.

7. See for example Lennard Davis's use of news reporting in *Factual Fictions: The Origins of the English Novel* (New York: Columbia University Press, 1983).

8. Thomas Palmer, *An essay of the meanes how to make our trauailes, into forraine countries, the more profitable and honourable* (London: Imprinted by Humphrey Lownes for Mathew Lownes, 1606).

9. Navigational details were paramount, but they were not the only instructions "very necessarie and needefull to be observed." Company travellers are instructed to draw and label pictures of the shoreline to assist in the creation of accurate maps, and to describe notable features of the land when sailing by or after having landed; the manner of the soil; the "manner, shape, attire and disposition of the people, and of the commodities they have, and what they most covet and desire of the commodities you carrie with you." In general, commodities for sale in local markets and guesses at which English wares would do well in particular areas are also emphasized as important to record, usually in the form of descriptions of homes, furnishings, clothing, and food. Finally, modes of warfare and defence, strategic islands and straights, and other military matters were also to be noted by company travellers. See Richard Hakluyt, *The principall nauigations, voiages and discoueries of the English nation made by sea or ouer land, to the most remote and farthest distant quarters of the earth at any time within the compasse of these 1500. yeeres: deuided into three seuerall parts, according to the positions of the regions wherunto they were directed. . . . Whereunto is added the last most renowmed English nauigation, round about the whole globe of the earth. By Richard Hakluyt Master of Artes, and student sometime of Christ-church in Oxford.* (London: printed by George Bishop and Ralph Newberie, deputies to Christopher Barker, printer to the Queenes most excellent Maiestie, 1589), 458–463. Richmond Barbour has also noted the importance of these letters and the regulation of their form in the development of the East India Company bureaucracy and eventually its role in establishing the British Empire: "To sustain profits, the London Company required corporate knowledge of the worlds its agents entered, and governing "adventurers"—investors—therefore insisted that principals on voyages maintain detailed journals to be surrendered on return. Agents posted abroad for longer periods reported their activities, and quarreled at length with associates, in letters. Strategic and tactical debates, data of commerce, daily developments abroad, minutes of meetings at home, commissions to mariners, were copied and archived in London. The East India Company managed a system of corporate discourse long before it ever thought to hold an empire, and it accumulated considerable acreage of text. At the British Library's India Office today, East India Company material occupies miles of shelving." See Richmond Barbour, *Before Orientalism: London's Theatre of the East, 1576–1626* (Cambridge University Press, 2003), 7–8; see also Richmond Barbour, *The Third Voyage Journals: Writing and Performance in the London East India Company, 1607–1610* (New York: Palgrave Macmillan, 2009).

10. For further discussion of "plats" and their links to drama, see John Gillies, "Introduction: Elizabethan Drama and the Cartographizations of Space," in *Playing the Globe: Genre and Geography in English Renaissance Drama*, ed. Virginia Mason Vaughan and John Gillies (Madison, NJ: Fairleigh Dickinson University Press, 1998), 27–28.

11. For the duration and intensity of English losses to captivity in North Africa, see Nabil Matar, "Introduction," in *Piracy, Slavery, and Redemption: Barbary Captivity Narratives from Early Modern England*, ed. Daniel J. Vitkus (New York: Columbia University Press, 2001), 1–52.

12. For further discussion of this domestic political context, see Nabil Matar, "English Accounts of Captivity in North Africa and the Middle East: 1577–1625," *Renaissance Quarterly* 54, no. 2 (2001): 553–572.

13. This phrase is historian David Goffman's description of the overarching intellectual project of the literary essays that constitute the collection *Remapping the Mediterranean World*. See David Goffman, Afterward, to *Remapping the Mediterranean World in Early Modern English Writings*, ed. Goran V. Stanivukovic (New York: Palgrave Macmillan, 2007), 274, emphasis mine.

14. This has not been the case with studies of travel writing as a whole. The work on Walter Raleigh's account of his trip to Guiana, for example, frequently analyzes the form of the text in conjunction with the type of work the author hoped it would perform domestically and the effect it did (not) have on its readers. One of the most thorough accounts is Mary C. Fuller, chapter 2 in *Voyages in Print: English Travel to America, 1576–1624*, (New York: Cambridge University Press, 1995) 55–84.

15. Gerald MacLean has recently called attention to an aspect of the English usage of the term "Turk" that has not been widely acknowledged in the literature—namely, that the term was not used or recognized by the Ottomans, except to refer "disparagingly to the Anatolian peasantry over whom they had come to rule." The Ottoman sultan was decidedly not the "Great Turk" and he did not rule over "Turkey." The word Turk, incorrectly used by early modern English authors to describe any Muslim, was equally erroneous as a designation for the Ottomans. See Gerald MacLean, *Looking East: English Writing and the Ottoman Empire Before 1800* (New York: Palgrave, 2007), 6.

16. Mayer, *History and the Early English Novel*, 2–3.

Bibliography

Andrea, Bernadette. "From Invasion to Inquisition: Mapping Malta in Early Modern England." In *Remapping the Mediterranean World in Early Modern English Writings*. Edited by Goran V. Stanivukovic, 245–271. New York: Palgrave, 2007.

———. "Lady Sherley: The First Persian in England?" *Muslim World* 95, no. 2 (April 2005): 279–295.

———. *Women and Islam in Early Modern English Literature*. Cambridge: Cambridge University Press, 2007.

Anghiera, Pietro Martire d'. *The [H]history of trauayle in the VVest and East Indies, and other countreys lying eyther way, towardes the fruitfull and ryche Moluccaes As Moscouia, Persia, Arabia, Syria, AEgypte, Ethiopia, Guinea, China in Cathayo, and Giapan: vvith a discourse of the Northwest passage. Gathered in parte, and done into Englyshe by Richarde Eden. Newly set in order, augmented, and finished by Richarde VVilles*. Translated by Richard Eden. Imprinted at London: By Richarde Iugge, 1577.

Anon. *A coranto Relating diuers particulars concerning the newes out of Italy, Spaine, Turkey, Persia, Bohemia, Sweden, Poland, Austria, the Pallatinates, the Grisons, and diuers places of the higher and Lower Germanie*. London: printed by T. Snodham for Nathaniel Butter, Nicholas Bourne, and William Shefford, 1622.

———. *Good newes from Florence of a famous victorie obtained against the Turkes in May last 1613. both by sea and land: By the great Duke of Florence, the earle of Candale, and diuers French commanders and gentlemen heereafter named. Translated faithfully into English out of the French copie, printed with priuiledge at Paris and taken out of the Italian discourse printed at Florence*. London: printed by Edward Griffin for Nathaniel Butter at Saint Austins gate, 1614.

———. *July. 16. Numb. 9. The continuation of the most remarkable occurrences of newes, since the 4 of Iune, vntill this present. 1630 Containing, amongst diuers others, these particulars. The preparation and landing of the King of Sweden in Germany, with a mighty army, against the emperour: together with a list of his whole army, horse and foot. A late skirmish and ouerthrow giuen by the States forces, to Count Iohn of Nassaw, himselfe being taken prisoner, being sore hurt: together with diuers men of note neare Wesel. Newes of the arriuall of the two Spanish plate fleets at the Havanna, with the Gargazin of their lading and riches. The great ielousie of the emperour, of the Turkes comming into Hungary, with the great cruelty of the said Turkes, vsed against certaine merchants of Hungary. The arriuall of diuers Dutch ships; richly laden, both from East-Indies, and from Farnambuco together with many other particulars, both from Italy Sauoy, France, and the Low-Countries*. London: printed by G. Purslowe for Nicholas Bourne, dwelling at the South entrance of the Royall Exchange, 1630.

———. *Newes from diuers countries as, from Spaine, Antwerpe, Collin, Venice, Rome, the Turke, and the prince Doria : and how the arch-duke of Austria is intended to resigne his cardinall hat through his marrying with the king of Spaines daughter*. London: Valentine Sims, 1597.

————. *Nevves from Rome, Venice, and Vienna, touching the present proceedinges of the Turkes against the Christians in Austria, Hungarie, and Heluetia, otherwise called Seuenbergh Also the true copie of a lamentable petition exhibited in the names of the afflicted Christians in those parts, to the Christian kingdomes in the vvest.* London: printed by Iohn Danter, for Thomas Gosson, and are to be sold at his shop adioyning to London Bridge Gate, 1595.

————. *Nevves from Turkie and Poland. Or A true and compendious declaration of the proceedings betweene the great Turke, and his Maiestie of Poland, from the beginning of the warres, vntill the latter end VVith a relation of their daily millitary actions; shewing plainly how the warre continued and ended, peace was concluded, the troubles appeased, the articles of agreement confirmed, and a full league of amity ratified. Translated out of a Latine copie, written by a gentleman of quality, who was an actor in all the businesse: and now with his consent published.* Printed at the Hage [i.e. London]: by Edward Allde, 1622.

————. *Newes from Vienna the 5. day of August. 1566. of the strong towne and castell of Tula in Hungary xi. myles beyond the riuer Danubius, which was cruelly assaulted by the great Turke, but nowe by Gods mighty working relieued, the sayd Turks marueilouslye discomfited and ouerthrowen. Translated out of hye Almaine into English, and printed in Augspurge by Hans Zimmerman.* Imprinted at London: by John Awdeley, dwelling in litle Britaine streete without Aldersgate, 1566.

————. *Novemb. 20. Numb. 4. The affaires of Italy, with the crowning and inauguration of the new Pope Barbarino a Florentine in Rome, and other accidents. The occurrents of Hungary, with the affaires of the Prince of Transsilvania, concerning his proceedings with the Emperour. Letters from Vienna, with the Emperours preparation against Bethelem Gabor. The seige of Lipstat in Westphalia, with the causes of the same, and many severall accidents arising from thence. News from the Hage, with the businesse of the provinces thereabouts. What they write from Antwerpe, with the particulars of Brussels, as the present time affords.* London: printed for Nathaniel Butter, 1623.

————. *Novem. 22. Numb. 42. The Continuation of our weekly Newes, Containing these particulers following. The warlike proceeding and good successe of the French and their Confederates in the Grisons and Valtoline. The great Victories which the Hollanders have gotten in Perne. The taking of seuerall Townes in the Land of Marke by the Forces of the Marquis of Brandenberg, and the States of the United Provinces. The Incursion of the Tartars upon Podolia, when the Turkes invaded Hungary. The Command of the Emperor to bring in all the protestant Bookes in Austria, and a summons of all the Protestant Preachers To appeere at Vienna whether private in Gentlemens houses, or others. Certaine Letters from Thurin concerning the meeting of seuerall Embassadors of France, of Venice, of England; with their consultations with the Duke of Savoy concerning the recovery of the Valtohne. The Death of the Lord of Southampton and his Sonne the Lord W___, with the valiant exploit of the Lord of Oxford and Essex upon the Enemies Convoy; whereupon the Lord of Oxford received some hurt, they seized of the Enemy some 20. wagons besides other spoiles With the Newes of diuers other parts of Christendome.* London: printed by E. A. for Nathaniel Butter and Nicholas Bourne, 1624.

————. *Nouemb. 28. Numb. 9. Briefe abstracts out of diuerse letters of trust Relating the newes of this present weeke, out of Persia, Egypt, Babylon, Barbary, Turkey, Italy, Spaine, Germanie, Silesia, France, and the Low Countries, with diuers passages from the sea. Wherein are remembered the troubles in the Turkish Empire, the strength of the pyrates of Argier, with a touch of the giuing vp of the towne of Glatz, and the holding out of Frankendale. With the victories of Count Mansfield in the land of Embden, and the flight of the Count of that countrey; and the going on of the Prince of Orange towards Lingen. Together with the sea businesses of the Spanish and Hollandish fleetes. In the end is added something of the French affaires, with some other occurrences.* London: printed by B. Alsop for Nathaniel Butter, Nicholas Bourne, and William Sheffard, 1622.

————. *October. 20. Numb. 44. The continuation of our late avisoes from forreine parts. Contayning amongst other things these particulars following. A more large and ample confirmation of the late overthrow given the Catholic army in Saxony, by his Majesty of Sweden and the D. of Saxony; with the death, the place, and manner of the burial of Mons. Tilly, (inferred in the front of our last newes) as wee have received it from the army of the Duke of Saxony (on the 25. of the last month) then before Leypsich, from Francford and Volchin, the 27. of the same. The names of some speciall commanders slaine on both sides. The proceeding of the King of Sweden since the battaile, with the taking of (these townes) Hall, Halverstadt, Morsenburgh, Weysenfels, Litsen, and other places Imperiall, which must yeeld a very large contribution to his Majesty. Two other passages of note, from Reginspurgh and Westphalia, which we will referre to the insuing avisoes. The continuation of the overthrow of the Imperialists in Silesia, by the Lord Marquis Hamleton.* London: printed for Nathaniel Butter and Nicholas Bourne, 1631.

————. *A primer of boke of priuate praier nedeful to be vsed of all faythfull Christians. Whyche booke is to be vsed of all out louyng subiectes.* Londini : ex officina VVilhelmi Seres typographi, 1560.

————. *A relation strange and true, of a ship of Bristol named the Iacob of 120. tunnes, which was about the end of Octob. last 1621. taken by the Turkish pirats of Argier. And how within fiue dayes after, foure English youths did valiantly ouercome 13. of the said Turks, and brought the ship to S. Lucas in Spaine, where they sold nine of the Turks for gally-slaues.* London: printed by Eliot's Court Press for Nathaniel Butter, and are to be sold at his shop, at the signe of the Pide Bull, neere S. Austins Gate, 1622.

————. *A true and credible report, of a great and very daungerous fight at sea, betwene certaine ships belonging to sundrye merchants of England, and fiue well approoued ships of warre of the King of Spaines: which fight hapned the 25. of May last past 1600. within the straightes of Gibraltare. The truth thereof beeing faithfully sent from one friend to an other.* London: printed by E. A. for VValter Burre, dvvelling in Paules Churchyard, at the signe of the Flower deluce, 1600.

————. *A true discourse vvherin is set downe the wonderfull mercy of God, shewed towardes the Christians, on the two and twenty of Iune. 1593 against the Turke, before Syssek in Croatia. Truly translated out of the high Dutch coppie. Printed at Vienna.* London: printed by J. Windet for Iohn Wolfe, 1593.

————. *A True relation of taking of Alba-Regalis in the German tongue, called Sfullweissenburgh [sic], the chiefe cittie in Nether-Hungarie, which was taken by the Christian armie, the twentith [sic] of September last past, 1601 / truely traslated [sic] out of the German tongue.* London: printed by Ralph Blower, for C. B., 1601.

————. *A true report of Sir Anthony Shierlies iourney ouerland to Venice fro[m] thence by sea to Antioch, Aleppo, and Babilon, and soe to Casbine in Persia: his entertainment there by the great Sophie: his oration: his letters of credence to the Christian princes: and the priuiledg obtained of the great Sophie, for the quiet passage and trafique of all Christian marchants, throughout his whole dominions.* London: printed by R. Blower for I. Iaggard, 1600.

————. *The estate of Christians, liuing vnder the subiection of the Turke And also the warres betweene the Christians and the Turke, beginning 1592. and continuing till the end of 1593.* London: printed by T. Scarlet for Iohn Wolfe, 1595.

———. *The fourth of September. Newes from sundry places, both forraine and domestique From Venice, Rome, Spaine, France, Naples, the Palatinate, and the Low-Countries. A relation of Count Mansfeilds progresse, (his battaile with Gonsalo in his passage) till his arriuall at Breda, with the Duke of Brunswicke his valiant pursuit of Gonsalo, (being wounded) and the slaughter of 500. of his men, and the taking of certaine waggons, and Gonsales owne coath. Whereunto is added, a true and certaine report, of the lamentable shipwracke which happened at Plimoth in Deuonshire, on Munday the 19th. of August last past, with other great harme done elsewhere, by lightning and thunder on the same day.* London: printed for Nathaniel Butter and are to be sold at his shop, at the signe of the Pyde Bull, at Saint Austins Gate, 1622.

———. *The tryumphant vyctory of the imperyall mageste agaynst the turkes: the xxvi day of Septembre in Steurmarke by a capytayne named Michale meschsaer. Cum privilegio.* London: translated and emprynted out of Frenche into englysshe by Robert Copland dwelling in Flete strete by Flete brydge at the sygne of the Rose garland, for Rychard bankes bookseller, 1532.

———. *True and most certaine nevves, sent from Vienna in Austria, the 17. of Iune last, 1595. Howe Ferdinand Earle of Hardeck, beeing generall over the strong citie of Raab in Hungaria, with Perlino his collonel, captaine over the Italia.* London: printed by P. Short for William Leake, 1595.

———. *True newes of a notable victorie obtayned against the Turkes.* London: printed by I. Roberts, 1598.

Arber, Edward, ed. *A Transcript of the Registers of the Company of Stationers of London, 1554–1640 A.D.* 5 vols. London: Privately Printed, 1894.

Archer, John Michael. *Old Worlds: Egypt, Southwest Asia, India, and Russia in Early Modern English Writing.* Stanford: Stanford University Press, 2001.

Atherton, Ian. "The Itch Grown a Disease: Manuscript Transmission of News in the Seventeenth Century." *Prose Studies* 21, no. 2 (1998): 39–65.

Bakhtin, Mikhail M. / Pavel N. Medvedev. *The Formal Method in Literary Scholarship: A Critical Introduction to Sociological Poetics.* Translated by Albert J. Wehrle. Baltimore: The Johns Hopkins University Press, 1978.

Barbour, Richmond. *Before Orientalism: London's Theatre of the East, 1576–1626.* Cambridge: Cambridge University Press, 2003.

———. *The Third Voyage Journals: Writing and Performance in the London East India Company, 1607–1610.* New York: Palgrave Macmillan, 2009.

Baron, S. A. "Gainsford, Thomas (bap. 1566, d. 1624)." In *The Oxford Dictionary of National Biography*, edited by H. C. G. Matthew and B. Harrison. Oxford: Oxford University Press, 2004. http://0-www.oxforddnb.com.library.unl.edu/view/article/10284 (Accessed January 9, 2010).

Bartels, Emily C. "Othello and Africa: Postcolonialism Reconsidered." *The William and Mary Quarterly* 3rd ser., 54, no. 1 (January 1997): 45–64.

———. *Speaking of the Moor: From Alcazar to Othello.* Philadelphia: University of Pennsylvannia Press, 2008.

Baumer, Franklin L. "England, the Turk, and the Common Corps of Christendom." *The American Historical Review* 50, no. 1 (October 1944): 26–48.

Beg, Uruch. *Don Juan of Persia, a Shi'ah Catholic, 1560–1604.* Edited by Guy Le Strange. New York: Harper & Bros., 1926.

Biagioli, Mario. *Galileo, Courtier: The Practice of Science in the Culture of Absolutism.* Chicago: University of Chicago Press, 1993.

Birchwood, Matthew. *Staging Islam in England: Drama and Culture, 1640–1685*. Cambridge: D. S. Brewer, 2007.

Bisaha, Nancy. *Creating East and West: Renaissance Humanists and the Ottoman Turks*. Philadelphia: University of Pennsylvania Press, 2004.

Blundeville, Thomas. *The true order and methode of wryting and reading hystories according to the precepts of Francisco Patricio, and Accontio Tridentino, two Italian writers, no lesse plainly than briefly, set forth in our vulgar speach, to the great profite and commoditye of all those that delight in hystories. By Thomas Blundeuill of Newton Flotman in Norfolke. Anno. 1574*. Imprinted at London: by VVillyam Seres, 1574.

Betteridge, Thomas, ed. *Borders and Travellers in Early Modern Europe*. Aldershot, England: Ashgate, 2007.

Boruchoff, David A. "Piety, Patriotism, and Empire: Lessons for England, Spain, and the New World in the Works of Richard Hakluyt." *Renaissance Quarterly* 62, no. 3 (2009): 809–58.

Bosworth, Clifford Edmund. *An Intrepid Scot: William Lithgow of Lanark's Travels in the Ottoman Lands, North Africa and Central Europe, 1609–21*. Aldershot, England: Ashgate, 2006.

Brancaforte, Elio Christoph. *Visions of Persia: Mapping the Travels of Adam Olearius*. Cambridge, MA: Harvard University Department of Comparative Literature, 2003.

Braudel, Fernand. *Civilization and Capitalism, 15th–18th Century*. Vol. 1, *The Structures of Everyday Life: The Limits of the Possible*. Translated by Sian Reynolds. New York: Harper & Row, 1991.

Brennan, Michael G., ed. *The Origins of the Grand Tour: The Travels of Robert Montagu, Lord Mandeville (1649–1654) William Hammond, (1655–1658), and Banaster Maynard (1660–1663)*. Works issued by the Hakluyt Society, 3rd ser., no. 14. London: Hakluyt Society, 2004.

Buonaccorsi, Andrea. *A Iewes prophesy, or, newes from Rome Of two mightie armies, aswell footemen as horsmen: the first of the great Sophy, the other of an Hebrew people, till this time not discouered, comming from the mountaines of Caspij, who pretend their warre is to recouer the land of promise, & expell the Turks out of Christendome. Translated out of Italian into English, by W.W. 1607*. London: printed by W. I. for Henry Gosson, and are to be sold in Pater noster rowe at the signe of the Sunne, 1607.

Burg, B. R. *Sodomy and the Pirate Tradition: English Sea Rovers in the Seventeenth Century Caribbean*. New York: New York University Press, 1995.

Burman, Thomas E. *Reading the Qur'an in Latin Christendom, 1140–1560*. Philadelphia: University of Pennsylvania Press, 2007.

Burton, Jonathan. "Emplotting the Early Modern Mediterranean." In *Remapping the Mediterranean World in Early Modern English Writings*, edited by Goran V. Stanivukovic, 21–40. New York: Palgrave, 2007.

———. "The Shah's Two Ambassadors: The Travels of the Three English Brothers and the Global Early Modern." In *Emissaries in Early Modern Literature and Culture: Mediation, Transmission, Traffic, 1550–1700*, edited by Brinda Charry and Gitanjali Shahani, 23–40. Burlington, VT: Ashgate, 2009.

———. *Traffic and Turning: Islam and English Drama, 1579–1624*. Newark: University of Delaware Press, 2005.

Calendar of the Manuscripts of the Most Honourable the Marquis of Salisbury. Part 19. Historical Manuscripts Commission. London: 1965.

204 BIBLIOGRAPHY

Cartwright, John. *The preachers trauels Wherein is set downe a true iournall to the confines of the East Indies, through the great countreyes of Syria, Mesopotamia, Armenia, Media, Hircania and Parthia. With the authors returne by the way of Persia, Susiana, Assiria, Chaldaea, and Arabia. Containing a full suruew of the knigdom [sic] of Persia: and in what termes the Persian stands with the Great Turke at this day: also a true relation of Sir Anthonie Sherleys entertainment there: and the estate that his brother, M. Robert Sherley liued in after his departure for Christendome. With the description of a port in the Persian gulf, commodious for our East Indian merchants; and a briefe rehearsall of some grosse absudities [sic] in the Turkish Alcoran. Penned by I.C. sometimes student in Magdalen Colledge in Oxford.* London: printed by William Stansby for Thomas Thorppe, and are to bee sold by Walter Burre, 1611.

Charry, Brinda, and Gitanjali Shahani, eds. *Emissaries in Early Modern Literature and Culture: Mediation, Transmission, Traffic, 1550–1700.* Burlington, VT: Ashgate, 2009.

Chaussinand-Nogaret, Guy. "Aux origines de la Révolution: noblesse et bourgeoisie." *Annales: Économies, Sociétés, Civilisations* 30, no. 2 (1975): 265–278.

Clegg, Cyndia Susan. *Press Censorship in Caroline England.* Cambridge: Cambridge University Press, 2008.

———. *Press Censorship in Elizabethan England.* Cambridge: Cambridge University Press, 1997.

———. *Press Censorship in Jacobean England.* Cambridge: Cambridge University Press, 2001.

Cleveland, John. *The character of a London diurnall.* London, 1644.

Cohen, Stephen. "Between Form and Culture: New Historicism and the Promise of a Historical Formalism." In *Renaissance Literature and Its Formal Engagements*, edited by Mark David Rasmussen, 17–41. New York: Palgrave Macmillan, 2002.

Collins, Arthur. *Letters and Memorials of State in the Reigns of Queen Mary, Queen Elizabeth, King James, King Charles the First, Part of the Reign of King Charles the Second, and Oliver's Usurpation.* New York: AMS Press, 1973.

Cortano, Ludovico. *Good newes for Christendome Sent to a Venetian in Ligorne, from a merchant in Alexandria. Discouering a wonderfull and strange apparition, visibly seene for many dayes togither in Arabia, ouer the place, where the supposed tombe of Mahomet (the Turkish prophet) is inclosed: by which the learned Arabians prognosticate the reducing & calling of the great Turke to Christianitie. With many other notable accidents: but the most remarkable is the miraculous rayning of bloud about Rome. Done out of the Italian.* London: printed by G. Purslowe for Nathaniel Butter, 1620.

Cribb, T. J. "Writing Up the Log: The Legacy of Hakluyt." In *Travel Writing and Empire: Postcolonial Theory in Transit*, edited by Steve Clark, 100–112. London: Zed Books, 1999.

Crowley, Robert. *An informacion and peticion agaynst the oppressours of the poore commons of thys realme compiled and imprinted for this onely purpose that amongest them that haue to doe in the Parliamente some godlye mynded men, may hereat take occation to speake more in the matter then the authour was able to wryte.* London: printed by John Daye, dwellyng in Sepulchres parish at the signe of the Resurrectio[n] a lytle aboue Holbourne Conduite, 1548.

Cust, Richard. "News and Politics in Early Seventeenth-Century England." *Past & Present* 112 (1986): 60–90.

Daborne, Robert. *A Christian turn'd Turke: or, The tragicall liues and deaths of the two famous pyrates, Ward and Dansiker As it hath beene publickly acted. VVritten by Robert*

Daborn, Gentleman. London: Printed by Nicholas Okes for William Barrenger, and are to be sold at the great north-doore of Pauls, 1612.

Dahl, Folke. *A Bibliography of English Corantos and Periodical Newsbooks, 1620–1642*. London: Bibliographical Society, 1952.

D'Amico, Jack. *The Moor in English Renaissance Drama*. Tampa: University of South Florida Press, 1991.

Daston, Lorraine. "Perché i fatti sono brevi?" *Quaderni Storici* 108, no. 3 (2001): 745–770.

———. "Why Are Facts Short?" *Max-Planck-Institut für Wissenschaftsgeschichte Preprint 174: A History of Facts*: 5–21.

Davies, David William. *Elizabethans Errant; the Strange Fortunes of Sir Thomas Sherley and His Three Sons, as Well in the Dutch Wars as in Muscovy, Morocco, Persia, Spain, and the Indies*. Ithaca, NY: Cornell University Press, 1967.

Davies, H. Neville. "Pericles and the Sherley Brothers." In *Shakespeare and His Contemporaries: Essays in Comparison*, edited by E. A. J. Honigmann, 94–113. Manchester: Manchester University Press, 1986.

Davis, Lennard. *Factual Fictions: The Origins of the English Novel*. New York: Columbia University Press, 1983.

Davis, Natalie Zemon. *Trickster Travels: A Sixteenth-Century Muslim Between Worlds*. New York: Hill and Wang, 2006.

Davis, Ralph. "England and the Mediterranean, 1570–1670." In *Essays in Economic and Social History of Tudor and Stuart England in Honour of R. H. Tawney*, edited by F. J. Fisher, 117–137. Cambridge: Cambridge University Press, 1961.

Davison, Roderic H. *Turkey: A Short History*. 3rd ed. Huntingdon, England: Eothen Press, 1998.

Day, John, William Rowley, and George Wilkins. *The trauailes of the three English brothers Sir Thomas Shirley Sir Anthony [Shirley] Mr. Robert [Shirley]. As it is now play'd by her Maiesties Seruants*. London: printed by George Eld for Iohn Wright, and are to bee sold at his shoppe neere Christ-Church gate, 1607.

Day, Matthew. "Hakluyt, Harvey, Nashe: The Material Text and Early Modern Nationalism." *Studies in Philology* 104, no. 3 (2007): 281–305.

Dimmock, Matthew. *New Turkes: Dramatizing Islam and the Ottomans in Early Modern England*. Aldershot, England: Ashgate, 2005.

Eden, Richard. *The decades of the newe worlde or west India conteynyng the nauigations and conquestes of the Spanyardes, with the particular description of the moste ryche and large landes and ilandes lately founde in the west ocean perteynyng to the inheritaunce of the kinges of Spayne. . . . Wrytten in the Latine tounge by Peter Martyr of Angleria, and translated into Englysshe by Rycharde Eden*. London: Guilhelmi Powell [for William Seres], 1555.

Edwards, Jess. "'Nature in Defect': Yielding Landscapes in Early Modern Discourses of Enclosure and Colonisation." *Studies in Travel Writing* 4 (2000): 1–28.

Elias, Norbert. *The Court Society*. Translated by Edmund Jephcott. New York: Pantheon Books, 1983.

Ellison, James. *George Sandys: Travel, Colonialism and Tolerance in the Seventeenth Century*. Cambridge: D. S. Brewer, 2002.

———. "Sandys, George (1578–1644)." In *Oxford Dictionary of National Biography*, edited by H. C. G. Matthew and B. Harrison. Oxford: Oxford University Press, 2004. http://0-www.oxforddnb.com.library.unl.edu/view/article/24651?docPos=11 (Accessed May 9, 2007).

"Fact." In *New Shorter Oxford English Dictionary*. Oxford: Oxford University Press, 1996.

Ferguson, Arthur. *Clio Unbound: Perception of the Social and Cultural Past in Renaissance England*. Durham, NC: Duke University Press, 1979.

Fleischman, Suzanne. "On the Representation of History and Fiction in the Middle Ages." *History and Theory* 22, no. 3 (October 1983): 278–310.

Fox, Adam. "Rumour, News and Popular Political Opinion in Elizabethan and Early Stuart England." *Historical Journal* 40, no. 3 (September 1997): 597–620.

Frank, Joseph. *The Beginnings of the English Newspaper, 1620–1660*. Cambridge, MA: Harvard University Press, 1961.

Frisch, Andrea. *The Invention of the Eyewitness: Witnessing and Testimony in Early Modern France*. Chapel Hill, NC: University of North Carolina Department of Romance Languages, 2004.

Fuchs, Barbara. *Mimesis and Empire: The New World, Islam, and European Identities*. Cambridge: Cambridge University Press, 2001.

Fuller, Mary C. "On Hakluyt's Dullness." Lecture for conference held at National Maritime Museum, Greenwich, London, May 15–17, 2008. "Richard Hakluyt (ca. 1552–1616): Life, Times and Legacy."

———. *Remembering the Early Modern Voyage: English Narratives in the Age of European Expansion*. New York: Palgrave Macmillan, 2008.

———. *Voyages in Print: English Travel to America, 1576–1624*. New York: Cambridge University Press, 1995.

Fussner, F. Smith. *The Historical Revolution: English Historical Writing and Thought, 1580–1640*. New York: Routledge and Paul, 1962.

Gagnon, Paul. "Why Study History?" *The Atlantic Monthly* 262.5 (Nov. 1988), 43–66.

Gillies, John. "Introduction: Elizabethan Drama and the Cartographizations of Space." In *Playing the Globe: Genre and Geography in English Renaissance Drama*, edited by Virginia Mason Vaughan and John Gillies, 19–45. Madison, NJ: Fairleigh Dickinson University Press, 1998.

Goffman, Daniel. "Afterword." In *Remapping the Mediterranean World in Early Modern English Writings*, edited by Goran V. Stanivukovic, 273–287. New York: Palgrave, 2007.

Grafton, Anthony. *New Worlds, Ancient Texts: The Power of Tradition and the Shock of Discovery*. Cambridge, MA: Harvard University Press, 1992.

Habib, Imtiaz. *Black Lives in the English Archives, 1500–1677: Imprints of the Invisible*. Burlington, VT: Ashgate, 2008.

Hadfield, Andrew, ed. *Amazons, Savages and Machiavels: Travel and Colonial Writing in English, 1550–1630: An Anthology*. Oxford: Oxford University Press, 2001.

———. *Literature, Travel and Colonial Writing in the English Renaissance, 1545–1625*. Oxford: Clarendon Press, 1998.

Hakluyt, Richard. *Diuers voyages touching the discouerie of America, and the ilands adiacent vnto the same made first of all by our Englishmen, and afterward by the Frenchmen and Britons: and certaine notes of aduertisements for obseruations, necessarie for such as shall heereafter make the like attempt, with two mappes annexed heereunto for the plainer vnderstanding of the whole matter*. London: printed by Thomas Dawson for Thomas VVoodcocke, dwelling in paules Church-yard, at the signe of the blacke beare, 1582.

———. *The principall nauigations, voiages and discoueries of the English nation made by sea or ouer land, to the most remote and farthest distant quarters of the earth at any time within the compasse of these 1500. yeeres: deuided into three seuerall parts, according to the positions of the regions wherunto they were directed. . . . Whereunto is added the last most renowmed English nauigation, round about the whole globe of the earth. By Richard Hakluyt Master of Artes, and student sometime of Christ-church in Oxford.* London: printed by George Bishop and Ralph Newberie, deputies to Christopher Barker, printer to the Queenes most excellent Maiestie, 1589.

Haynes, Jonathan. *The Humanist as Traveler: George Sandys' Relation of a Journey begun an. Dom. 1610.* London: Associated University Press, 1986.

Heal, Felicity and Clive Holmes. *The Gentry in England and Wales, 1500–1700.* Stanford: Stanford University Press, 1994.

Helfers, James P. "The Explorer or the Pilgrim? Modern Critical Opinion and the Editorial Methods of Richard Hakluyt and Samuel Purchas." *Studies in Philology* 94, no. 2 (1997): 160–186.

Helgerson, Richard. *Forms of Nationhood: The Elizabethan Writing of England.* Chicago: University of Chicago Press, 1992.

Hotson, Leslie. *The First Night of Twelfth Night.* New York: Macmillan, 1954.

James I, King of England. *His Maiesties Lepanto, or heroicall song being part of his poeticall exercises at vacant houres.* London: printed by Simon Stafford and Henry Hooke, 1603.

Jonson, Ben. *Volpone.* In *Ben Jonson's Plays and Masques*, edited by Richard Harp, 3–110. New York: W. W. Norton, 2001.

Kintgen, Eugene. *Reading in Tudor England.* Pittsburgh: University of Pittsburgh Press, 1996.

Lee, Sidney. "Gainsford, Thomas (d. 1624)." In *Dictionary of National Biography*, edited by Leslie Stephen and Sidney Lee, 7:808. Oxford: Oxford University Press, 1917.

Leth, Göran. "A Protestant Public Sphere: The Early European Newspaper Press." In *Studies in Newspaper and Periodical History*, edited by Michael Harris, 67–92. Westport, CT: Greenwood Press, 1994.

Levine, Joseph. *Humanism and History: Origins of Modern English Historiography.* Ithaca: Cornell University Press, 1987.

Levy, Fritz. "How Information Spread Among the Gentry, 1550–1640." *Journal of British Studies* 21, no. 2 (Spring 1982): 11–34.

Lloyd, Christopher. *English Corsairs on the Barbary Coast.* London: Collins, 1981.

MacCrossan, Colm. "New Journeys through Old Voyages: Literary Approaches to Richard Hakluyt and Early Modern Travel Writing." *Literature Compass 6.1* (2009): 97–112.

MacLean, Gerald. *Looking East: English Writing and the Ottoman Empire Before 1800.* New York: Palgrave Macmillan, 2007.

———. *The Rise of Oriental Travel: English Visitors to the Ottoman Empire, 1580–1720.* New York: Palgrave Macmillan, 2004.

———. ed. *Re-Orienting the Renaissance: Cultural Exchanges with the East.* New York: Palgrave Macmillan, 2005.

MacNutt, Francis Augustus, ed. & trans. *De Orbe Novo: The Eight Decades of Peter Martyr D'Anghera.* New York: B. Franklin, 1970.

Mancall, Peter C. *Hakluyt's Promise: An Elizabethan's Obsession for an English America.* New Haven: Yale University Press, 2007.

Matar, N. I. *Britain and Barbary, 1589–1689*. Gainesville: University Press of Florida, 2005.

———. "English Accounts of Captivity in North Africa and the Middle East: 1577–1625." *Renaissance Quarterly* 54, no. 2 (2001): 553–572.

———. "English Renaissance Soldiers in the Armies of Islam." *Explorations in Renaissance Culture* 21 (1995): 81–95.

———. *Islam in Britain, 1558–1685*. Cambridge: Cambridge University Press, 1998.

———. *Turks, Moors and Englishmen in the Age of Discovery*. New York: Columbia University Press, 1999.

———. "'Turning Turk': Conversion to Islam in English Renaissance Thought." *Durham University Journal* 86.55, no. 1 (January 1994): 33–41.

Mayer, Robert. *History and the Early English Novel: Matters of Fact from Bacon to Defoe*. Cambridge: Cambridge University Press, 1997.

Mc Elligott, Jason. "Watts, William (c.1590–1649)." In *The Oxford Dictionary of National Biography*, edited by H. C. G. Matthew and B. Harrison. Oxford: Oxford University Press,2004.http://0-www.oxforddnb.com.library.unl.edu/view/article/28895?docPos=2 (Accessed January 9, 2010).

McJannet, Linda. *The Sultan Speaks: Dialogue in English Plays and Histories About the Ottoman Turks*. New York: Palgrave Macmillan, 2006.

McRae, Andrew. *God Speed the Plough: The Representation of Agrarian England, 1500–1660*. Cambridge: Cambridge University Press, 1996.

Meserve, Margaret. *Empires of Islam in Renaissance Historical Thought*. Cambridge, MA: Harvard University Press, 2008.

Middleton, Thomas. *Sir Robert Sherley, sent ambassadour in the name of the King of Persia, to Sigismond the Third, King of Poland and Swecia, and to other princes of Europe his royall entertainment into Cracovia, the chiefe citie of Poland, with his pretended comming into England : also, the honourable praises of the same Sir Robert Sherley, giuen vnto him in that kingdome, are here likewise inserted*. London: printed by I. Windet, for Iohn Budge, and are to bee sold at his shop at the great south doore of Pauls, 1609.

Mitsi, Efterpi. "A Translator's Voyage: The Greek Landscape in George Sandys's Relation of a Journey (1615)." *Studies in Travel Writing* 12, no. 1 (March 2008): 49–65.

Morgan, Edmund S. *American Slavery, American Freedom: The Ordeal of Colonial Virginia*. New York: Norton, 1975.

Muldrew, Craig. "Interpreting the Market: The Ethics of Credit and Community Relations in Early Modern England." *Social History* 18, no. 2 (May 1993): 163–183.

Munday, Anthony. *The admirable deliuerance of 266. Christians by Iohn Reynard Englishman from the captiuitie of the Turkes, who had been gally slaues many yeares in Alexandria The number of the seuerall nations that were captiues follow in the next page*. London: printed by Thomas Dawson, and are to be sold by P. Harrison at the little shop at the Exchange, 1608.

Neville-Sington, Pamela. "'A Very Good Trumpet': Richard Hakluyt and the Politics of Overseas Expansion." In *Texts and Cultural Change in Early Modern England*, edited by Cedric C. Brown and Arthur F. Marotti, 66–79. New York: St. Martin's Press, 1997.

Nixon, Anthony. *The three English brothers Sir Thomas Sherley his trauels, vvith his three yeares imprisonment in Turkie: his inlargement by his Maiesties letters to the great Turke: and lastly, his safe returne into England this present yeare, 1607. Sir Anthony*

Sherley his embassage to the Christian princes. Master Robert Sherley his wars against the Turkes, with his marriage to the Emperour of Persia his neece. London: printed by Adam Islip, and are to be sold by Iohn Hodgets in Paules Church yard, 1607.

———. *The travels of three English brothers 1. Sir Thomas Sherley. 2. Sir Anthony Sherley. 3. M. Robert Sherley. With Sir Thomas Sherley his returne into England this present yeare 1607.* London: 1607.

Palmer, Thomas. *An essay of the meanes hovv to make our trauailes, into forraine countries, the more profitable and honourable.* London: printed by Humphrey Lownes for Mathew Lownes, 1606.

Parker, Patricia. "Fantasies of 'Race' and 'Gender': Africa, *Othello* and Bringing to Light." In *Women, 'Race,' and Writing in the Early Modern Period,* edited by Margo Hendricks and Patricia Parker, 84–100. London: Routledge, 1994.

Parks, George Bruner. *Richard Hakluyt and the English Voyages.* New York: American Geographical Society, 1928.

Parr, Anthony. "Foreign Relations in Jacobean England: The Sherley Brothers and the 'Voyage of Persia.'" In *Travel and Drama in Shakespeare's Time,* edited by Jean-Pierre Maquerlot and Michèle Willems, 14–31. Cambridge: Cambridge University Press, 1996.

———. *Three Renaissance Travel Plays.* Manchester: Manchester University Press, 1995.

Parry, William. *A new and large discourse of the trauels of sir Anthony Sherley Knight, by sea, and ouer land, to the Persian Empire Wherein are related many straunge and wonderfull accidents: and also, the description and conditions of those countries and people he passed by: with his returne into Christendome. Written by William Parry gentleman, who accompanied Sir Anthony in his trauells.* London: printed by Valentine Simmes for Felix Norton, 1601.

Payne, Anthony. *Richard Hakluyt and his books.* London: Hakluyt Society, 1997.

———. "'Strange, Remote, and Farre Distant Countreys': The Travel Books of Richard Hakluyt." In *Journeys Through the Market: Travel, Travellers, and the Book Trade,* edited by Robin Myers and Michael Harris, 1–37. New Castle, DE: Oak Knoll Press, 1999.

Payne, Anthony and Pamela Neville-Sington. *An Interim Census of Surviving Copies of Hakluyt's Divers Voyages (1582) and Principal Navigations (1589; 1598/9–1600).* London: Hakluyt Society, 1997.

Peckham, George. *A true reporte, of the late discoueries, and possession, taken in the right of the Crowne of Englande, of the new-found landes: by that valiaunt and worthye gentleman, Sir Humfrey Gilbert Knight Wherein is also breefely sette downe, her highnesse lawfull tytle therevnto, and the great and manifolde commodities, that is likely to grow thereby, to the whole realme in generall, and to the aduenturers in particular. Together with the easines and shortnes of the voyage. Seene and allowed.* London: printed by Iohn Charlewood for Iohn Hinde, dwelling in Paules Church-yarde, at the signe of the golden Hinde, 1583.

Pincombe, Michael, ed. *Travels and Translations in the Sixteenth Century: Selected Papers from the Second International Conference of the Tudor Symposium (2000).* Aldershot, England: Ashgate, 2004.

Pocock, J. G. A. *The Ancient Constitution and the Federal Law: A Study of English Historical Thought in the Seventeenth Century. A Reissue with a Retrospect.* Cambridge: Cambridge University Press, 1987.

Preuost, Fleuri. *Letters sent from Venice. Anno. 1571 Containing the certaine and true newes of the most noble victorie of the Christians ouer the armie of the great Turke:*

and the names of the lordes & gentlemen of the Christians slaine in the same battell. Translated out of the Frenche copie printed at Paris by Guille[. . .]d Niuerd, with the kings priuiledge. London: printed by Henrie Bynneman, and are to be sold in Paules churchyard by Anthonie Kitson, 1571.

Purchas, Samuel. *Hakluytus Posthumus, or, Purchas His Pilgrimes: Contayning a History of the World in Sea Voyages and Lande Travells by Englishmen and Others.* Glasgow: J. MacLehose and Sons, 1905.

Quinn, David, ed. *The Hakluyt Handbook.* London: The Hakluyt Society, 1974.

Rabb, Theodore K. *Enterprise & Empire; Merchant and Gentry Investment in the Expansion of England, 1575–1630.* Cambridge, MA: Harvard University Press, 1967.

———. "Investment in English Overseas Enterprise, 1575–1630." *The Economic History Review,* n.s., 19, no. 1. (1966): 70–81.

Raleigh, Walter. *The discouerie of the large, rich and bevvtiful empire of Guiana with a relation of the great and golden city of Manoa (which the spaniards call El Dorado) and the prouinces of Emeria, Arromaia, Amapaia, and other countries, with their riuers, adioyning. Performed in the yeare 1595. by Sir W. Ralegh Knight, Captaine of her Maiesties Guard, Lo. Warden of the Stanneries, and her Highnesse Lieutenant generall of the countie of Cornewall.* London: printed by Robert Robinson, 1596.

Raleigh, Walter Alexander. "The English Voyages of the Sixteenth Century." In *The Principal Navigations Voyages Traffiques & Discoveries of the English Nation, etc.,* by Richard Hakluyt, 12: 1–120. Glasgow: James MacLehose & Sons, 1905.

Report on the Manuscripts of Lord De l'Isle & Dudley Preserved at Penshurst Place. London: H. M. Stationery Office, 1934.

"Rowland Whyte to the Earl of Shrewsbury, September 17, 1607." *The Sussex County Magazine* 9 (1935): 708.

Rudolf II. *A Great and Glorious Victorie Obtained by the Emperour Rodolph the Second Against the Turke. Verbatim According to the Dutch Copies Printed at Augspurg.* London: Eliot's Court Press, 1595.

S., R. *Late nevves out of Barbary In a letter written of late from a merchant there, to a gentl. not long since imployed into that countrie from his Maiestie. Containing some strange particulars, of this new Saintish Kings proceedings: as they haue been very credibly related from such as were eye-witnesses.* London: printed by George Eld for Arthur Ionson, 1613.

———. *The nevv prophetical King of Barbary Or The last newes from thence in a letter vvritten of late from a merchant there, to a gentl. not long since imployed into that countrie from his Maiestie. Containing some strange particulars, of this newe saintish Kings proceedings: and how hee hath ouerthrowne Mulley Sidan twice in battell, as hath been very credibly related from such as were eye-witnesses.* London: printed by George Eld for Arthur Ionson, 1613.

Sandys, George. *A relation of a iourney begun an: Dom: 1610 Foure bookes. Containing a description of the Turkish Empire, of AEgypt, of the Holy Land, of the remote parts of Italy, and ilands adioyning.* London: printed by Richard Field for W: Barrett, 1615.

Saunders, Thomas. *A true discription and breefe discourse, of a most lamentable voiage, made latelie to Tripolie in Barbarie, in a ship named the Iesus vvherin is not onely shevved the great miserie, that then happened the aucthor hereof and his whole companie, aswell the marchants as the marriners in that voiage, according to the curssed custome of those barbarous and cruell tyrants, in their terrible vsage of Christian captiues: but also, the great vnfaithfulnesse of those heathnish infidels, in not regarding their promise. Together, with the most wonderfull iudgement of God, vpon the king of Tripolie and his sonne, and a great number of his people, being all the tormentors of those English captiues. Set foorth by Thomas Saunders, one of those captiues there at the same time.* London: printed by Richard Iones, for Edward White, dwelling at the signe of the Gun, by the little North doore of Paules, 1587.

Sebek, Barbara, and Stephen Deng, eds. *Global Traffic: Discourses and Practices of Trade in English Literature and Culture from 1550 to 1700.* New York: Palgrave Macmillan, 2008.

Sell, Jonathan P. A. *Rhetoric and Wonder in English Travel Writing, 1560–1613.* Aldershot, England: Ashgate, 2006.

Shaaber, Matthias. *Some Forerunners of the Newspaper in England 1476–1622.* Philadelphia: University of Pennsylvania Press, 1929.

Shakespeare, William. *Twelfth Night, Or What You Will.* Edited by Elizabeth Story Donno. Cambridge: Cambridge University Press, 2003.

Shand, G. B. "Source and Intent in Middleton's Sir Robert Sherley." *Renaissance and Reformation/Renaissance et Réforme* 7 (19), no. 4 (November 1983): 257–264.

Shapin, Steven. *A Social History of Truth: Civility and Science in Seventeenth-Century England.* Chicago: University of Chicago Press, 1994.

Shapiro, Barbara J. *"Beyond Reasonable Doubt" and "Probable Cause": Historical Perspectives on the Anglo-American Law of Evidence.* Berkeley: University of California Press, 1991.

———. *A Culture of Fact: England, 1550–1720.* Ithaca, NY: Cornell University Press, 2000.

———. *Probability and Certainty in Seventeenth-Century England: A Study of the Relationships Between Natural Science, Religion, History, Law, and Literature.* Princeton: Princeton University Press, 1983.

Sherley, Anthony. *Sir Antony Sherley his relation of his trauels into Persia The dangers, and distresses, which befell him in his passage, both by sea and land, and his strange and vnexpected deliuerances. His magnificent entertainement in Persia, his honourable imployment there-hence, as embassadour to the princes of Christendome, the cause of his disapointment therein, with his aduice to his brother, Sir Robert Sherley, also, a true relation of the great magnificence, valour, prudence, iustice, temperance, and other manifold vertues of Abas, now King of Persia, with his great conquests, whereby he hath inlarged his dominions. Penned by Sr. Antony Sherley, and recommended to his brother, Sr. Robert Sherley, being now in prosecution of the like honourable imployment.* London: printed by Nicholas Okes for Nathaniell Butter, and Ioseph Bagfet, 1613.

Sherley, Thomas. *A true discourse, of the late voyage made by the right worshipfull Sir Thomas Sherley the yonger, knight: on the coast of Spaine, with foure ships and two pinnasses: no lesse famous and honourable to his country, then to him selfe glorious and commendable. Wherein is shewed the taking of three townes, Boarco, Tauaredo and Fyguaro, with a castle and a priorie. / VVritten by a gentleman that was in the voyage.* London: printed for Thomas Pauyer, and are to solde [sic] at the signe of the Cat and two Parrets, neere the royall Exchange, 1602.

———. *Discours of the Turkes.* Edited by E. Denison Ross. Camden miscellany v. 16 [no. 2]. London: Offices of the Royal Historical Society, 1936.

Sidney, Philip. *An Apology for Poetry, or, The Defence of Poesy.* Edited by Geoffrey Shepherd and R. W Maslen. 3rd ed. Manchester: Manchester University Press, 2002.

Stanivukovic, Goran V., ed. *Remapping the Mediterranean World in Early Modern English Writings.* New York: Palgrave, 2007.

Stone, Lawrence. *The Crisis of the Aristocracy, 1558–1641*. Oxford: Clarendon Press, 1965.

Taylor, E. G. R., ed. *The Original Writings & Correspondence of the Two Richard Hakluyts*. London: Printed for the Hakluyt Society, 1935.

Virginia Company of London. *The Records of the Virginia Company of London*. Washington, D.C.: Government Printing Office, 1906.

Vitkus, Daniel J. "The Circulation of Bodies: Slavery, Maritime Commerce and English Captivity Narratives in the Early Modern Period." In *Colonial and Postcolonial Incarceration*, edited by Graeme Harper, 23–37. New York: Continuum, 2001.

———. *Turning Turk: English Theater and the Multicultural Mediterranean, 1570–1630*. New York: Palgrave Macmillan, 2003.

———. "Turning Turk in *Othello*: The Conversion and Damnation of the Moor." *Shakespeare Quarterly* 48, no. 2 (Summer 1997): 145–176.

Vitkus, Daniel J, ed. *Piracy, Slavery, and Redemption: Barbary Captivity Narratives from Early Modern England*. New York: Columbia University Press, 2001.

Willes, Richard. See Anghiera, Pietro Martire d'.

Winnerlind, Carl. "Credit-Money as the Philosopher's Stone: Alchemy and the Coinage Problem in Seventeenth-Century England." In *Oeconomies in the Age of Newton*, edited by Margaret Schabas and N. De Marchi, 234–261. Durham, NC: Duke University Press, 2003.

W. S. R. *True newes of a notable victorie obtayned against the Turkes, by the right honourable Lorde, Adolph Baron of Swartzburg, the 18. day of March last past, anno 1598 vvhen as he and his armie three houres before day, came before Raab, and tooke in that strong and well fenced hold and cittie / translated out of the high Dutch coppy ; printed first at Nurnbergh &c. ; by W.S.R.* London: printed by I. R. for Richard Oliue, and are to be sold at his shop in Long-lane, at the signe of the Bible, 1598.

Index

213